DATE DUE

Can Government Go Bankrupt?

Can Government Go Bankrupt?

RICHARD ROSE

UNIVERSITY OF STRATHCLYDE

&

GUY PETERS

TULANE UNIVERSITY

Basic Books, Inc., Publishers   New York

Library of Congress Cataloging in Publication Data

Rose, Richard, 1933–
    Can government go bankrupt?

    Includes bibliographical references and index.
    1. Finance, Public. 2. Debts, Public.
3. Bankruptcy. I. Peters, Guy, joint author.
II. Title.
HJ141.R64   336.3'4'01   78–54493
ISBN: 0–465–00834–8

T O

Mrs. McGlone & Mrs. West

who can cope with any loads

There is no such thing as a free lunch.

CONTENTS

Contents

[x

ACKNOWLEDGMENTS

THE STUDY of comparative politics, to borrow a phrase from *Guys and Dolls*, is the "oldest established permanent floating crap game" in the social sciences. It moves freely across the boundaries of academic disciplines as well as nation-states. The pioneers of comparative politics, from Aristotle to Alexis de Tocqueville, were born too long ago to have had their thoughts confined by the narrow boundaries of a single academic discipline, or by a single national culture. We have tried to follow the example of such pioneers, drawing upon concepts from three academic disciplines—politics, economics, and sociology —as well as from the experience of two continents. Only in this way could we capture the reality of a political economy problem that belongs to society as a whole.*

In crossing international boundaries, students of comparative politics become members of an invisible university that is the more stimulating because its members live in different countries. The rewards drawn are commensurate with the uncertainties of contemporary travel, and the unwelcomeness of absences from family.

While this book is the sole responsibility of two authors, the effort involved in research and writing on both sides of the

---

* For a justification of our methodology, see Richard Rose, "Disciplined Research and Undisciplined Problems," *International Social Science Journal* 29 (1976): 1, 99–121; and Richard Rose, "Why Comparative Policy Studies?" *Policy Studies Journal* 1 (1972): 1, 14–17.

Acknowledgments

Atlantic inevitably required institutional support. Our research in comparative public policy was initially supported by separate grants to each of us from the Ford Foundation. Richard Rose's was awarded in his role as Secretary of the Committee on Political Sociology of the International Political Science and International Sociological Associations. Committee members have always set high standards for intellectual rigor and fellowship. Guy Peters was a joint recipient at Emory University, Atlanta, of a Ford grant to analyze the quality of life in North American and European cities. The two authors met when the United States-United Kingdom Educational Commission awarded a visiting Fulbright professorship to Peters for research at the University of Strathclyde in 1975–76. In the long nights of a Scottish winter we had ample time to talk together, and discover the mutuality of interest leading to this book.

The institutional mechanisms by which comparative research is advanced are multiple, and depend heavily upon the imagination and good will of individuals therein. A founding member of the Committee on Political Sociology, Giovanni Sartori, then of Florence and now of Stanford University, provided initial stimulus and encouragement to ponder the consequences of overloaded government. Rudolf Wildenmann, Rector of the University of Mannheim, organized the conference at the Werner-Riemens Stiftung, Bad Homburg, that provoked the idea. An Anglo-American work group on The Crisis of the Welfare State, organized by Arnold J. Heidenheimer and Theodore Marmor on behalf of the Council of European Studies, confronted us with the pressures for government to spend more and more. Richard Rose's spell as a visiting fellow at The Brookings Institution, Washington, D.C., in 1976 afforded an opportunity to listen to economists seeking technical solutions to the problems discussed herein. Rose's residence at the European University Institute, Florence, in 1977 was especially useful in providing insights into transnational dimensions of political

[*xii*

economy. At the Institute, two Belgian economists, Professor Louis Duquesne de la Vinelle and Visiting Professor E. S. Kirschen, were congenial companions in intellectual travels crossing national and disciplinary boundaries. Officials of the Organization for Economic Cooperation and Development (OECD), Paris, helpfully provided unpublished information, and their data base has made possible the systematic analysis of long-term trends.

In the course of writing this book, we have discussed its ideas at seminars and conferences in all of the six countries studied. Materials from this book were presented at international conferences organized at the European University Institute, Florence, in December 1976; at Berlin, in March 1977; and at Paris, in November 1977, as part of Rose's study of overloaded government, financed by a grant from the Volkswagen Foundation to the European Consortium for Political Research; and at a well-timed Summer School of the Australian Institute of Political Science, Canberra, in January 1978.

Among individuals who have repeatedly discussed ideas of mutual interest, we are particularly indebted to Diane A. Dawson of the Adam Smith Building at Glasgow University, a true professional in analyzing economic concepts and statistics, especially those that do not always align readily with real world problems. Philippe C. Schmitter of the University of Chicago provided incisive criticisms of our argument from a fund of knowledge that is as broad as it is engaged with major problems of the social sciences. Many individuals have contributed to the development of ideas through informal discussions, formal interviews, or written comments on portions of the draft manuscript. They include the Rt. Hon. Joel Barnett MP, Dr. Jeremy Bray MP, James Cornford, J. A. T. Douglas, J. E. S. Hayward, Brian W. Hogwood, Dennis A. Kavanagh, Michael Keating, Rudolf Klein, Jacques Leruez, T. T. Mackie, Alan T. Peacock, Paolo Roberti, Charles Schultze, Robert J. Schweich,

Acknowledgments

Sir Andrew Shonfield, Ezra Suleiman, Alan A. Tait, Daniel Tarschys RM, Gunter Wёhrmann, Aaron Wildavsky, and Jack Wiseman.

In preparing the manuscript for publication, we have benefited from the resources of the Center for the Study of Public Policy at the University of Strathclyde. The manuscript could not have seen the light of day half so quickly but for the specific and general assistance that Mrs. M. McGlone and Mrs. R. West provided for two overloaded professors. Institutional assistance was also provided by the University of Delaware, the Centre for Environmental Studies, London, and Tulane University. As a publisher, Martin Kessler responded promptly and positively to this idea for a basic book, and made many constructive editorial comments.

The main issues of this study involve political judgments about real life problems; they are not confined to the abstract world of that mythical beast, economic man. Therefore it is particularly important to stress that none of the institutions named above is in any way responsible for the ideas contained herein, and that every individual mentioned above disagreed with us about specific points of interpretation, and sometimes about basic premises too.

Since each reader already knows his or her political outlook, it may be useful to mention that of the authors. We are each Democrats from border territories—Missouri and Virginia— with all that implies in terms of complex views that do not fit easily into familiar ideological boxes, whether manufactured in California, New York, London, Paris, or Berlin. We have seen enough at first hand of the ups and downs of politics in the United States and Europe to reject the idea that any one political party or nation has an easy answer to the problems analyzed here. The ideal political system would almost certainly combine some elements borrowed from America, Britain, France, Germany, Italy, and Sweden. But this ideal is not attainable. Each of us should face the fact of where we start from in the here and now.

Richard Rose   Guy Peters
University of Strathclyde   *Tulane University*

Can Government Go Bankrupt?

INTRODUCTION

The End of an Illusion

Let every nation know, whether it wishes us well or ill, that we shall pay any price, bear any burden, meet any hardship, support any friend, oppose any foe to assure the survival and success of liberty. This much we pledge—and more.
President John F. Kennedy,
Inaugural address, 1961

We have learned that more is not necessarily better, that even our great nation has its recognized limits, and that we can neither answer all questions nor solve all problems. We cannot afford to do everything.
President Jimmy Carter,
Inaugural address, 1977

SOMETHING is happening to government and to our faith in government, after a generation of expectations in excess. With the confidence of riches behind him, President Kennedy could proclaim that the United States had infinite resources to spend in pursuit of global aims. And President Johnson could launch his war on poverty by assuring Americans that government had "the abundance and the ability to free every man from hopeless want." [1] The Viet Nam War also expressed this boundless confidence of America's governors in an economy that could produce both more guns *and* more butter. The era climaxed with the ultimate in technology: landing a man on the moon. Man's control of matter was displayed before the universe. It was a triumph of government as well as astrophysics, driven by White House ambitions and brought about by innovative bureaucrats of the National Aeronautics and Space Administration, translating great aspirations into real achievements.

Today, people who once looked to government to resolve problems no longer look to it with confidence. The global economic recession of the 1970s has deflated expectations everywhere. The devaluation of the once almighty dollar in August 1971 symbolized the end of America's economic hegemony, just as surely as defeat in Viet Nam marked the end of its military hegemony. The years since the devaluation have witnessed inflation, economic stagnation, and unemployment far beyond the government's expectations or control. By the time of the 1976 American Presidential campaign, both the incumbent Gerald Ford and the challenger Jimmy Carter were proclaiming that government had neither the skills nor the money to do everything that might be demanded of it. President Carter's Inaugural address echoed John F. Kennedy's phrasing, but rejected his boundless optimism, concluding, "We cannot afford to do everything."

Pessimism has replaced optimism as the political fashion of the moment. The difficulties of governing have produced a plethora of books warning of disasters ahead. Americans are invited to contemplate *The Crisis of Democracy*; Britons, *The Future That Doesn't Work*; Frenchmen, *Le Mal Français* (The French Malady); and Germans examine critically the very idea of *Regierbarkeit* (Governability).[2] Sweden, once praised as a model of the "middle way," is now depicted as the home of *The New Totalitarians*.[3] Italians, after generations of political difficulties, now face *La Scelta Italiana* (The Italian Choice), in which none of the alternatives is palatable.[4] Even in Switzerland, long a haven of peace and prosperity, writers today raise the question: *Wird die Schweiz Unregierbar?* (Is Switzerland Becoming Ungovernable?).[5]

When writers refer to *the* crisis of Western government, it is assumed that everyone knows what is meant. But do we? Our difficulties may not consist of a single easily identified and

[4

quickly resolved problem. They may instead reflect the emergence of chronic tensions that can have no resolution, generating an unending series of crises without solutions. Conceivably, the world may be changing less than the way that we think and feel about it. Perhaps talk of crisis only reflects the bankruptcy of language that inflates everyday problems of governing into issues of cosmic significance.

Prophecies of the downfall of civilization are as old as civilization itself. Since the decline and fall of the Roman Empire took centuries to consummate, any announcement of the imminent death of Western civilization is likely to be premature. It can be argued that the troubles of contemporary Western societies are not evidence of an inability to govern, but instead reflect the overloaded expectations of citizens who ask government to do more than any human institution can achieve.[6]

A reasonable person scrutinizes prophecies of doom as severely as promises of eternal abundance. An assertion that the end of the world is nigh no more deserves intellectual respect than a claim that prosperity is "just around the corner," the phrase with which President Herbert Hoover greeted the worldwide depression of the 1930s. In this book we examine theories of hope and despair, and test them against the evidence of events to see whether government's difficulties today are a brief interruption in the march of progress, the portent of greater difficulties ahead, or simply a time of transition in a world that can never be static.

WHAT IS THE PROBLEM?

This book starts from the assumption that there *is* something different and potentially troubling in the world of today. The challenge that faces major Western nations today is a challenge of political economy. It is *political* because it concerns the very authority of government; it is *economic* because a major cause is the failure of national economies to grow as rapidly as government commitments to spend money.

The greatest challenge facing the governors of every Western country today is the maintenance of political authority in the face of economic difficulties greater than at any time since the worldwide depression of the 1930s. Political authority is a priceless asset. In Western countries we take it for granted that government will do what citizens want, and that citizens will do what government wants. We only worry about political authority when it is absent and disorder reigns, or when it is threatened by authoritarian leaders or popular disaffection.

To suggest that a country with economic difficulties could become ungovernable is literally to talk nonsense. In the career of a political system, a so-called state of ungovernability can only be a temporary phase of anarchy until order is once again established by the voluntary consent of the governed or the coercive actions of governors. A modern Western society can no more do without political authority than it could do without money as a medium of exchange. The question is not whether we shall be governed, but how?

Political bankruptcy is the fate that faces a government that so mismanages its economy that it loses popular consent as well as economic effectiveness. The distinctive feature of a politically bankrupt regime is that citizens are indifferent to it. An indifferent citizen is not up in arms against authority; instead, he just shrugs his shoulders and turns his back on government, using the sophistication of the city streets or the wiles of a peasant to evade government's commands.

Indifference to authority is now widespread in the home, in schools, and in religion. There is no reason why it cannot become manifest in politics as well. An indifferent citizen will do what government wishes if it is in his interest to do so, or if government convincingly threatens punishment for inaction. Otherwise, authority will be ignored at will. Civic indifference offers a cheap, easy, and safe alternative to organized rebellion for individuals who no longer have a positive allegiance to their regime, yet can see no satisfactory alternative.

A politically bankrupt government is not consigned to the dustbin of history, like a regime overthrown by violence. Politicians remain in office, but they are bereft of authority, existing in a limbo of ineffectiveness. The weakness of government will be welcomed by those who see its economic failings as the cause of their personal troubles. Yet every citizen will suffer some loss, for a bankrupt government cannot maintain the education, health, pensions, and other services that citizens expect as the benefits of public policy.

A government cannot go bankrupt in the normal commercial sense of the term. A business firm that goes bankrupt can be dissolved and its assets sold for the benefit of its creditors. An individual who goes bankrupt suffers temporary financial difficulties, but a court order can legally discharge a debtor from future obligations for past overspending. The bad news is that, unlike an individual citizen, a government cannot go bankrupt and be discharged from responsibility for its past liabilities. A government carries its past commitments forward into the future. Even when a regime collapses under military defeat, its successor is expected to assume many of its obligations.[7] A politically bankrupt government can remain in business—but not as before.

In the Age of Empires, weak African or Asian countries did go into bankruptcy, becoming colonies of creditor nations that formally annexed their territory, or else, as in Imperial China or Egypt under the Khedive, extracted trade and military concessions from governments unable to meet their debts to foreign lenders.[8] The last time a European nation temporarily lost its sovereignty because of indebtedness was in 1922, when French and Belgian troops occupied the industrial Ruhr in an attempt to coerce Germany into continuing reparations payments for the losses of war. The effort failed and failed spectacularly.[9]

Contemporary politicians have no wish to take over the responsibilities of a government if its leaders and its citizens are indifferent to their fiscal future. When New York City faced fiscal bankruptcy in 1975, both the state and the federal government did their best to keep the municipal government in business, notwithstanding its manifest fiscal shortcomings, for to have forced New York City into bankruptcy would have compelled state and federal officials to attempt what was beyond the power of the city's natives, namely, managing its finances effectively.[10] For better or worse, a national government faced with fiscal bankruptcy cannot expect other countries to take over its political liabilities, as might have happened a century ago. It must live with the future consequences of its past mistakes.

BANKRUPTCY IS NOT INEVITABLE

To govern is to choose. No government would consciously choose political bankruptcy. But this can be the unintended consequence of decisions taken for short-term political advantage. To avoid sliding into political bankruptcy, politicians must be aware of the unhappy consequences of following the line of least resistance when faced with immediate and hard decisions about their political economy. To understand the causes and consequences of contemporary difficulties does not make them any less unpleasant when the cost of long-term security is short-term sacrifice. Because the actions necessary to avoid bankruptcy are hard for politicians to take, there is no assurance that politicians will adopt unpopular policies in order to avoid worse in the future.

It is past success that today puts government at risk. The first part of this book analyzes the growth of the mixed-economy welfare state and the role of this state in creating treble affluence: a steady growth in the aggregate national product, in the benefits of public policy, and in real take-home pay. Every member of society has benefited from the growth of government programs, whether as a recipient of cash welfare benefits, as an employee of the welfare state, or as a businessman with government as his chief customer. But because the benefits of public policy must be paid for by taxes, every member of society also pays some of the costs of the contemporary welfare state.

The second part of this book addresses the trillion-dollar question of politics today: can government continue on a business-as-usual basis if the economy no longer produces the goods as in the past? The answer of this book is no. The reason is simple: past commitments to future spending threaten to overload government, requiring it to spend more money than can be provided by the fruits of economic growth. As and when this happens, politicians will be faced with the full force of the economic aphorism, "There is no such thing as a free lunch." Government must then put the brakes on public spending or else cut the take-home pay of its citizens. If it decides to cut rather than protect take-home pay, it faces the prospect of political bankruptcy.

If past trends continue, American politicians have upwards of a decade in which to act before political bankruptcy becomes an immediate threat. The same is true of the governors of Germany and France. By contrast, in Italy, Sweden, and Britain, the threat of bankruptcy is near at hand.

The first instinct of politicians faced with a problem is to buy time. But papering over the problem by inflation does not increase national wealth; it simply makes inflation the immediate anxiety of citizens. Governments can try, like King Canute, to hold back the inevitable waves of price and wage increases. But even if a nation's citizens continue to support an economically incompetent government, foreigners can effectively vote their lack of confidence by selling its currency short in the international money market.

In the concluding chapters, we review the alternative choices of a government forced to accept the limits of its political economy. The easiest course is also the least attractive: to do nothing and drift into political bankruptcy. Secondly, it could choose to make government programs sacrosanct, giving absolute priority to providing more and more benefits of public policy, even though the resulting tax increases would produce a cut in take-home pay. The third alternative is easy to identify but difficult to carry out: protecting real take-home pay by limiting the growth of spending on public policies.

We do not raise unpleasant prospects because of a taste for doom-mongering or an aversion to the mixed-economy welfare state. We do so because our world is full of threatening as well as hopeful signs. Unfortunately, the mention of undesirable alternatives risks an unthinking response.* Yet the bankruptcy of political authority is not made less likely by those who search vainly for a philosopher's stone to resolve all problems, or turn their backs on the future and utter the most disconcerting of reassuring words: "It can't happen here." Fortunately, to identify a risk is also to show that the worst is not inevitable. Government *can* cope with the problems that we describe, but only if politicians have the will to recognize and respond to them for what they are.

In a democratic age, one cannot assume that problems involving ordinary people are beyond their understanding. Be-

* After reading a draft of this manuscript, a perceptive social scientist wrote the authors from Paris, "Politically, I have not the slightest doubt that the book will be used *and misused* by those who want to look for a simple thesis and a simple remedy."

cause the subject matter of this book is important to ordinary citizens as well as to social science specialists, we have written it in straightforward language. Obscurity in phrasing invites obscurity of thought, and an excess of academic abstractions can encourage remoteness from reality. This study is not an economic treatise. It concentrates instead upon those uncomfortable and nonquantifiable political problems that economists usually ignore.

The chief issues facing government today are not abstruse points of economic theory but gut questions of practical politics. Who is to bear the cost of letting present trends continue, or the cost of changing public policies? Which party is to risk electoral defeat by promising voters hard times rather than happy times? In a democratic political system, politicians cannot keep these issues to themselves. Having shared in the benefits of affluence, governors and governed must together pay the costs if the cupboard is someday found bare.

A CHALLENGE TO EVERYONE

No citizen can be indifferent to the difficulties of government, because today each person's livelihood depends directly or indirectly upon the success of government economic policies. When the economy is in trouble, a businessman worries about falling profits and rising taxes, and a factory worker is anxious about losing his job because no one will buy the goods he makes. Students worry about the value of their education in the market place and what kind of job, if any, they will be able to find after graduation. Because of inflation, many people find that while their nominal wages go up, their real standard of living goes down.

Can Government Go Bankrupt?

When the economy goes as much awry as it has done in the 1970s, citizens lose confidence in the elected leaders and technocratic experts who are supposed to be managing it on their behalf. National leaders have not succeeded in directing the economy as their followers want. Economic experts have planned what individuals ought to earn and buy, but not what they can earn and buy. Differences between ordinary individuals and the politicians and economists managing affairs in their interest cannot be explained away as a mere failure of communication. It may be a sign that something is wrong with the institutions of representative democracy. Or there may be a conflict between what citizens want as individuals (e.g., higher wages and living standards) and what they want collectively (e.g., stable prices and full employment).

However much abuse individuals heap upon government, they cannot do without it. If economic problems were only the result of individual failings, a person could work harder, take a new job, move where the economy was booming, or simply worry less. If the problems were only the fault of individual politicians or parties, a citizen could respond by voting for a change, whether turning to a conventional party of left or right, or gambling that an unconventional party might be better suited to deal with novel problems. Individuals may adopt either or both strategies in an effort to find shelter from the difficulties of their national economy. But the consequences of inflation, unemployment, and rising taxes will find them out nonetheless.

Politicians cannot be indifferent to the loss of public confidence in their capabilities, for an erosion of popular confidence could ultimately undermine political authority itself. In the affluent 1960s, many thinkers assumed that government's success in managing the economy would strengthen its political authority.[11] An unpleasant implication of such reasoning is that economic recession could lead to a decline in political authority, with threats to material prosperity becoming political threats as well.

Privately, politicians in every national capital are anxious about what has gone wrong with their ability to give the people what they want. A stoic British Cabinet minister can define the problem as evidence that "the laws that we studied in the textbooks of economics have not been suspended just because our party is in office." An aggressive White House staff man can blame a President's difficulties on the system, asserting that "Everybody believes in democracy until he gets to the White House and then you begin to believe in dictatorship because it's so hard to get things done." [12] A quick-witted politician such as Pierre Trudeau, Prime Minister of Canada, can charge that government appears inadequate only because it is today expected to achieve the impossible. "I deny that my own government is weak. If I asked you to lift this hotel and you couldn't do it, that wouldn't mean you were weak. It would mean the hotel was too heavy. That's the way it is with government. We all face problems which we cannot easily solve." [13]

Economists too face anxieties; the world recession of the 1970s has created a crisis in economics as well as in national economies. For a generation, many economists have believed that the intellectual innovations of J. M. Keynes assured an end to economic depression, and they looked forward to the glowing prospects of unlimited growth. When launching the attack that overturned the conventional wisdom of the 1930s, Keynes had savagely described the so-called "practical men" presiding helplessly over the worldwide depression as "the slaves of some defunct economist." [14] As we face the unexpected troubles of the 1970s, we must remember that now Keynes too is a defunct economist, having died in 1946. Today his teachings suffer the vulgarization of Holy Writ, as epigoni and critics debate what Keynes really meant.

A conventionally optimistic view of the contemporary difficulties of the political economy is that they reflect "an unusual bunching of unfortunate disturbances unlikely to be repeated on the same scale, the impact of which was compounded by some avoidable errors in economic policy." [15] This is the conclusion of a major international report to the Organization for Economic Cooperation and Development (OECD) produced by a group of well-known economists headed by Professor Paul A. McCracken, former economic advisor to Presidents Eisenhower and Nixon. Left-wing economists interpret the world recession of the 1970s as another sign of Karl Marx's long-awaited collapse of capitalism. Yet left-wing economists are conspicuously silent about how a Socialist or Communist takeover of the means of production would reconcile the basic problem of matching potentially infinite human wants and inevitably finite resources. After all, Eastern European governments too face big problems of effectively managing their economies and governing with consent. In the words of a sympathetic Swedish critic, new-left economists lack "an awareness of the enormous difficulties involved in solving the problems which arise in any social and economic system." [16]

Some analyses of contemporary difficulties stand athwart conventional categories of left and right. For example, Peter Jay, the British political economist appointed Ambassador to the United States in 1977, has argued that "the very survival of democracy hangs by a gossamer thread" because of "the gap between the minimum economically necessary and the maximum politically possible." Unless a radical change is made by Western nations, introducing workers' control in industry and strengthening consumer sovereignty, Jay forecasts ". . . the dread familiar cycle of multiplying ineffectual regulations, rampant inflation, falling employment, industrial decay, administrative breakdown, social and political chaos, the emergence of a strong man of the right, revolution, and a self-perpetuating nominally left-wing oligarchy." [17]

The threat of political bankruptcy is worldwide. At a time

when governments need greater growth to meet the rising cost of public policy, the global recession of the 1970s confronts every government with the prospect of lower rates of economic growth in future. A generation of free and expanding international trade has made all major Western nations interdependent through the multilateral exchange of imports and exports. To meet the rising cost of imports such as oil, a country must export more. Yet some Western nations, the United States and Britain for example, find that their exports are increasingly less competitive internationally. Successful exporters, such as Germany, worry because their customers find it more and more difficult to pay for the goods that they want to buy from them. The rapid fluctuations in the exchange rates of currencies, increasing the international value of the Deutsche mark and devaluing the dollar, reflect the resulting imbalance. No national government can by itself resolve its economic difficulties in a world of economic interdependence.

When economic problems are global, they cannot be explained as the fault of individual politicians or national character. Nor can they be resolved by the actions of individual citizens or by the legislature of a single nation. If Americans or Europeans had the choice between using their votes to change the government of their own country or to change the leaders of the Organization of Petroleum Exporting Countries (OPEC), they would do their own country more immediate good by breaking up OPEC.

To understand how great the risk to public policy is in any one country we must compare it with other lands. To tell citizens of Boston or Bonn that they are better off than citizens of Bristol or Bologna may not cause general satisfaction, but it does provide a comparative basis for assessing how well a country is doing. This book systematically compares six major Western countries: America, Britain, France, Germany, Italy, and Sweden. All are democratic and all are affluent. In terms of gross national product, America ranks first in the world, and

Can Government Go Bankrupt?

Germany, France, Britain, and Italy are among the world's eight richest nations. Because of its small population, Sweden has less total wealth, but Sweden now ranks ahead of America in gross national product per head. The average Swede has become the richest citizen in the Western world. Collectively, the 235 million people of these five rich European nations and the 215 million people of the United States dominate the political and economic affairs of the Western industrial world. The national problems of the six countries analyzed here are of international significance, and international problems have an immediate domestic impact.*

The world recession of the 1970s has divided the major nations of the Western world. Faced with a common challenge, countries have not made a common response. Politicians can learn how to avoid mistakes by studying the example of countries where things have gone wrong. In the 1970s, Britain and Italy have competed for the dubious distinction of being the best example of how *not* to manage a political economy. For example, in a farewell interview as President, Gerald Ford cautioned Americans, "It would be tragic for this country if we went down the same path and ended up with the same problems that Great Britain has." [18]

Insofar as comparisons emphasize differences between major Western nations, citizens of politically successful countries can take comfort from the fact that they are not as others, and citizens of misgoverned lands can look abroad for instruction. Insofar as comparison emphasizes common failings, we should not ask "What's wrong with my country?" but rather "What's wrong with democratic government everywhere?"

---

* Because this book is a study of the problems of democratic political systems, we do not attempt to incorporate analysis of Japan, with its very different past political tradition, or the Soviet Union, with very different contemporary political and economic institutions.

CHAPTER 1

Undermining Political Authority

In some measure, governability and democracy are warring concepts.
Crozier, Huntington, and Watanuki,
The Crisis of Democracy, 1975

To restore confidence is perhaps the most important though least tangible facet of the tasks facing government.
OECD, *The McCracken Report*, 1977

THE MISMANAGEMENT of the economy only costs a nation money; the mismanagement of the polity threatens a government with the loss of political consent as well. In political terms, the government's direction of the economy is but a means to a more general end, namely, maintaining political authority.[1] In the past decade, governors of many Western nations have realized that this authority is vulnerable. It has been challenged by confrontations between radical students and police everywhere from Berkeley to Berlin, by *les événements* in Paris in 1968, by the intimidation and murder of judges, public officials, and journalists in Italy, and by civil war in Northern Ireland.

When ineffectiveness in managing the economy makes citi-

[17]

zens indifferent, then political bankruptcy is at hand. A politically bankrupt regime suffers from the tyranny of weakness; it is crippled but not destroyed. Conventional analyses of government assume that whoever controls government can effectively make citizens do what government wants. Our approach emphasizes the political weakness of government once citizens become indifferent to its demands and cease to rely on it to realize their wants. In a politically bankrupt regime the major division is not between different parties competing for office, but between those who are meant to govern and the mass of citizens indifferent to who governs.

In this chapter, we examine the conditions that could cause the economic inadequacies of government to undermine political authority. The first section explains why it is no longer meaningful to think of separate political and economic systems and why the growing power of political as against market choices has made the authority of government more vulnerable. The second section identifies the limits of political economy and how a government may try to exceed these limits in vain efforts to consume more than it produces. If a government persists indefinitely in such a course, it faces the prospect of political bankruptcy. Because this outcome is no more inevitable than it is desirable, the concluding section reviews the choices open to a government wishing to safeguard its political authority.

FROM MARKET CHOICE TO POLITICAL CHOICE

Since the Second World War there has been a great shift from market choice to political choice in every major Western society. The economy is no longer thought to be governed by natural inequalities, impersonal fate, or a vengeful God. Instead, the economy is considered the responsibility of the government of the day, and governments are expected to benefit their citizens by avoiding depression and promoting economic growth. Sanctioned by popular election as well as law, the state has become the central directing institution of contemporary society.

The century-old rhetoric of Capitalist and Socialist ideologies is hardly meaningful in the contemporary Western world. We do not live in societies characterized by the stark alternatives of individual choice in the Capitalist market place, or decisions made by the organized political choices of a Socialist state. We live in a mixed economy, in which government and market decisions are interrelated. At one extreme, some sectors of the economy depend upon private production for private consumption (e.g., baked goods or clothing). At the other extreme, there are government factories producing goods for government consumption (e.g., the mint or, in European countries, arms factories). In one important intermediate sector, government-owned industries produce goods for sale to private consumers (e.g., electricity or nationalized airways), and in another, private manufacturers sell their goods to government (e.g., American manufacturers of space equipment, or European doctors supplying medical care to a national health service). A significant portion of every major Western economy is in each of these four categories. Moreover, groupings are not rigid, for private firms may have both private- and public-sector customers, and the same is true of government-owned firms.

The contemporary mixed economy is an ideological hybrid. It is conservative, insofar as private property and profits remain important in the economy and insofar as the mixed economy strengthens established political institutions. It is liberal, inasmuch as free trade between nations is encouraged as a stimulus of economic growth and as a surety of peace between formerly warring nations. It is Socialist, because government makes major economic decisions that pervasively influence the economy and allocates a large portion of the national product. A variety of compound catchwords have been coined in efforts to describe our contemporary political economy. One author refers to a "conservative socialist" state, another to "laborist capitalism," and a third to a "business-government state." [2]

The wealth created by the mixed economy has financed the growth of the welfare state. Today, citizenship underwrites an individual's well-being from womb to tomb, for public programs guarantee such fundamentals of individual welfare as schools, hospitals, and a pension in old age. Anything that disturbs the mixed economy endangers the financial basis of the welfare state.

The rise of the mixed-economy welfare state has greatly expanded the scope of government. The nineteenth-century Nightwatchman state did not do much, yet the things it did attempt—maintaining an Army and Navy, building roads, and collecting customs—were usually well within its competence. Today politicians of every political color or none are ready to proclaim a war on poverty, a war on crime, or even a global war on want, and to devise laws pledging government to seek full employment and economic growth, as if legislating for wealth was bound to make it appear.

The growth of government's responsibilities has not been matched by an equivalent growth in its capabilities. In the days of the Nightwatchman state, government needed only simple technologies to do such things as build bridges or hang criminals. But many goals of the contemporary mixed-economy welfare state cannot be achieved by any engineering technology; they result from complex social and economic relationships that government can influence but not control. For example, welfare is not the product of a welfare department; it results from a "cooperative game" in which those being helped must play their part. Education not only requires school buildings and teachers, but also students willing to learn. Health not only requires hospitals and doctors to care for the ill, but also individuals willing to follow a healthy routine in their daily lives.

The total value of all the goods and services produced by a nation's economy is the result of an infinite variety of actions, some determined or influenced by government, but others reflecting choices made within the domestic or international market place. Politicians do not decide about the economy; instead, they preside over it.

By expanding their commitments, contemporary Western governments have exchanged the authority of command for the uncertainties of influence. Governments no longer concentrate upon doing the things that large organizations can effectively do. Instead, they try to influence social processes that are only imperfectly understood by public officials or social scientists. While government can influence these processes through inputs of money, manpower, and laws, these inputs do not by themselves determine the outputs of society. The social engineer may regard it as bad news that societies are "incapable of being shaped"; [3] but citizens may regard this as good news, a reminder that there are limits to the ability of any government to gain total control of society.

Even the most efficient and imaginative government finds that when it seeks to determine what the economy does, its authority is vulnerable from three directions—from below, sideways, and from above.

Governments are immediately vulnerable to the erosion of their electoral base if they fail to make the economy produce what they have promised. But the governors of the world's wealthiest country can no more vote themselves immunity from the buffetings of worldwide economic trends than citizens of the poorest country can vote themselves immunity from poverty. Voters can turn against the governing party of the day, whatever its political color, if the economy for which it is formally responsible heads downwards. Since the 1973 oil crisis, the governing party of every major Western nation has lost votes, and in America, Britain, and Sweden, it has lost office as well.

To register disgust with all party alternatives, citizens may vote with their feet, using market-place pressures to defend or advance their economic interests. In the market, an individual does not need to rely upon the imperfections of representative democracy; persons can make their own choices, deciding what to buy, where to work, and whether to follow politicians' exhortations or to spend money when saving is commended and to ask for higher wages when wage restraint is government policy.

Governments are also vulnerable to a sideways leakage of authority because they require the cooperation of business and labor to steer the economy in desired directions. As governments try to extend their influence upon business and trade unions, these organizations simultaneously seek to influence government. Corporations want favorable tax treatment before investing in accord with national plans, and unions want government to increase welfare spending as the price of cooperating in programs of wage restraint.

The interpenetration of government, business, and unions reflects the interdependence of major societal organizations in a mixed economy. It is not a simple transfer of power. Government exchanges its unilateral power for a share of influence in a complex network of interdependent institutions. Bargaining replaces sovereign authority as the means of resolving differences between these major institutions of society.

The leakage of authority upwards is the result of conscious national political decisions to promote free trade in goods and money through such means as the General Agreement on Tariffs and Trade, the International Monetary Fund, and the

European Economic Community. The promoters of free trade seek both peace and prosperity by encouraging economic inter-dependence and political cooperation. The internationalization of trade has brought great economic benefits to the world's major trading nations, and to the multinational corporations that have grown up in their wake. Politically, it has created a world market vastly beyond the power of any one nation to control.

The opening of economies to international influence has happened concurrently with governments taking responsibility for the management of their national economy. National governments are now more and more involved in economic affairs at a time when their economy is less and less sovereign.[4] Today, if a government wishes to stimulate the economy to produce a pre-election boom, it may find that this will also precipitate a crisis of confidence among foreign holders of its currency. If a government wishes to protect a depressed industry to reduce unemployment, the tariffs or import quotas that it considers may violate international treaty agreements, and it may find its exporters threatened with retaliation if the tariffs or quotas are put into effect. A rueful British Cabinet minister remarked, when asked to do something that would promote short-term domestic popularity, "We can't. Too many people are watching us now."

The shift from market choice to political choice has bene-fited both governors and governed. Citizens have enjoyed higher standards of living, and governors have gained credit from the provision of many welfare benefits. However, the economic recession of the 1970s now forces politicians to face the full logic of their position. When public policy and take-home pay are at risk, politicians who claimed the credit in good times must also expect to take the blame for bad times.

ON TRYING TO CONSUME MORE
THAN WE PRODUCE

If democratic politics is about giving people what they want, then economics is about telling people what they can have with the resources at hand. In an era of economic growth, politics is a happy science, promising to give people more and more of the goods that contribute to a better life. Economics is always a dismal science, for its central assumption is that everybody cannot have everything at once. The relative scarcity of goods forces people to limit what they consume, for there is no such thing as a free lunch.

In managing the mixed-economy welfare state, politicians must learn to balance the competing claims of the happy science of politics and the dismal science of economics. Economics sets limits within which politicians can make effective choices. While there are no restrictions upon how a nation's resources may be spent, there are restrictions upon how much can be spent. The votes that give politicians office do not assure them the resources needed to meet the expectations raised in the enthusiasm or desperation of an election campaign.

The simplest way to think about the limits of political economy is to visualize the total national product of a society as a pie. The national pie can come in many different sizes and it can be divided many different ways, but once it is cut and the pieces consumed, there is no more. Politicians are sometimes prepared to give away slices of national income that may not be there. For example, in the 1976 Presidential campaign, Gerald Ford and Jimmy Carter each made generous promises, Ford emphasizing the prospect of tax cuts, and Carter emphasizing new public programs without a tax increase. Both candidates were relying upon future economic growth to underwrite these benefits. In the words of a *New York Times* headline, "Ford, Carter Plan Spending Money They May Not Have." [5]

Money measures the size of the national pie. To say this is not to deny the advantage of ample oil and mineral resources, or of such intangible assets as social altruism or a well-educated population. But a government that has a well-educated citizenry draws no benefit if large numbers of educated people are unemployed rather than working at jobs commanding high salaries and paying high taxes. Money has the great advantage of being fungible, that is, it can be used for anything that money can buy. Whereas a small Arab sheikdom has a limited appetite for petroleum products, it has a virtually unlimited appetite for the things that oil money can buy.

Government has first claim upon the national product by virtue of its political sovereignty. It takes the first slice of the national pie to meet the costs of public policy, which encompasses the public money spent to provide a manifold of government programs covering everything from aerospace to zoos. While the importance of a policy cannot be judged solely by the amount of money spent upon it, we should not lose sight of the fact that nearly everything government wants to do has some cost. The most distinctive activities of the contemporary state, its welfare programs, are especially costly commitments.

To carry out its policies, twentieth-century government cannot rely upon nineteenth-century philanthropy or upon the medieval practice of *corvée*, that is, labor given government as a supplement to taxes. A modern government must levy taxes to gain the money needed to pay teachers and nurses, and to pay cash benefits to old-age pensioners and the unemployed. The costs of public policy reflect past decisions more than the current choices of the government of the day.* Spending com-

---

* Chapters 5 and 10 explain in detail why our model of the growth of public policy is grounded upon an observed propensity of government to spend more and more on public policy, a "ghost within the machine," rather than upon a putative popular expectation of more and more public benefits.

mitments are embodied in thousands of pages of already enacted laws. In theory, a newly elected government might annul the laws of its predecessors. In practice, few politicians wish to take away specific benefits, for the recipients will protest their loss. The beneficiaries of government programs range from aeronautical engineers to zoologists, and embrace the whole of society several times over.

The other slice of the national pie constitutes the take-home pay of citizens, the earnings that individuals have as of right after income tax and compulsory social security taxes are subtracted to meet the costs of public policy. An individual does not regard take-home pay as a leftover, but rather as the deserved reward of individual effort and skill. Whereas the benefits of public policy are determined by collective political choice, take-home pay is preeminently a private good, to be spent as each individual wishes. This is not to argue that individual choice is invariably superior to collective choice, but simply to emphasize that it is different.

In a mixed economy, government and individuals each claim a part of the national pie. The taxes that a government levies on gross earnings limit a citizen's take-home pay, for individuals only control that portion of their earnings that government does not appropriate in taxes. Because we are concerned with the control of the national product and not with individual consumption, cash transfer payments (e.g., pensions and unemployment) are part of the cost of public policy. To provide such transfer payments, a government must first levy taxes that reduce gross earnings. The consumption financed by government transfer payments depends upon government decisions, and not upon market-place earnings. And at any one point in time, these cash welfare benefits require the government to reduce the disposable income of some citizens in order to increase that of others.

The first claim of the tax man to earnings is analogous to the *droit du seigneur* of medieval times, the claim of the lord of the manor to spend the first night with the newly married bride of a vassal. Every individual must pay some taxes as part of the dues of citizenship. For example, old-age pensioners pay tribute to government every time they buy goods subject to sales tax. In the case of gasoline, tobacco, or drink, the government tax can be greater than the cost of manufacturing the product. Taxes can be levied even in the absence of profits. Sales taxes and European Value-Added Taxes give government a percentage of the gross revenue of financial transactions, whether those involved are making a profit or loss.

The limits of the political economy can be summed up in a simple equation:

$$\textit{The National Product} =$$
$$\textit{The Costs of Public Policy} + \textit{Take-Home Pay.}$$

With a given national product, government can only increase take-home pay if it cuts the costs of public policy. Alternatively, it can increase spending on public policy by cutting the take-home pay of citizens. It cannot provide more public programs and more take-home pay if the national pie remains constant in size. As and when the national product grows faster than the established commitments of public policy and take-home pay, government is in the fortunate position of being able to provide more of both.[6]

Government today is responsible for allocating the national product between the costs of public policy and take-home pay, as well as for the size of the national pie. When sharing out the national product, politicians are squeezed from two sides.[7] On the one side, they face claims from citizens concerned about their take-home pay, while on the other, they face demands from parties and pressure groups to provide more tax-financed public benefits. In the short run, it is politically appealing to spend more money to provide more public benefits. But government must eventually increase taxes to pay for those benefits. Politicians are not on top of the economy; they are caught in the middle, wanting the popularity of delivering more benefits without the unpopularity of exacting higher taxes.

The standard economic prescription to resolve these conflicting pressures is to invest more money to make the national product grow. Increased investment can be financed in a number of ways: by savings accumulated from take-home pay, by public expenditure, by government lending to private industry, or by foreign loans or grants. Insofar as investment requires individual consumers to forego immediate public and private benefits, it is politically less appealing than other uses of the national product. Yet only if investment continually increases the national product can take-home pay and spending on public policy grow. Some economists argue that the growth of spending on public policy actually makes it harder for the national product to grow.[8]

Managing the political economy is a continuing process that cannot be summarized in the annual budget of government or in a single year's national income accounts. Politicians are not expected to balance their books at the end of each fiscal year; laws that require American cities to do this generate a pathological pattern of public expenditure, as public officials imaginatively meet the letter of the law while evading its spirit.[9] Governments can finance deficits by borrowing from their own citizens, if citizens will devote some of their take-home pay to government bonds rather than to personal consumption. Governments can also finance deficits by borrowing money from abroad, thus temporarily augmenting their national product by importing that of other countries. Governments can use their power of printing money to invoke the illusion of economic growth, but a big increase in the money supply does not produce a big increase in the goods and services that citizens can consume.

Just as a government needs the consent of its citizens, so too it needs credit, whether from its own citizens or foreign banks, if it is to continue to borrow money. In principle, there is no limit to the amount of money that a government might borrow. In practice, the limit is set by the amount of credibility that lenders grant to the government. Once credibility is lost, a crisis of political economy abruptly follows, as New York City learned in 1975.

Government borrowing does not free politicians from the constraints of the dismal science of economics. Loans made to government at one point in time must later be paid back by a growing national product, by an increase in taxes levied upon citizens, or by new loans. The more money a government borrows, the more the costs of public policy will rise, for more must be paid in interest on government loans.

Managing the political economy is a continuing feedback process. At a given moment, a government may face one of the following three positions:

1. *A fiscal dividend:* When the national product is growing faster than the fixed commitments of public policy, the government of the day is in the happy position of having a fiscal dividend to spend. Politicians have the congenial task of deciding how much should be spent collectively to finance the growth of public policy and how much should be left in the pockets of individuals as extra take-home pay. The growth of the national pie means that there can be something for everybody.

2. *No dividend:* If there is zero growth in the national product, or if growth only meets fixed commitments to public policy and take-home pay, there is no surplus to distribute. In such circumstances, the easiest thing to do politically is to confirm the status quo, and hope that the national product soon produces another fiscal dividend. A no-dividend situation is unlikely, for the margin of error in human affairs makes it virtually impossible to achieve so fine a balance by design.

3. *An overloaded political economy:* A political economy is overloaded when the national product grows more slowly than the costs of public policy and the claims of take-home pay, and there

Can Government Go Bankrupt?

is not enough money in hand to meet both public and private claims. Because raising and spending money is a continuous process, there can be a time when a government is temporarily overloaded, whether from an excess of spending zeal directed at winning an election, an unexpected downturn in the economy, or public deficits intentionally created to prime the Keynesian engine of economic growth. But no government can indefinitely spend more than its country produces. Sooner or later, it must reduce the excess load. It can do this by the politically appealing course of increasing the size of the national pie, or by the politically unpalatable course of reducing spending on public policy or cutting take-home pay or doing both.

The direction in which the political economy is heading is as important as its position at a given moment. If politicians correctly interpret danger signals, an overloaded economy can, with temporary discomfort, be guided to safety by controlling the growing cost of government programs, thus matching government's commitments to resources. Equally, a seemingly prosperous system can be headed for trouble, if commitments race ahead of the growth of the national product. In Britain, for example, for more than two decades governments have specialized in rapid reversals of economic policies, to prevent the full logic of their dilemma choices—to stimulate growth and overload the economy, or to reduce overloading and depress growth—from becoming "too disastrous."

"There is a lot of ruin in a nation," Benjamin Disraeli once remarked. Politicians responsible for steering the economy expect to be blown off course from time to time as events beyond their control turn risk into failure. Sooner or later, however, a government trying to consume more than it produces must deal with the causes of overloading by returning to what economists would call an "equilibrium." But the use of so antiseptic a term should not lead one to overlook the political problems that face a government trying to fit the growing costs of public policy to a finite national product.

[30

THE PROSPECT OF POLITICAL BANKRUPTCY

Political authority rests upon two essentials in the relationship between governors and governed—effectiveness and consent.[10] As long as a government enjoys both the consent of its citizens and effectiveness in action, it is a fully legitimate regime. While no government can expect to be completely effective or enjoy the consent of every one of its citizens, this is the ideal by which it is judged. Many regimes fall far short of this ideal. If a government lacks the consent of its citizens and also loses effectiveness, it will be repudiated. Most modern European states have arisen from the ruins of a predecessor regime repudiated by external invasion or internal revolt. A regime that loses popular consent may coerce citizens to do what it wants. Eastern European countries offer examples of coercive regimes exercising effectiveness without consent.

Effectiveness is the first concern of governors. Government is not only about good intentions; it is also about getting things done. In many parts of the world today effectiveness is the sole concern of governors; instead of courting consent through popular measures, a regime strengthens its army and police. To exercise political authority, a government must effectively organize control of its own maze of institutions. To be effective in society, government must also raise taxes and allocate money for public policies.

Effectiveness is undermined if governors attempt to spend more than their society can produce. When a political economy becomes overloaded, public policies lose effectiveness, because the total resources allocated are inadequate to their purposes. The more activities a government finances, the greater the risk of organized overcomplexity, with one hand of an N-handed octopus not knowing what the other hands (or other octopuses) are doing. In addition, the more policies a government pursues, the greater the risk that its manifold of programs will incorporate all the contradictions of society.

Consent is the primary concern of citizens. In a modern democratic society, individuals are not automatically prepared to do whatever government commands. Only if citizens consent to a regime will they voluntarily comply with its basic laws, whether or not they approve of particular laws or the government of the day. Consent is important to governors too, for when citizens *freely* consent to authority, a government gains effectiveness without coercion or bribes. The consent of citizens characterizes what we think of as good government today. In Germany, it dates only from the success of the Federal Republic founded in 1949. In postwar France and Italy, both right and left have challenged the authority of regimes established in the wake of political dissensus and military defeat. In America, crises in race relations and the Viet Nam War led some Americans to register dissent in the streets. Englishmen cannot take for granted the political authority of the United Kingdom as long as Northern Ireland is governed without consensus and a substantial number of Scottish Nationalists oppose rule from London.

The most obvious challenge to consent consists of rebellion against the regime of the day. The rebellion may be expressed in illegal but not necessarily violent protests, or in violent acts by armed guerrilla groups. Rebels take the authority of the state seriously; they wish to overthrow it and establish another in its place. They seek to undermine a particular regime, but not political authority in general.

Political bankruptcy, by contrast, undermines constitutional authority by joining civic indifference to institutional ineffectiveness, without putting anything else in its place.[11] A politically bankrupt government is not immediately threatened with repudiation; its very weakness limits the antagonism it engenders, and discourages hopes of a successor governing better. A politically bankrupt government differs from a coercive regime, for it lacks the capacity to force citizens to do what they do not want to do. It can still collect a substantial portion of the national product in taxes and spend a lot on public policies, but citizens can scoff at its policies if they choose. An ordinary citizen might prefer the weakness of a politically bankrupt authority to the unrestrained power of a coercive regime. But those who have lived under a fully legitimate authority would undoubtedly prefer government as they have known it.

Political bankruptcy is reached in stages. The first stage occurs when a government progressively overloads its political economy, allocating more money for public programs and take-home pay than the national economy produces. This can be a consequence of a nation's economic growth rate declining, or of a continuing and unrestrained demand by citizens for more of everything.[12] The argument of this book emphasizes another danger, namely a "ghost within the machine" of government that continuously increases the costs of public policy without conscious choice. For example, the open-ended commitments of government to spend money for pensions and education are legally binding, and these costs can grow by an increase in the number of old people and young people in society.

A government reaches a second stage in the progress to political bankruptcy if the overloading of the economy forces a steady fall in the take-home pay of most of its citizens. Ordinary citizens are not particularly concerned about the percentage of the national product devoted to the costs of public policy, whether it be 25 or 60 percent.[13] Citizens will accept a smaller percentage share of the national product *if* their take-home pay is still growing in absolute terms. But citizens are not prepared to finance additional government programs by accepting a cut in the absolute value of their take-home pay.

Can Government Go Bankrupt?

Just as workers resist more strongly an employer who tries to cut wages than one who refuses a wage increase, so citizens will react strongly against a government that cuts their take-home pay instead of protecting it. Take-home pay has fallen at least once in every major Western nation in the 1970s (cf. Table 7.1), a reminder that no government is foolproof against becoming "too" overloaded.

The final stage of the undermining of political authority is reached when masses of citizens realize that their government no longer protects their interests as they wish. They cannot launch a frontal challenge to the authority of the modern state, as disaffected peasants could stone a tax collector in a primitive society, for the modern state has the power to break up any large force that masses against it. Individuals can, however, invoke elusiveness and indifference in order to undermine the authority of government.

In a politically bankrupt regime, government goes on—but not as before. Since a politically bankrupt regime cannot rely upon indifferent citizens to comply voluntarily with its laws, it may try to bribe citizens into paying taxes by the promise of benefits, e.g., social security. It may offer economic aid to boost the take-home pay of disaffected regions or groups of workers. But by definition a politically bankrupt regime lacks the money to buy consent wholesale; it needs to restrain rather than accelerate public spending. Nor is coercion likely to succeed, since a politically bankrupt government cannot rely upon public officials to do what it commands. Policemen, public prosecutors, and tax officials will be subject to a squeeze on their take-home pay like everyone else. They may go on strike or work to rule, reducing further the effectiveness of government. Some public officials may go into business for themselves, supplementing inadequate salaries by selling exemption from prosecution to citizens whose indifference leads them to violate the law.

In a politically bankrupt society, individuals do not doubt

government's claim to rule—insofar as it can. But they are not prepared to do voluntarily what government asks. The tacit premise of the indifferent citizen becomes "exclude the government." One immediate way to demonstrate indifference to authority is by avoiding and evading taxes. This effectively increases the take-home or "keep-home" pay of individuals, while simultaneously making it harder for government to meet the costs of public policy. The motto of the typical citizen in a politically bankrupt country is *"Sauve Qui Peut"* (Every man for himself).

When a government goes bankrupt, market choices can be preferred to political choices, because the market place is a free-for-all in which each citizen can try to protect himself by his own actions, or collectively with the help of family, friends, and trade union or business associates. Union and management can bargain with each other about wages and costs free from government interference. Those unions and industries with a strategic position in the economy, such as suppliers of energy, can be satisfied with the results of a free-for-all. Their real wages may actually rise, and profits can be protected too by passing higher costs on to consumers. But doing this does not resolve the problems of an overloaded political economy; it only shifts the burden to other members of society.

Any government's vulnerability to political bankruptcy is affected by its past history, as well as by the present-day management of its political economy. A government that has long enjoyed full legitimacy has an unquantifiable but real reserve of authority that can arrest but not necessarily prevent the growth of civic indifference and political bankruptcy.[14] Among major Western nations, Sweden is the country with the greatest historic reserve of legitimacy. Swedes have not only avoided the trauma of war and occupation, but also the worst ravages of the 1930s depression, developing sophisticated techniques to promote social welfare and economic growth. In America, the authority of government was probably weaker in the affluent

1960s than in the depression days of the 1930s. Today, there is little evidence of a general challenge to authority; anxieties focus upon minority groups within American society such as young blacks in urban ghettos. In England no party significantly challenges political authority, but the Scottish National Party uses the state of the British economy and the presence of North Sea oil as arguments to break up Great Britain. In Northern Ireland, Protestant Loyalists and Catholic Republicans demonstrate that class war is relatively placid compared to their seventeenth-century form of uncivil war. In Germany, the commitment of the citizenry to the Federal Republic is strong, not out of custom, but in reaction against the totalitarianism of Hitler's Reich.

It is in France and Italy that the authority of government is most vulnerable, for even in periods of prosperity, each country has experienced political disaffection. The Fifth French Republic was established by General de Gaulle in 1958 amidst the ruins of a popularly elected government of the Fourth Republic. The Gaullist regime appears to have reduced to insignificance the once formidable anticonstitutional right, but its political dominance has intensified a sense of exclusion among the Socialist and Communist left. A high rate of economic growth has prevented the overloading of the French political economy, but a residue of political distrust exists among left-wing political groups, and there is also a tradition of *incivisme*.

Italy has the unfortunate distinction of combining a long tradition of citizen indifference to government with a highly vulnerable contemporary political economy. According to one Italian expert, a *sottogoverno* of personal and interest group connections can insulate society from its governors, keeping "a country running when government in the accepted sense of the term is lacking." [15] The world recession of the 1970s has imperilled the position of the dominant Christian Democratic Party by reducing the public funds it has relied upon to buy

support with porkbarrel politics. The 1976 Italian election resulted in the return of a Christian Democratic government
without a majority in Parliament. It holds office in default of any
agreed alternative, being sustained by a parliamentary vote of
Non Sfiducia ("Not no confidence"). Outside Parliament, political bombings, shootings, and kidnappings by small groups of
left- and right-wing terrorists underline the fragile authority of
Italy's government.[16]

Political bankruptcy is a risk that every government faces,
but the risks are not the same in every country. Some major
Western nations, such as Germany, France, and Italy, entered
the world recession of the 1970s with a record of great economic achievements from the preceding twenty years. Neither
Sweden nor the United States has owed its prosperity to rapid
economic growth; unlike the major Continental countries, both
have long been secure in their political authority. While
Britain's economic growth has been slow, it could draw political
confidence from a long and uninterrupted tradition of the
authority of Parliament.

WHAT CAN BE DONE?

In the contemporary welfare state, the risk of political bankruptcy is the price paid for making many commitments of
public policy that anticipate the continuance of economic
growth. It is neither practical nor desirable for a government
to eliminate all risk by denying the presumption of economic
growth and adopting a "stand pat" position on public spending.
If politicians assumed zero growth, whether from economic
pessimism or ecological purity, their difficulties would intensify, for then they could only provide more for some citizens by

taking something from others.[17] Nor can the directors of the contemporary welfare state easily secure support for cutting costly programs, for these provide benefits for nearly everybody. Any attempt to dismantle the policies of the contemporary welfare state would be a response out of all proportion to the cause of the problem.

A government trying to reduce the overloading of its political economy might initially try any or all of three broad strategies. The first and most tempting is to do nothing, hoping that the risk of political bankruptcy will disappear. In its pure form, a government might pursue a Micawber policy, hoping like this Dickensian character that "something will turn up." But a Micawber policy is unsatisfying in a rational age, for it offers no theory to explain why conditions should get better rather than worse. Intentionally or unintentionally, a government might seek a placebo that promised solace without solution. "Planning" and "'increased government efficiency" are two placebos often prescribed to remove an imbalance between resources and commitments. Unfortunately, these policies offer reform without change. The economy remains overloaded; only those taking the placebos feel better.

A second alternative is to increase the growth of the national product, thus reducing the loads upon government by producing more resources. But this is to solve a problem by stipulating the condition that could remove it. Governments do not need to be told what to do, but how to do it. Governments that have failed to produce a high rate of economic growth cannot simply be told "Don't fail again." Moreover, in only one of the six major Western nations—Britain—is authority at risk because of a comparatively low rate of economic growth. Usually, a political economy becomes overloaded by an escalation in the cost of public policy.

Buying time is a third alternative for an overloaded government. This postpones the moment at which unpalatable actions must be taken to deal with the causes of difficulties. Politicians can buy a little time with inflation. The money illusion makes the national product appear bigger, even if it isn't. The illusion does not last long. Citizens soon realize that nominal wage increases do not match real price increases. Inflation, itself a symptom of an overloaded political economy, then becomes the immediate problem of governors. In an effort to contain inflation, governments can introduce laws to control wages and prices, or organize tripartite corporate institutions of government, business, and unions to decide how much (or how little) wages and prices should increase. But these controls invite failure through success. If wages and prices are effectively constrained while the costs of public policy rise faster than the national product, then real take-home pay will fall, and workers and businessmen alike will try to evade or break government's constraints. Loans from abroad can also buy time—until the burden of repaying the loans becomes onerous.

If time runs out on an overloaded government, then it can find itself backing into political bankruptcy, as falling take-home pay encourages citizen indifference. At such a juncture, politicians have two broad alternatives: they might proclaim the fall in take-home pay a good in itself, resulting from the socialization of wealth by government, or necessary as a means to the end of financing desirable public policies; alternatively they could protect take-home pay by putting the brakes on the costs of public policy. The latter would not require a cut in government spending; but as long as the world recession continues, it would mean a very low rate of growth in future spending commitments. Protecting take-home pay is easy to endorse as a principle, but difficult to implement in practice, for a continuing expansion of public policies is an institutionalized characteristic of the contemporary welfare state.

To identify unpalatable choices is not to doom governments to political bankruptcy. While the logic of doom-mongers is often clear, their assumptions are often false to history. For example, the fashionable attempt to extrapolate revolution from economic recession overlooks the fact that governments in America, Britain, and Scandinavia preserved their political authority intact in the face of the worldwide depression of the 1930s. The attempt to extrapolate Nazism from inflation misreads the history of twentieth-century Germany; the political authority of the Weimar Republic was flawed at birth, and not by the inflation of 1923.

Our object in considering the future is to contradict rather than predict trends. Just as a doctor may advise an overweight patient to count calories to lessen the risk of a heart attack, so a social scientist may note that if politicians do not count the cost of public policy, then political bankruptcy can result. It is far better to avoid trouble by anticipating it than to be wise after the event.

The future is open, but not unconstrained. Past events have future consequences. The greater the weight of past spending commitments, the more restricted and the less palatable are the choices of an overloaded government. Because there is scope for choice, no government is necessarily driven to political bankruptcy; but no government can hope to avoid the consequences of past follies by relying upon a "hidden hand" mechanism to ensure that all will turn out for the best.

This book links time past with time future. Just as each year's economic growth reflects past investment, so too the costs of public policy reflect commitments made by politicians who have long since departed office. Each increases by a process of compounding. An annual growth rate of 4 percent a year may sound small, but it adds up to 48 percent change in 10 years, and 100 percent in 17 years. This is true whether it is the national product, the costs of public policy, or take-home pay that is compounding. Government today must relate past commitments to present resources to avoid political bankruptcy in the future.

Far too much of our thinking is backward looking. To refer to the 1970s as a postindustrial era is to define it by contrast

with economic conditions dating from the Industrial Revolution a century ago. To refer to our time as the postwar era is
to imply that the events of 1939 to 1945 are dominant in the
1970s. Neither label tells us anything positive about current
circumstances. The same is true of a description of the political
economy as post-Keynesian. Such a label does not tell us
whether we are heading for a revival of the classical free-market
economy, toward a centrally planned Socialist economy, or
some third alternative. Everyone, whether anxious or hopeful
about the future, wants to know what our current circumstances are a prelude to.

CHAPTER 2

Treble Affluence: The Three Faces of Growth

Economic growth has been a political solvent. While growth invariably raises expectations, the means of financing social welfare expenditures and defense without reallocating income (always a politically difficult matter) or burdening the poor (which has become an equally difficult affair) has come essentially from economic growth.

Daniel Bell, *The Public Household: On Fiscal Sociology and the Liberal Society,* 1974

THREE FACES of growth have become familiar in every major Western nation in our time: growth in the national product, growth in public policy, and growth in the take-home pay of individual citizens. There is no logical necessity for all three of these crucial measures of economic well-being to grow at the same rate, or even to move in the same direction. Yet in each year since 1951, the national product of major Western nations has usually grown larger, and spending on public policy and take-home pay have both grown too. The result has been treble affluence.

Treble Affluence: The Three Faces of Growth

The road to treble affluence was long and hard. In the 1930s, many Western governments lacked full popular consent, and in every country the national product fell because of the world depression. During the Second World War, governments were not judged by economic statistics, but by whether they could produce arms and use them effectively in a war for survival. In 1945, the reconstruction of political authority was the first priority of governors; it could not be taken for granted in Continental Europe. Economic reconstruction came second. Among the war-ravaged nations, Italy did not regain its 1939 level of production until 1949 and France did not equal its 1929 standard until 1950. Germany did not attain prewar levels of national production until 1952; and in austerity Britain a return to prewar standards was delayed until 1953.[1]

Western governments did not wish to maintain the boom-and-bust economic conditions of the 1920s, or accept the view that the depression of the 1930s was caused by an excess of goods for people to buy. Growth-oriented Keynesian techniques for managing the economy were congenial on political as well as economic grounds. They did not require comprehensive direct controls, as in the command economies of Communist Eastern Europe. Instead, Keynesian prescriptions employed classic public finance mechanisms to influence market conditions, without involving government intimately in the details of the private sector of the mixed economy. By the mid-1960s, Milton Friedman, an economic advisor to Republican Presidential candidate Barry Goldwater, could proclaim, "We are all Keynesians now." [2]

In the past generation major Western nations have succeeded, and succeeded spectacularly, in sustaining economic growth far beyond that required to reconstruct war-ravaged economies. France, Germany, Italy, and Sweden have enjoyed decades of growth greater than at any time previously in their modern history, and growth in America and Britain has been higher than at any earlier period of the twentieth century.

Can Government Go Bankrupt?

Since the economic base of every Western nation was greater in 1951 than in 1901 or 1851, higher rates of growth have produced much more national wealth in absolute terms. For example, average real annual growth rate in America in the 1960s was worth six times more to the average citizen than a typical year's growth in the 1890s.[3]

Mass affluence has followed in the wake of economic growth. In the 1930s the average citizen's standard of living involved simple, even minimum wants: food, shelter, and clothing. Many who considered themselves to be comfortable then were without goods that the majority take for granted today, such as a radio, refrigerator, or automobile. Moreover, many consumer goods important today, such as television or charter-flight holidays, were not available then. Mass affluence has resulted from the pervasive distribution of consumer goods that were once the prerogative of the few. In 1950, only in America was there an average of one automobile for each family. There was one car for every four families in France, five in Britain, seven in Sweden, twenty-one in Germany, and thirty-six in Italy. By the mid-1970s conditions had been transformed. There was an average of one car for each family in every European nation, and two cars per family in America. In 1950, television broadcasting was in its infancy; few families had television sets and there were few programs to view. A quarter-century later, there was a television set in the home of the great majority of European families, and two in the average American home.[4] Mass affluence was matched by an end to mass unemployment, which had historically accompanied the downturn in the business cycle. In the mid-1930s, unemployment ranged from 10 to 20 percent in major Western nations. During most of the era of affluence it has been about 2 or 3 percent in major European nations. Even at the worst moments of the 1975 recession, unemployment was at a level that would have been considered full employment before 1939.[5]

Public affluence has developed simultaneously with private

affluence. In the 1950s J. K. Galbraith captured much attention by arguing that individual take-home pay would inevitably grow much faster than government spending on public policy. He predicted that affluent citizens would successfully resist any increase in the amount or rate of taxation, leading to an era of private affluence and public squalor.[6] Events have proven him spectacularly wrong. Everywhere public expenditure on pensions, health, and education has grown faster than take-home pay or the economy as a whole. Government itself has become the most affluent institution of the affluent society.

Treble affluence has been a solvent of many potential political difficulties. Questions about the distribution of wealth have not so much been answered as swamped. Politicians have not been forced to choose between raising taxes to spend more on government programs or else lowering taxes and cutting back on program spending. A more prosperous economy generates more tax revenue and can simultaneously increase take-home pay. Politicians have thus been able to claim credit for creating conditions of both public and private affluence.

The pages that follow demonstrate the cumulative importance of the slow, steady annual growth of the national product, public policy, and take-home pay. But the upward trend of each has not been equal. If present trends continued in future, this would mean the end of treble affluence and the onset of political bankruptcy.

SLOW BUT STEADY:
THE GROWTH OF THE NATIONAL PIE

A nation's wealth is dynamic, not static. A factory or a farm is not valued for its land and buildings, but for what it will produce. An economy must continuously produce new wealth to replace what it has just consumed. Government is not much concerned with nonproductive wealth such as art treasures or Crown jewels; it gives first priority to the rate at which new wealth is produced each year. Each year's national product is important because it is needed to finance the current costs of public policy. Governors not only consider the current cash value of the national product, but also whether it is growing, static, or even contracting by comparison with a year ago.*

Of course, money is not the measure of all things.[7] Individuals can value family, friends, and leisure more than the material rewards of work, and government offers its citizens such priceless benefits as freedom of speech and public order. But any institution that raises and spends billions of dollars each year—and every major Western government does just that —cannot be indifferent to the material conditions of its society.

Government is concerned about the production of wealth because it needs money to finance its activities and it cannot tax what does not exist. There cannot be a tax on increased happiness, as long as happiness is not measured in money terms. The greater a nation's product, the more money a given tax raises; for example, a tax of 1 percent of the national product of Germany will yield about three times as much revenue as the same percentage tax in less affluent Italy. A growing national product generates extra public revenue by increasing the wages, profits, and sales that can be taxed. A more affluent society will have more people in higher income tax brackets and fewer paying little tax because of low earnings. In a booming economy, a government may even be able

---

* Economists have developed measures of constant or "real" prices, so that the effects of inflation can be discounted when making comparisons within an economy across time. Unless otherwise stated, all cross-time comparisons in this book use constant-value currencies. On the political advantages and hazards of the technique, see pp. 144–49.

to cut its tax rates and still collect more revenue in total, for a 25 percent tax on rising incomes will soon bring in more money than a 27 percent tax on static incomes.

Government also wants the economy to grow because it is now held responsible for the prosperity of its citizens. Insofar as prosperity is no longer regarded as a static condition (being as well-off next year as last) but rather as a dynamic status (being better-off next year than last), economic growth is necessary to increase both take-home pay and the benefits of public policy.

The quarter-century since 1951 has seen booms and recessions. The long-term trend in the national product, measured by the economist's yardstick of the Gross Domestic Product (GDP),* has everywhere registered great material growth (see Appendix, Table A2.1):

Growth is real. In each major Western nation the national product has increased greatly over the past quarter-century. Real growth has increased as much as 6.1 percent in Germany and 4.8 percent in France and Italy. While the growth rates of America and Sweden are less, this has been offset by the fact that each country was already wealthy by 1951. Thus, a 3.3 percent increase in the American Gross Domestic Product in 1976 is equivalent to $52 billion, about twice the value of a much higher average increase in the smaller German national product. Cumulatively, economic growth has quadrupled Germany's national product in the past quarter-century, trebled that of France and Italy, and more than doubled the national product of Sweden, America, and Britain.

Growth is continuing. Nearly every year every major Western

---

* The Gross Domestic Product (GDP) is a standard measure of economic output in publications of national governments, OECD, and the United Nations. In this book it is taken at factor cost to remove the effects of government subsidies and indirect taxes upon the value of goods and services. GDP differs from Gross National Product (GNP) because the latter includes net property income received from abroad.

nation enjoys some benefits from a growing national pie. In France, Italy, and Sweden, the national product has grown in twenty-four of the past twenty-five years, and in Germany, the economy has only failed to grow twice. Notwithstanding its relatively low annual rate of economic growth, Britain has enjoyed at least some economic expansion in twenty-two years. The United States has seen its national product fall in five of the past twenty-five years: after the end of the Korean War in 1954, in the domestic recession of 1958, under pressure from the Viet Nam War in 1970, and after the world oil crisis in 1974 and 1975.

Growth is big in total. A large population creates large concentrations of wealth, and continuing growth augments this even more. The compounding of small annual percentage increases in the national product cumulatively produces vast sums of money. In the past quarter-century, the American economy has grown by more than $850 billion at current prices, a figure almost double the total national product of Germany in 1976, and about fourteen times the total national product of Sweden. The United States is a trillion-dollar economy heading for two trillion. Germany is a trillion-Deutsche mark economy and France has a trillion-franc economy.[8]

Growth in per capita income is big. If the average citizen's standard of living is not to fall, then the national pie must grow at least as fast as the population. Every major Western nation has had some increases in population since 1950. The United States' has been extreme; its population increase of 65,000,000 is greater than the total population of any major European country today. Growth in the American economy has provided extra jobs and then some for a greatly enlarged population. The national product has increased by 65 percent per head in the past quarter-century. In Europe, slower rates of population growth have allowed per capita income to increase faster. In Italy, France, and Sweden, the national product per head has more than doubled, thanks to a high rate of economic growth and a low rate of population growth, and in Germany it has trebled.

The national product is growing at a declining rate. While Gross Domestic Products have grown almost continuously during the past quarter-century, their rate of growth has been slowing down. The slowdown cannot be attributed solely to the world oil crisis, for growth was already beginning to slow down before Autumn 1973. The pattern is clearest in Germany, where the national product averaged growth at 8.5 percent annually in the reconstruction years of 1951–56. The German growth rate has declined in every five-year period since, falling to an annual average of 2.5 percent for the period 1971–76. The United States, France, and Sweden reached their peak rate of growth in the first half of the 1960s; growth slowed down in the second half of the decade, and the deceleration has continued in the 1970s. Italian growth has been exceptionally steady, fluctuating between 4.8 and 5.4 percent in each five-year period from 1951 through 1970. But Italian growth has fallen sharply since, dropping to 2.7 percent from 1970 through 1976. Britain's growth rate has been relatively steady but also very low. The annual 1.9 percent increase in Britain's national product in the 1970s is the lowest five-year figure of any major Western nation in the past quarter-century.

All major Western nations have grown greatly in wealth since 1951, but they have not grown equally. Seemingly small percentage differences in annual growth rates can mask big real differences. At the extreme, the German economy has grown more than twice as much as the British. The 1.5 percent difference in the annual growth rates of France and America has cumulatively resulted in the French economy trebling in size, while America's simply doubled. The 0.4 percent annual advantage of Sweden over America means that the Swedish economy has cumulatively grown one-quarter more than the American in the past quarter-century.

Differences in national growth rates have not removed historic differences in wealth between countries, but they have much narrowed the gaps. The per capita national product of Germany and Sweden exceeded that of the United States ($7,315) in 1976. The competition to come first is now determined by the fluctuating exchange rates of the dollar, the Deutsche mark, and the krona, and not by intrinsic industrial advantages. The French national product per capita was about four-fifths that of the United States in 1976, Britain about half, and Italy about one-third. Today, the major differences in national wealth are within Europe, and not between Western Europe and the United States.

Comparison of patterns of growth emphasizes that there is no single, simple explanation for the differences found among major Western nations.[9] There are differences in the ways governments manage their political economies,[10] but these do not appear to correlate with rates of economic growth. Both the American and German governments have tended to allow market forces to operate free from government direction. Yet the results have been very different in Germany and America. In the homeland of Keynes, recurring attempts by the British Treasury to apply his techniques have led to complaints about the resulting "stop-go" policy stimulating, then restraining the British economy. Since the 1960s the British have sought to imitate the French strategy of *dirigisme* (i.e., specific and vigorous short-term government economic action) without success. Swedish Social Democratic governments have enjoyed a reputation for governmental efficiency and economic sophistication in marked contrast to that of Italy. Yet in spite of this, Italy's economy has cumulatively grown half again as much as the Swedish economy in the past quarter-century. Important as the differences between nations are, they do not detract from the common element in their postwar experience, namely, an unprecedented growth in national wealth in the third quarter of the twentieth century.

NEITHER STEADY NOR SLOW: THE GROWTH OF PUBLIC POLICY

To write about public policy rather than public spending is to emphasize the purposes as well as the costs of governing.[11] The tax revenues that governments raise are spent on policies intended to benefit the public, individually and collectively. Officials paid from public funds provide services for citizens, such as teaching children, collecting rubbish, and protecting public order. The goods that government buys with tax revenues—highways, hospitals, or books for libraries—benefit citizens too. Money paid to citizens as pensions or unemployment benefits is cash in hand that individuals can spend themselves. Public expenditure is large because citizens of the mixed-economy welfare state benefit greatly from such government programs.

The most general indicator of the scope and scale of public policy is the money that government spends. The most costly programs of government are of great importance to society: promoting welfare through health, education, and old-age pensions; national defense; managing and stimulating the economy; and paying interest on government debts accumulated in years past. Slowly but surely, the growth of the welfare state has increased the relative and absolute costs of public policy. For example, in 1876 it was equivalent to 3.6 percent of the national product in America; by 1976 it was 36 percent. In Sweden, public policy was equivalent to 6.2 percent of the national product in 1876; a century later, it had risen to 54 percent.[12]

Public spending is itself neither good nor bad, notwithstanding the efforts of Socialist and private enterprise propagandists to give it a moral significance. Socialists argue that government provision of a service makes that service more equitable and morally superior, because it is provided on the basis of common citizenship, rather than on the ability to pay. Proponents of private enterprise argue that government provision of services reduces a citizen's choice and increases the power of government. The middle-of-the-road view of public spending was aptly summed up by President Lyndon Johnson in his 1965 budget message:

> I have been guided by the principle that spending by the Federal Government, in and of itself, is neither bad nor good. It can be bad when it involves overstaffing of government agencies, or needless duplication of functions or poor management, or public services which cost more than they are worth, or the intrusion of government into areas where it does not belong. It can be good when it is put to work efficiently in the interests of our national strength, economic progress and human compassion.[13]

Just as the benefits of public policy are distributed among the general public, so too are the costs. To speak of the growth of public policy is also to speak of more and more taxes being paid, more money being borrowed by government, and government consuming more of the nation's fixed capital. Governments try to hide some of these costs in what are called "off-line" budget entries in Washington, or aptly described in French as *debudgetisé*.[14] For example, in France, Germany, and Italy, the national budget does not show social security payments; but bookkeeping tricks cannot conceal the fact that public benefits involve public costs.

We emphasize the costs of public policy, because each government program, however meritorious or popular, must be paid for from public revenue.* A significant portion of public

---

* The cost of public policy is here defined as total current receipts plus deficits plus capital consumption at all levels of government. Nationalized industries and other trading corporations are included only insofar as taxes are levied to pay them subsidies; their borrowing from nongovernmental sources is excluded. Capital as well as current expenditure is included. OECD accounts normally exclude joint-stock companies of which government is the sole or part owner, and we follow their practice.

spending returns to private hands as the wages of public employees or welfare payments. But the wages of teachers and
policemen and the pensioner's check must be met by taxes
upon the earnings of everyone not on the public payroll, and
in part by the taxes of those who are.

Here are the facts about how the costs of public policy have
everywhere been rising in the past quarter-century (see also
Appendix Table A2.2):

The growth in public policy is real.   In every major Western
nation, annual increases in the costs of governing have cumulatively compounded into extra billions in whatever currency
a government does its accounts. The cost of public policy has
grown most rapidly in Italy. An annual increase of 9.4 percent
has cumulatively increased the total real cost of government
programs by nearly eight times since 1951. France ranks second,
with an annual increase of 8.8 percent compounding into an
increase of nearly six times in a quarter-century. In Germany
government spending has risen five times, and in Sweden by
four-and-one-half times. The costs of American public policy
have risen relatively slowly; an average annual increase of 5.3
percent cumulatively totals a growth of two-and-one-half times.
Britain, often cited as a country spending too much on public
policies, has had costs rise less than in any other major Western
nation in the past quarter-century, 185 percent.

The growth in public policy is continuing.   The cost of
public policy has risen in real terms in every one of the past
twenty-five years in Italy and Sweden and every year for
twenty-four years in France and Germany. In America and
Britain costs have risen every year for twenty-two years in the
past quarter-century. The fact that the government's claim
upon the national pie can occasionally be reduced is important,
for it shows that there is no mechanism that automatically
pushes up the cost of public programs each year. But cuts in
government spending have been infrequent, occurring only in
exceptional circumstances, such as prevailed in the 1950s. Over-

all, the dominant theme is the continuing growth in the costs of governing.

The growth in public policy is big in total. Government today is the biggest business (*sic*) in every major Western country. Following the Second World War, governments were spending billions to further public policy. Today, the cost of governing is measured in hundreds of billions. In absolute terms, government spending is highest in America, notwithstanding the nominal private enterprise ideology of both Republicans and Democrats. In 1976, the total bill for government programs at all levels of government was $597 billion, and rising annually by tens of billions of dollars in real terms, a sum further increased by inflation. The cost of public policy in European nations only appears less in aggregate because of the difference in population. To Europeans, hundreds of billions of Deutsche marks, francs, or kronor is a lot of money. The big boost in public spending reflects government providing more goods and services for each citizen and every family.

The growth in public policy is big per capita. Population growth accounts for less than one-third of the increased cost of public policy in European nations, and for little more in the United States. In 1976, Swedes were the costliest citizens in the Western world. The government spent an average of more than $4,500 per Swede, or $18,000 for a family of four. In Germany, the cost of public policy was equivalent to $4,000 a head, and in France nearly $3,000. Americans rank fourth, as public spending was $2,776 a head in 1976. Britons and Italians appear to have less spent on them by government only because national living standards are lower.

The costs of public policy are growing at an accelerating rate. On the face of it, the costs of government programs appear to be rising at a steady rate: in the 1970s, as in each of the two decades previously, the increase among Western nations has averaged a little above 6 percent each year. But such an analysis obscures a fundamental fact: as the total cost of public policy increases, then the same percentage increase represents a much larger sum in absolute terms and as a proportion of the national product. For example, in the United States the average increase in the cost of government programs represented 1.5 percent of the national product in 1951, or about $4 billion; by 1976, the same percentage increase equalled 2.1 percent of the national product, that is, $31 billion.

The steady and great growth in the cost of public policy reflects conditions general to every Western country; there is no statistically significant relationship between the growth of public spending and a Socialist government.* Public spending has grown most in Italy, yet Italy has been governed continuously by a conservative Christian Democratic party since World War II. The countries next highest in spending, France and Germany, have been dominated for most of the past quarter-century by anti-Socialist governments of Christian Democrats and Gaullists, respectively. While Sweden has been under a Socialist government for more than four decades, its costs have grown less in percentage terms than in the three major continental European countries. The lowest rate of increase in public spending is found in Britain, where the Labour Party has won five of the nine elections since 1950. The anti-Socialist parties of the United States have cumulatively increased public spending by one-third more than the more interventionist British governments.

---

* Multiple regression analysis showed that the growth of the national product consistently explained far more of the variance in the costs of public policy than did party control in government. The respective figures for the influence of economic growth and partisanship are: the United States, 48 and 14 percent; Britain, 42 and 9 percent; France, 51 and 11 percent; Germany, 76 and 8 percent; Italy, 44 and 1 percent; and Sweden, 67 and 10 percent. Only in the United States is the influence of partisanship (measured as Democratic control of both the White House and Congress) statistically significant at the 0.05 level.

REAL GROWTH AND RELATIVE DECLINE: THE TRAJECTORY OF TAKE-HOME PAY

At the beginning of the century a nation was considered wealthy if its government owned colonies or could command a massive military machine. A rich country was a country with a number of rich citizens who were to be respected and taxed lightly, for fear that otherwise the source of national riches might be lost. National wealth did not mean mass affluence. A speaker in London's Hyde Park who praised the riches of the British Empire invited the heckler's gibe: "Then why are so many people poor?"

Today both winners and losers of wars have retreated from the dreams of national glory that national wealth was once meant to support. Sweden and Britain have sought international prestige by promoting innovations in welfare services. Germans and Italians, deprived of large standing armies by military defeat, have found that it pays better to concentrate upon the industrial sinews of peace. Under General de Gaulle, France sought to pursue *la gloire*, but it has gained far more international repute for its *économie concertée* than for its nuclear striking force. The Viet Nam War made evident the limits of America's political economy, as well as of its military effectiveness.

Instead of national glory, individual well-being is today the central object of a nation's political economy. In a mixed economy, this well-being is guaranteed partly by the benefits of public policy, and partly by what each individual earns as take-home pay. While an economist may be indifferent about whether the money an individual spends comes from his own earnings, or from such cash transfer benefits as pensions or unemployment compensation, politically there is a crucial difference. Transfer benefits are controlled by government. As the

[56

name indicates, they are sums of money paid by government to citizens. Financing these benefits necessarily requires transferring money *from* citizens *to* government. The government determines who receives transfer benefits, how much is paid, and how taxes are levied to finance these payments. A person who wants a bigger transfer benefit cannot earn it by working harder or longer hours; it can only be gained by political action. An individual who wishes more benefits of public policy must resort to the time-consuming procedures of representative government. By contrast, an individual's take-home pay is not controlled by government. A person who wants more take-home pay can try to increase earnings by initiatives in the market place.

The growth of take-home pay is the best measure of individual affluence. Take-home pay is here defined as wages, salaries, profits and property income, net of deductions for income tax, employee contributions to social security, and incidental direct taxes.* The growth of an individual's take-home pay depends not only upon individual effort and the growth of the total national pie, but also upon how fast the costs of public policy increase, for take-home pay is simply what the individual has left over after the government's claims upon the national product have been met. For example, in presenting its 1976 budget estimates, the British government gave a fixed value to its claims upon the national product, while noting that the national product could grow less than its median growth forecast of 3.4 percent. The lowest of the three forecasts given, growth at 2.4 percent per annum, allowed an increase of only 0.5 percent annually in take-home pay. This figure, the British Treasury noted, "should be regarded as purely illustrative and not necessarily as a lower limit." In actuality the economy

---

* The effect upon take-home pay of changes in indirect taxation is included in our analysis, for the GDP deflator used to convert currency into constant-value take-home pay incorporates the effect of indirect tax changes upon overall price levels.

grew by only 1.5 percent. The government needed to devote all of this and then some to meet the rising costs of public policy, and take-home pay thus fell.[15]

The growth in take-home pay is real. The total amount of money left for citizens after government has taken its cut from the national pie has grown everywhere in the Western world in the past quarter-century (see Appendix, Table A2.3). In any one year, take-home pay tends to grow slowly. The annual increase has been greatest in Germany (4.5 percent) and France (4.3 percent). It has been least in Sweden (2.5 percent) and Britain (2.1 percent). Small increases in take-home pay can have disproportionately big effects, for once an individual's earnings meet basic needs, any increase in take-home pay adds to the discretionary income that an individual can freely spend as he or she wishes. In an era of treble affluence, individuals have also earned more leisure, by getting the same cash wages for working up to one-third fewer hours.[16]

Growth in take-home pay is continuing. Take-home pay is vulnerable if growth slows down, if the costs of public policy rise unexpectedly, or both. Yet take-home pay consistently rose in every year in every major Western nation except Britain throughout the 1950s and 1960s. In Britain it fell seven times in the past quarter-century, because of downturns in the economy. Except for Britain, the average Western citizen is likely to have had an increase in take-home pay in eleven years in twelve, or in seven years in eight, including the British record.

The growth in take-home pay is big per capita. Any figure showing per capita increases in earnings underestimates the real growth in the living standards of a family. While a family may have only one wage-earner, it will on average have about four members, important in relating per capita to total family income.* Thus, the per capita take-home pay of $5,619 for each

---

* It is not practicable to convert per capita take-home pay into earnings per employed worker, for the definition of an employed person varies from country to country; and in lands where agriculture has historically been

of 213 million Americans in 1976 is equivalent to an annual income of more than $22,000 for a family of four. Even after making the necessary allowances for inflation and population growth, take-home pay per head has everywhere grown greatly in the past quarter-century. In Germany, per capita income has increased by 175 percent; in France by 147 percent; and in Italy by 135 percent. Lower rates of economic growth have made the increase of per capita take-home pay in Sweden and Britain less than half these figures. The great population increase in the United States has meant that per capita take-home pay has grown by only 48 percent in America.

Take-home pay is growing at a declining rate. The 1950s was the decade in which take-home pay rose most quickly, increasing an average of 4.2 percent annually in major Western nations. In the 1960s, because of the increased cost of public policy, take-home pay rose less, averaging an annual increase of 3.5 percent. Take-home pay has grown much more slowly from 1971 to 1976—0.9 percent a year on average—because of the slower growth in the national pie and the growing claims of public policy. In major Western nations, take-home pay has on average fallen in two of the past six years, and in three of the past six years in Italy and Sweden (see Table 7.1).

Because the claims of the taxman are less in the United States than in any major European country, Americans, on average, enjoy the biggest annual after-tax earnings. Post-tax earnings are one-sixth higher than in Sweden and slightly higher than in Germany, even though the per capita national product of both these European countries is higher at current exchange rates. American earnings are also ahead of the average Frenchman's earnings, and well ahead of the slow-growing British and the fast-growing but historically poor Italians.

----

large, especially France and Italy, statistics are subject to significant error margins. Moreover, the proportion of adult men and women in work has varied within each nation, as well as between nations, in the past quarter-century.

National politicians are fortunate that the great bulk of citizens judge their prosperity by national rather than international standards. For example, few Englishmen emigrate to France and Germany to enjoy higher Continental growth rates and higher standards of living; nor is money the primary reason that leads young Americans to move to London, Paris, or Rome. Individuals tend to judge their current well-being by comparing it with their past standard of living. And when Americans or Europeans compare their own take-home pay today with what they or their parents earned a quarter-century ago, invariably they see a steady and real increase in wealth.

While take-home pay is the face of affluence that is most important to the individual citizen, it is also the most vulnerable face of affluence. The size of take-home pay depends upon how much the economy has grown and how restrained the government is in its first claim upon the fiscal dividend of growth. The pressures of the 1970s have tended to flatten out the upward trend in its growth. They are a reminder that a trend upwards can, in the fullness of time, show a falling trajectory.

SQUEEZING AFFLUENCE

Affluence has had a pervasive influence upon the politics of Western nations in the past quarter-century. In a no-growth political economy, the only way to finance new or expanded public programs would be by reducing spending upon some established programs, or increasing taxes and cutting take-home pay. Any proposal to cut the take-home pay of the average citizen would invite a massive popular reaction threatening political bankruptcy. A policy of redistributing income by protecting the take-home pay of the relatively poor and raising taxes on the well-to-do could only be at the cost of intense political conflict. In the circumstances of Europe in 1951, redistributing income would not have made the masses affluent; it would simply have made the wealthy poor.

The continuing and unprecedented growth of the national product in the past quarter-century has produced something for almost everybody. Moreover, the prospect of future growth has allowed politicians to promise bread and butter today, jam tomorrow, and a nice big cake on Sunday. The Couéist doctrine— "Day by day in every way I am getting better and better"— ceased to be regarded as the wishful delusion of a bemused psychotherapist and became a description of the blissful reality of continuing growth.

The political solvent of treble affluence eroded old political divisions between left and right, or Catholic and Protestant. Activity replaced ideology among a new generation of hyperthyroid politicians who believed in doing things for their own sake and for the credit this reflected upon the individual mover. Political office, instead of being a status requiring motionless dignity of its incumbent, has become a challenge to do something. Almost everything that can be done costs money. John F. Kennedy inaugurated the 1960s by campaigning for the Presidency with the slogan "Let's get America moving again." No indication was given about the direction of change. In Britain, the Labour Party of Harold Wilson endorsed movement for its own sake with the ideologically directionless slogan "Let's Go with Labour," and six years later the British Conservatives under Edward Heath responded with the equally vague exhortation "Action not Words." In Germany, the Christian Democratic Union abandoned emphasis upon the traditional values of German Protestantism and Catholicism to concentrate upon spreading consumer goods and what Germans call *Konsumterror* (keeping up with the Joneses). In a Gaullist regime established to defend France's traditional virtues, the telephone service was suspect as an example of American cultural penetration; yet Frenchmen too have come to have a healthy appetite for American-style consumer goods, including telephones. In Italy, Christian Democratic governments devoted so much of the fiscal dividend of growth to paying off political debts through porkbarrel politics that the Communist Party has proclaimed the need to reduce government intervention in the economy. Early in the 1970s Swedish Social Democrats worried less about ideological issues than about coping with a continuous growth of affluence in a postindustrial society.[17]

When the 1970s produced a squeeze on affluence, this caught by surprise politicians who had banked on an unending cornucopia of benefits. The squeeze reflects the accumulation of trends during the past quarter-century: the three faces of affluence have not grown at an equal rate.

The basic problem is this: In every major Western government the costs of public policy have increased at a faster rate than the national product. During a recession there are pressures to increase public spending to stimulate the economy and to meet increased welfare claims with more people in need. Additional spending can be justified in boom years with the argument "After all, the money is there." Yet a government cannot make the national product grow simply by passing laws, as it can increase the costs of public policy.

In a given year, the cost of public policy normally grows much faster in percentage terms than the national pie. In percentage terms, the cost of public policy has grown at a faster rate than the national product in twenty-one of the past twenty-five years in Sweden, in twenty in Italy, eighteen in America and France, sixteen in Germany, and fifteen in Britain. Cumulatively, the cost of public policy in the past quarter-century has grown by more than five times as much as individual take-home pay in Sweden; by four-and-one-half times in Italy; by about two-and-one-half to three times in the United States, Britain, and France; and by twice as much in Germany.

As long as government spending claimed a relatively small part of the national pie, then a large percentage increase in spending did not take the whole of the fiscal dividend of growth. For example, in an economy with a 4 percent increase in national product and an 8 percent increase in public spending, take-home pay could increase as much as the cost of public policy if the latter claimed only one-quarter of the total national product.

Because public spending was relatively small in 1951, allocating a diminishing proportion of the fiscal dividend of growth to take-home pay could still give citizens more money in absolute terms. For example, if a national product of $500 billion grew by 4 percent, and half that growth was devoted to take-home pay, this would place an extra $10 billion in the pockets of citizens. If the national product grew to $1,000 billion and one-third of a 4 percent fiscal dividend was devoted to take-home pay, this smaller share of a larger product would put more money in total in the pockets of citizens.

Good news like this cannot last forever. The squeeze on affluence is increasingly felt as the government's claims on the national pie grow. When public policy is equivalent to 50 percent of national product, then an 8 percent increase in its cost accounts for *the whole* of a 4 percent fiscal dividend of growth. If public policy rises further, say to 60 percent of the national product, then the same percentage increase would account for *the whole of the dividend of growth and then some*, forcing a cut in take-home pay.

In the past quarter-century, the government's claim upon the national pie has grown greatly in every major Western nation.* In 1951 the government allocated an average of 29 percent of the national product. By 1976 its average share was

---

* OECD economists have calculated that the elasticity of the increase in public expenditure relative to the increase in Gross Domestic Product has averaged 1.20 from 1960 to 1975 and 1.30 from 1970 to 1975 in our six major Western nations.

TABLE 2.1

*The Growing Importance
of Public Policy*

	1951	1976	Change
(Public Policy as a Proportion of the National Product)			
America	27%	36%	+9%
Britain	34%	49%	+15%
France	33%	41%	+8%
Germany	31%	46%	+15%
Italy	23%	46%	+23%
Sweden	27%	54%	+27%

Sources: The cost of public policy, calculated as in Table A2.2, is divided by Gross Domestic Product at market prices as reported in OECD statistics cited in Table A2.1.

45 percent—and *growing* (see Table 2.1). At the beginning of the era of affluence, the costs of public policy were equivalent to about one-quarter of the national product in America, Italy, and Sweden, and nowhere did they account for more than one-third. By contrast, in 1976, the relatively low share going to American public policy (36 percent) was more than the largest share claimed in any country in 1951. In the extreme case of Sweden, the share of the national pie claimed by government has doubled: it is now 54 percent, and rising. In Italy, the claims of public policy have also doubled in the past quarter-century.

There is nothing fixed or sacred about the share of the national pie devoted to public policy or to take-home pay. Under certain circumstances a great growth in government's claims upon the national product can be consistent with treble affluence. Those who look only to the past may see no cause for alarm. But the differences in the three faces of growth imply that a continuation of past trends into the future would sooner or later force a cut in take-home pay, thus threatening a country with political bankruptcy.

CHAPTER 3

Everybody Benefits

The frontiers of European and American social
policy are not a combat zone between pro- and
anti-welfare state forces, because there is no
defensible line between the armies. The modern
welfare state intermingles benefits, dispensations
and transfers to such an extent that it is
practically impossible to separate dependents and
nondependents.

A. Heidenheimer, H. Heclo, and C. Adams,
Comparative Public Policy, 1975

IN THE CONTEMPORARY welfare state, citizens cannot be
divided neatly into Us and Them, that is, those who draw
benefits and those who pay taxes. That is its political strength;
the welfare state provides something for everybody. Nearly
every citizen benefits from the money that government spends
upon education, health, and pensions, as well as from such
collectively provided services as water, roads, fire, and police.
Without the services of contemporary government, a complex
modern society could not continue as we know it. In big cities
with deteriorating public services such as New York, the only
thing worse than bad government would be the anarchy and
disruption of no government.

Government does not provide the same thing for each person when it offers something to everybody. The demands of
individuals and organizations differ greatly. Farmers want dif-

ferent programs than city dwellers; children have different needs than working adults or pensioners; and business corporations and labor unions make different demands about the economy. The art of designing a new public policy lies in particularizing benefits, that is, determining who or what organization will benefit, by how much, and under what circumstances.

In deciding what benefits to provide, politicians balance two sets of considerations: the needs of individual citizens and their own needs as officeholders. The definition of what is needed and who is needy cannot be resolved by measuring the number of calories an individual requires to stay alive, or the monetary stimulus that an economy needs to grow. It is a political question, determined by political bargaining, and enshrined in public laws.

Politicians encourage the growth of public spending by emphasizing the benefits rather than the costs of the welfare state. Instead of talking about higher income taxes or motoring charges, they prefer to speak of bigger pensions, newer schools, or broader highways. They know that the citizen who complains about taxes while speeding along a highway in a Cadillac or a Mercedes-Benz does not want the highway taken away for the sake of a slight reduction in taxes. As long as the tax cost of a program is disassociated from the delivery of public benefits, then public benefits can appear as "gifts." Few people wish to shoot Santa Claus—even if they do not believe in him.

The profile of public policy can be analyzed in three different ways. First of all, one can examine the pattern of public spending to see what are the main programs that public funds support. Secondly, we ask: who benefits from the contemporary welfare state, and how? Finally, we look at the problems of spreading the jam: should the contemporary welfare state give benefits to every citizen, including those able to look after themselves, or should it concentrate resources selectively upon those most in need?

WHAT THE MONEY BUYS

To ask "What does government do?" is to state a plain man's question in plain man's language. The answer is by no means simple, for the mixed-economy welfare state does so many different things.

In terms of political significance, these activities can be grouped under three broad headings.[1] First come the *defining* activities of the state: protecting national security through military and diplomatic means; enforcing law through the courts and police; and controlling the supply of money and raising taxes to pay for public programs. If a government cannot do these things, then it can no longer claim the effectiveness of George Washington's first Cabinet, or the French government in Napoleon's time. *Mobilizing economic resources*—e.g., building canals, railroads, and highways to promote communications and the growth of agriculture, trade, and industry —came second in the rise of the modern state. In Prussia and in mercantilist France, the state itself was a prime agent of industrialization, by contrast with *laissez-faire* Britain and America. Finally, *social policies* such as education, health, and pensions, accepted as a government concern for up to a century, in the post-1945 era have come to dominate spending in every major Western country.

From an individual citizen's perspective, the activities of government differ greatly in the directness of their personal effect. Social policies are intimately related to individual concerns. A pensioner, a person receiving medical care, or a young person in school can see immediately what government is doing for him or her. When government looks after the economy by mobilizing economic resources—for example, promoting exports or encouraging capital investment—the benefits to individuals are often indirect or less immediately visible. The defining activities of government, such as military defense and foreign policy, are not directed at citizens as individuals, but rather at the nation as a whole.

Social policies are preeminent in the contemporary welfare state. In every major Western nation they rank first in spending importance, on average accounting for 53 percent of the total cost of public policy. Mobilizing economic resources and defining policies are of secondary importance in the budget. Most European countries tend to spend more on mobilizing resources than on defining policies, whereas the United States tends to spend more on defining policies, because of its greater defense commitments. Overall, mobilizing economic resources ranks second in importance, accounting on average for 25 percent of the cost of public policy, with defining policies a close third, taking 22 percent (see Appendix, Table A3.1).

It is easy to see why *social policies* rank first in government spending. They provide education, health, and pensions to millions of citizens. These are "good" goods, that is, things that citizens like to have, and want more of. Moreover, they are benefits that go directly to individuals, unlike investment subsidies to industries or such collective goods as military defense.

The United States demonstrates that many services of the welfare state need not be provided by government; churches, philanthropic bodies, or profitmaking companies can run hospitals and schools. But an affluent mixed economy encourages politicians to use government's powers to allocate a substantial proportion of the national product to social benefits.

As a result, every major Western government today devotes large sums of money to social policies. In Sweden, three out of every ten kronor of the national product are directed by government to pay for social benefits. Other European governments spend from one-fifth to one-quarter of their national product on social programs. The United States spends the smallest proportion (16 percent) of its national product on social policies, but this came to about $250 billion in 1976, and the sum is growing annually.

Governments differ significantly in the priority given particular social programs. France and Germany, for example, devote much more money to pensions than to education; whereas Britain and Sweden devote much more to education than pensions. The United States not only spends less than European countries on social policies; it also spends its share differently. Education looms much larger in the United States social budget, reflecting the nation's historic concern with giving opportunities to citizens, rather than helping those who cannot readily take care of themselves. Americans do spend lots of money on their own welfare—but they do not trust the government to spend it all for them. Health costs consume almost 9 percent of the United States national product, a *higher* proportion than in any major European country. However, most of these dollars are *not* provided by government, but come from take-home pay or private health insurance programs.

Government today spends far more money on social programs than it spent on public policy in total a quarter-century ago, even after discounting for the effects of cost inflation. Spending on social policy has increased more than twelve times in Italy, and more than nine times in Germany and Sweden. It has increased "only" five times in Britain, because by 1950 Britain had already established a relatively high level of social benefits, and expansion since then has been inhibited by its low rate of economic growth.

Historically, every major Western government has encouraged the *mobilization of economic resources* in the national interest. The promotion of railroads in nineteenth-century Europe and the United States depended upon government actions as well as upon the initiative of economic entrepreneurs. Today, governments are concerned with the specifics of trade and industry, as well as with the much more general and diffuse problems of managing the economy. Governments own and operate both quasi-monopolistic utilities, such as telephones, electricity, or gas, and firms that must compete internationally for markets, such as steel, automobiles and aircraft. In Europe, railroads and airlines are owned by government, as well. Investment and operating subsidies of government are given to so-called private enterprises. For example, the price that farmers receive for their food not only reflects market conditions of supply and demand, but also government decisions about price subsidies, tariffs, and import quotas. City dwellers may pay twice for their food: once at the shop and again through taxes.

The Italian government is foremost among major Western nations in mobilizing resources, devoting 35 percent of public spending to this in 1975. This is more than one-sixth of the total national product. Government's involvement in the economy derives in part from Italy's historic poverty, and also from measures that Mussolini took between the wars to promote economic growth for military ends. In addition to spending on *autostrada* and making cash grants to private industry, the Italian state is directly involved in trade and commerce through the major banks and two large holding companies, IRI (*Istituto per la Ricostruzione Industriale*) and ENI (*Ente Nationale Idrocarburi*).[2] The United States, Germany, Sweden, and Britain each devote about one-quarter of total public spending to mobilizing resources. Britain is distinctive for its emphasis on nationalized industries. The British government owns the whole of some industries, e.g., coal, steel, and electricity, and shares in individual firms throughout the economy, including automobiles, airplanes, computers, and Cook tours.

Any attempt to measure the importance of public policy in mobilizing resources inevitably underestimates its role, because government can exert influence without formally incurring a charge in its budget. Through tax policy as well as by spending policy, governments can encourage investment and growth. The power of government today is such that its informal discussions with businessmen also exert significant influence. In Sweden, for example, the Social Democratic government did not rely upon state ownership and investment to direct the economy, but negotiated agreements with privately owned companies to invest their resources in accord with national economic priorities.[3] Similarly, the French government intervenes selectively to give direction to particular firms or industries when deemed appropriate.

In principle, mobilizing economic resources is important for social policy, because only by a growth in the national product can government easily collect more taxes to finance increasingly costly social policies. In fact, differences in government spending on mobilizing resources do not appear to bear a direct relationship to economic growth rates. While Italy gives a high priority to such policies and has grown quickly, France, which spends less than half the Italian share, has also grown rapidly. Party politics appears to have little influence upon spending. The two countries devoting the largest proportion of their national product to resource mobilization—Italy and Germany —have been dominated by anti-Socialist governments in the postwar era.

In the race to get more public funds, departments of commerce, industry, agriculture, transportation, and natural resources have increased their budgets substantially in absolute terms, and usually as a proportion of the total national product, as well. But they have fallen behind social welfare agencies in the race to claim a larger share of the public purse. The proportion of public spending devoted to mobilizing resources has been declining in every major Western nation since 1950.

In terms of survival, the *defining* activities of government come first. If a government does not maintain public order at home and promote national interests abroad, it will cease to govern in the most literal sense of the term. But the cost of defining activities is relatively low in major Western nations today. Foreign affairs is cheap in money terms—unless mistakes are made that lead to war. While maintaining a diplomat is costly, the total number of diplomats that a country requires is small. Similarly, although judges and lawyers are well paid individually, the total cost of running the courts is small, and police and fire services cost less than education or health services. Collecting taxes and printing money are unusual governmental activities, for they produce revenue far greater than their costs.

Most of the money spent for defining activities goes for military defense. It claims one-sixth of public spending in the United States; and, if the cost of paying interest on war debts and caring for the widows, orphans, and wounded of past wars is included, the burden is even greater. Among major Western nations, the United States devotes the largest share of its public spending to defining activities. It bears the major burden of military defense in Western Europe and the North Atlantic, and in the Pacific as well. In 1975, the United States devoted 17 percent of public spending to military defense, nearly double the share spent by Britain, which ranked second; and nearly four times that of Italy, which spends least on military defense.

Traditionally, debts were to be contracted only to preserve the nation in time of war, and the balanced budget was a sign of governmental probity. But the respectability conferred upon deficit financing by the Keynesian revolution has cumulatively increased the debts and interest charges that governments must pay annually. Today, Britain has the dubious distinction of devoting the largest portion of its budget (8 percent) to interest on its debts. In 1975 debt interest cost the British government almost as much as maintaining its Army, Navy, and Air Force.

If contemporary Western governments concentrated solely upon defining activities, like their predecessors a century or more ago, today there would be no overloading of the political economy. About a tenth of the national product is devoted to the original defining activities of the state, and the cost of these policies has risen little or not at all since 1950. If a contemporary government only looked after its necessary defining concerns and did nothing else, its claim to one-tenth of the national product would leave citizens with 90 percent of their gross earnings as take-home pay. But people would then need more personal income, for if this came to pass they themselves would have to pay directly for all the social and economic benefits that are now provided by government.

SPREADING THE BENEFITS

In the field of public policy, social benefits stand out because they are numerous, important, and given directly to individuals and families at all stages of life. The young receive education; their parents get children's allowances; the elderly are given pensions; and in Europe, citizens of all ages enjoy health services.

Each year government provides tens of millions of social benefits to its citizens; some in cash such as pensions, and others as services in kind, such as education and health care. A simple tabulation of the annual total of social benefits shows that in Europe, they are greater than the national population (see Appendix, Table A3.2). This means that each European on average receives at least one major social benefit each year from government. In Sweden, citizens average almost two benefits per person each year. In the United States, where the ideology of individual independence of the state is relatively strong, government annually provides an average of four social benefits for every five Americans.

Any attempt to count the number of people benefiting from social policies inevitably underestimates the total. One reason for this is that many benefits affect a whole family and not just an individual. For example, parents benefit when their children receive education, and middle-aged adults as well as elderly parents benefit from pensions, for the former do not need to support the latter from their earnings. If a social policy immediately affects all four members of a typical family, the scope of social benefits is greatly expanded. The average Swede, personally or through his or her family, would thereby receive more than seven social benefits each year, and citizens elsewhere in Europe would receive four to five benefits. In America, the family impact of social benefits is equivalent to three benefits for the average citizen.

A second reason why merely enumerating benefits underestimates their significance is that most social benefits are not enjoyed once a year, like the right to vote, but are of frequent or continuing importance. Elderly people need their pension check to pay for the things they buy to eat each day; children spend half the days of the year in school; and anyone in hospital has an illness indefinitely affecting health. No simple tabulation of the number of social benefits can properly emphasize their duration and intensity.

Thirdly, many citizens enjoy a sense of security thanks to the insurance elements of social policies, e.g., unemployment compensation or health services, even when they are healthy and fully employed, and thus do not cost the government a penny. If these "uncashed" benefits were also reckoned in our tabulations, the numbers reckoned to benefit from the welfare state would be multiplied much more.

Contemporary welfare states spread much the same benefits among their citizens: education, a pension, an income if in need, and hospital or medical care if ill. But there remain significant differences in coverage and emphasis within the broad common framework (see Appendix, Table A3.2 for detailed calculations):

Education. Educating young people is everywhere a major spending commitment of government because education is regarded as a merit good, that is, something that every citizen must have. The minimum years of compulsory school range from eight in Italy to eleven years in Britain, and twelve years in some American states. The actual numbers receiving education reflect the age structure of the population; the greater the proportion of young people in a society, the higher the proportion benefiting from a public education. Education figures also reflect the desire of young people to get more than a minimum secondary education. The United States has the largest proportion of its population in school because of the relative youthfulness of its population and virtually open access to college.

Health and hospital care. In every major European country, all citizens are covered by a comprehensive national health service for routine visits to the doctor and hospital treatment for such routine occasions as childbirth or appendicitis, as well as catastrophic illnesses. The government also provides cash payments to individuals absent from work because of illness. Because the government must bear most of the cost of ill health, there are major public programs of preventive medicine, such as care for expectant mothers and "well-baby" clinics. The United States stands alone among major Western nations in providing no comprehensive health service for its citizens. Medicare and Medicaid cover about one-sixth of the population, those too old to be accepted as insurance risks by private companies and those too poor to buy insurance. The proportion of a nation's population benefiting each year from hospital treatment or cash sickness payments varies substantially among Western nations. In Sweden, the number of benefits annually is equivalent to 98 percent of the population. This is not because the Swedes are fond of going to hospital, but because sickness benefits are provided generously. In other European countries, from one-third to one-half of the population on average receives a major benefit each year from health services; the proportion depends upon the availability of hospital beds and the leniency of qualifications for sickness benefits. In the United States, a noteworthy proportion of the elderly and poor claim health care from government—but altogether they constitute only 9 percent of the population.

Pensions. The number of pensions that a government pays is determined first of all by the age structure of the population. A smaller proportion of Americans claim pensions than Europeans, because the elderly are a smaller fraction of the total population of the United States. The second major determinant is the age at which citizens become eligible for retirement with full benefit. The lowest qualifying age for a pension is fifty-five for some Italian women; men and women can usually retire at sixty in France and Italy. Elsewhere the usual retirement age for men is sixty-five. Thirdly, the value of a pension varies between countries. In Sweden the minimum national pension is about one-third the average wage; in the United States it is about one-sixth. Among major Western nations, France has the most citizens drawing a pension—19 percent— because of the relatively large proportion of its population that is aging, and because men and women both qualify for a pension at the relatively low age of sixty.

Other income maintenance grants. The elderly are not the only members of society who cannot earn enough to keep alive. The unemployed, the blind, the disabled, the prematurely widowed, and others in dire need look to government for a regular income. Governments sometimes pay supplementary income maintenance grants to those who cannot live on their pensions or support their family on a low wage. The United States is unusually high in the proportion of the population (17 percent) receiving income maintenance grants because of the high percentage of unemployed workers drawing benefits, and the high proportion of single-parent families receiving aid for dependent children. Every European country also has programs aiding families with dependent children;[4] but unlike America, the issue has not become embroiled in race. Income maintenance payments are lowest in France, covering 6 percent of the population and highest in Italy, reaching 26 percent of the population, because they are administered liberally as a form of state patronage.

Children's allowances. Family needs vary with the number of children, but wages do not. To assist large families, every European country makes cash payments to parents. The United States is the odd land out because it makes no such payments, and British coverage is low because it did not pay parents an allowance for the first child until 1977. France has the broadest coverage as well as the most generous range of family allowances.[5] Family allowances were originally promoted to compensate for the decline in the French birth rate because of husbands and fathers lost in World War I. The specter of depopulation has passed, but the tradition of generously providing family allowances continues. The cash value of benefits is much less than a pension. In Germany, for example, parents with two children may draw 125 Deutsche marks (about $60) monthly.

Special national programs. While the broad outlines of the welfare state are similar, some programs are distinctive to one nation. Housing is everywhere a concern of government, but government assistance is usually provided indirectly, by allowing generous tax write-offs of construction or purchase costs, or a tax reduction for mortgage interest payments.[6] Britain is distinctive in that an ad hoc policy of low-rent housing adopted after World War I has ballooned into a program making local governments the owner of nearly one-third of all British housing. They are loss-making rather than nonprofit landlords, offering subsidized rents to 18 million Britons of a wide range of incomes. France, Germany, and Italy give housing aid, but like the United States the benefits are confined to low-income tenants. In some European countries, rent controls effectively make housing cheap for some tenants and do so at the expense of landlords, rather than the public purse. Sweden's most distinctive policy involves labor-market policies—job retraining, and cash benefits and assistance in moving house to take a new job. In the United States, the Food Stamp program, originally intended to help government dispose of embarrassing surpluses of agricultural products in the 1960s, has grown to subsidize the diet of nearly 19 million Americans by the mid-1970s.

The clients of welfare programs are not the only people who benefit directly from government. In every major Western nation today, government is by far the nation's biggest employer, and public employees depend upon government for their income just as much as do pensioners or the unemployed. There are four groups of workers who depend upon government for their take-home pay. First and most obviously are those who work for the national government. The most prominent and prestigious government jobs are always few. The big public employers of labor tend to be relatively routine departments, such as the post office and the military. Collectively, local governments can be a bigger employer of labor than the central government; the great growth of education has been particularly influential, for teachers are usually locally employed, even if their pay and qualifications are often regulated by nationwide legislation and labor negotiations. Nationalized industries are a third sector of public employment. Long established nationalized industries can sometimes develop a civil service mentality among their work force, but industries that had trade union bargaining before nationalization or have unions combining public- and private-sector workers can differ from the traditional civil-service ethos. Last and not least among beneficiaries of the welfare state are employees in private firms whose goods and services are bought by government. The armaments and aerospace industries are most immediately dependent upon government for customers; it would be illegal or impractical for them to sell their products to private buyers.

Firms manufacturing everything from computers to paper clips also find government a substantial customer for their products.

In total, persons depending upon government for their take-home pay constituted 58 percent of the total work force in Sweden in 1975, and the proportion has risen since because of the government support for lame-duck Swedish firms following the country's major recession of 1977. Nearly two-fifths of British and Italian workers are directly or indirectly on the public payroll. The proportion is least, 29 percent, in the United states (see Appendix, Table A3.2).

The distribution of public employment differs substantially among major Western countries. The United States is distinctive because a larger portion of its public employees are in state and local government than in any other country. Along with Germany, another federal state, it has the smallest proportion of central government employees. The United States is also outstanding for the contribution that public spending makes to the covert public sector, that is, private enterprise firms selling government everything from highways and military equipment to management consultancy advice about how to cut out waste in public spending.[7] The so-called military-industrial complex is not the sole reason for so much of American private sector employment depending upon government. Germany has a relatively small military force, but it too is a big customer for private suppliers. It is the bigness of government—and, in both countries, an aversion to manufacturing supplies in government-owned factories—that accounts for the scale of government purchases from private industry.

In the centralized governments of France, Italy, and Sweden, the national government is itself the major employer of public-sector workers. In France and Italy, more than half of public officials are employed by the central government in some form or another, and another quarter are selling goods and services to central government. Britain, with a strong tradition of local government delivery of services and central government control of program standards and finance, falls midway between highly centralized Continental countries and the two federal systems in its distribution of public employees.

If the numbers who earn their take-home pay from government, directly and indirectly, are added to those who receive social benefits from governments, the total benefits that the contemporary welfare state provides are increased still further.* Altogether, Sweden provides an average of 2.3 benefits for every citizen, other European countries provide about 1.5 benefits for every citizen, and in the United States, government provides more than one benefit on average for every citizen.

GIVING AWAY MONEY ISN'T AS EASY AS IT SOUNDS

Delivering the benefits of the welfare state sounds both simple and popular. But in practice, the more money that a government tries to give away, the more difficulties it creates. The very act of giving away money creates demands from individuals and pressure groups. Since there can never be enough benefits to meet every potential demand, controversies arise about who should benefit and how.

The chief programs of the welfare state are universal in scope. Because every citizen can expect to benefit at some time from public education, health services, and a pension, such programs have a very broad base of popular support. But, while every citizen can count on receiving social benefits at some

---

* Because the number of workers cannot be related precisely to family composition, the figures in this paragraph are necessarily approximate estimates.

stages of the life-cycle, they are not enjoyed all at once and all the time. At some stages of the life-cycle, a citizen does not draw any major benefits from government.

Broadly speaking, individuals are likely to be "net gainers" when they are married couples with children in school, or when they are retired on a pension and vulnerable to chronic health problems. Within a family, parents can have children benefiting from a free public education for fifteen to twenty years. Retired persons have the sure knowledge that their income will continue however long they live, and that it should be protected against inflation as well. Among the elderly, women particularly benefit; for they may retire at an earlier age than men, and can expect to live longer in retirement.

In a complementary manner, the largest number of "net losers" are likely to be middle-aged persons with children through school but who are not old enough to retire. Pensions experts can rightly argue that such citizens are only temporarily without a major benefit; the money that they and their employers contribute in social security taxes is held for later payment of a pension. In other words, individuals may be disadvantaged in the short term, but not permanently. To argue thus is to assume that ordinary taxpayers are as farsighted as pensions experts, and do not suffer from what OECD economists have described as "defective telescopic vision," that is, an unwillingness to pay present taxes for future benefits.[8] The permanent losers in the welfare state are those who remain single, married couples without children to benefit from public education, and those who die before they can collect their old-age pension. Each group is a minority, but collectively their numbers are substantial in every society.

It is often overlooked that the chief benefits of the welfare state are not confined to the poor. Parents who can pay for their children's education are not charged tuition; their children receive free schooling just like the offspring of the poor. Similarly, national health services are provided without a means test of income. Citizens who can afford to pay for private schooling or health care may choose to do so, but they are not excluded from the benefits of public policy. In the extreme case of French and German pensions, the top fifth of the nation's wage earners can expect to receive one-fifth or more of the total sum paid out in pensions.[9]

The contemporary welfare state is intended to help every citizen, and not just the poorest and neediest members of society. One incidental consequence is that its benefits do not redistribute income to a substantial degree.[10] The relatively small sums of money paid as unemployment benefits do not make their recipients well-to-do, and may be worth less than the educational subsidies given the children of the well-to-do. The object of the welfare state is not the equalization of income after taxes and the distribution of welfare benefits; instead, it is to provide something for everybody. By doing this it builds the widest possible base of popular support for the high costs of public policy. People receive public benefits whatever their income, because they are due them as citizens. The benefits of the welfare state are meant to go to every citizen within society. Laws do not authorize free education only for the poor, but for everyone. And citizens who pay average or above average taxes and cast votes at elections expect to receive benefits in return for paying high taxes to government.

If a government wished to reduce the cost of public policy, it might confine benefits selectively to those deemed needy. As a statement of principle, such a goal may receive broad endorsement. But in practice, it creates many difficulties. The laws determining eligibility for selective benefits identify those who are ineligible, as well as those who are eligible. For example, any program providing publicly subsidized housing does not benefit home-owners or tenants of private landlords. Those who have no wish to live in public housing may dislike paying taxes for benefits that they do not think desirable, and those who would like subsidized housing but fail to secure a tenancy may resent the fact that others get what they want.

In some cases, people may claim benefits because they meet legal criteria of need, but may still be thought undeserving by many citizens. For example, the Aid to Families with Dependent Children (AFDC) program in the United States is often criticized, not because recipients do not need the money, but because some are thought undeserving, having earned [*sic*] welfare payments by becoming unwed mothers.

The recipients of selective welfare benefits may resent such policies too. One reason is that selection is usually on the basis of financial means. The administration of a means test requires public officials to ask probing questions about family circumstances and finances, as concern for public monies makes officials try to detect and prevent fraudulent claims. Those who are on the borderline of qualification may find that they lose a large amount of benefit for a small amount of earnings. For example, a mother on AFDC can earn $30 a month without losing any public benefit, but for every extra dollar earned, the benefit is reduced by two-thirds, an effective marginal tax on earnings of 67 percent.[11] Public services provided only to poor people are likely to be poor services, because they are confined to a politically inarticulate and disadvantaged minority. Municipally run free hospitals in America bear grim testimony to this fact.

The existence of a dilemma gives government a choice. It can continue to provide more welfare benefits at proportionately higher costs; or alternatively, it can become cost-conscious, reducing the total claim of welfare programs by providing them selectively. This may mean depriving some citizens of benefits they have previously enjoyed (free university education in the City of New York, or free prescriptions on the British National Health Service), or limiting benefits only to those who meet means tests, dividing citizens into welfare recipients and those whose ability to pay taxes disqualifies them from receiving the benefits that their taxes finance.

When the benefits of public policy are impersonal, government does not have the problem of discriminating between citizens in distributing them. The most clear-cut examples of impersonal benefits are collective goods that government provides to every citizen but not for anyone in particular such as military defense. Many resource mobilization policies are also relatively impersonal. For example, investment in energy resources indirectly provides benefits for individuals. The investments are not directed at identifiable individuals, but at the environment, and at organizations that can exploit environmental resources.

The impersonal benefits of government are massive in scale, accounting for upwards of half the total spending of government. A rough allocation of 1976 federal spending in America suggests that about 51 percent is directed to individual recipients (principally income maintenance benefits), about 30 percent spent on collective goods (principally defense), and another 19 percent immediately directed at corporate recipients (e.g., aids to business). In Sweden, the greater prominence of social policies shows 56 percent of public spending directed immediately at individual beneficiaries.[12]

The British government has demonstrated the difficulty of tracing the recipients of many benefits of public policy by an annual household survey of the beneficiaries of public policies.[13] Its careful statistical study can allocate only 40 percent of the total cost of public policy (principally social benefits) to individuals and families. The official British study could not identify individual beneficiaries of three-fifths of public spending, including such major programs as defense, debt interest, environmental services, and aids to trade and industry. Insofar as the targets of these impersonal programs are part of society, individuals benefit indirectly or collectively; but because these programs provide benefits for everybody, they also provide benefits for nobody in particular.

The cost of major welfare benefits is proportionate to the numbers receiving them. The more people who benefit from a program, the more expensive it is in total. For example, the baby boom of the postwar years has everywhere increased the aggregate amount of money spent by governments on education as the total number of children in school increased, and a rapid increase in the demand for education led suppliers to raise educational standards and costs.[14] The fewer people who benefit from a program, the less the cost in aggregate. For example, a policy to give tape recorders free to the relatively few who are blind would cost far less than paying cash sickness benefits to the great number off work each year because of a common cold. As the cost of a program increases with the breadth of its coverage, resistance to it may also increase as citizens realize that they must also pay for everything that government does in their name.

CHAPTER 4

Everybody Pays

Those old-fashioned values of liberty, equality and
fraternity come with massive bills for education,
health and social services.
K. Newton, *The Politics of Public
Expenditure Studies*, 1977

IN THEORY, taxation can be evaluated in many different
ways: by whether taxes are acceptable to the electorate and
administratively practicable; by what effects they have upon
economic growth and the consumption of goods and services;
by "fairness," as reflected by their impact upon those most and
least able to pay and upon the overall distribution of national income. But the practical justification of taxation today
is very different: government needs the money to meet the
costs of the contemporary mixed economy welfare state.

The problem facing politicians today is "not how to limit the
welfare state, but how to finance it." [1] When government provides costly welfare benefits, its need for revenue grows greatly.
The benefits of the welfare state are popular with citizens who
no longer need pay a poll tax as a condition of getting a
vote; instead they can use their vote to get the benefits of
public policy.

Citizens are schizophrenic in their approach to the costs and
benefits of public policy. As one academic expert on public
finance confesses, "We vote cheerfully enough for better hospitals, pensions and so on, but we are not prepared to accept

the implications for our own real take-home pay." [2] Taxes are necessary as a means to the end of the benefits of public policy. The money that government collects in taxes is not burned; it goes into the public purse to pay for the goods and services that citizens receive individually and collectively.

Because there is rarely a fixed relationship between what people pay in taxes and the value of the benefits that they draw from government, the politics of the welfare state is as much about who pays for benefits as it is about who receives them. Individuals and groups can effectively get something for nothing—if their fellow citizens pay most or all of the cost of what they consume. Individuals do not receive benefits from government in exact proportion to their taxes. Every citizen is to some extent a loser, that is, some taxes must be paid whether or not he or she receives any direct personal benefits. In the race for public benefits, a limited fraction of citizens end up net gainers, whereas most find, however much they may consume, that the cost of their taxes is not equalled by benefits directly attributable to themselves and their family.

To understand the politics of taxation, we must first of all examine how government raises money to pay for public policies. Next, we must see who pays taxes, and how widely the burdens of taxation are spread. Because every citizen is liable to pay taxes, in effect they constitute the dues of citizenship. But these dues differ from the subscription an individual might make to a club, for a club is a voluntary organization, whereas the taxes of the state are compulsory.

HOW THE MONEY IS RAISED

The goods and services that citizens consume must be paid for, whether by taxes or by charges levied directly upon consumers by private or public agencies. An earmarked social security tax may be said to differ little in principle from a contribution to a private pension scheme, except that the former buys a pension guaranteed by the full faith and credit of government. And the payment that a motorist makes for a tankful of gasoline not only pays the company that produces it, but also contributes to the government that builds the roads equally necessary for motorized mobility.

No government in the world meets all the costs of public policy from a single tax, nor would citizens be happy if they saw the total costs of public policy expressed in a single very sizeable bill. Government takes its cut from the national pie by a wide variety of taxation techniques. Politically, the most important features of a tax are *visibility* (how conscious are citizens that money is taken for government's use?) and *earmarking* (is tax revenue set aside for a specific purpose, such as paying pensions or building highways, or merged in a general revenue fund?).[3] In the long run, the effects of taxes cannot be hidden from citizens and sophisticated public officials. But the politics of taxation is not about final settlements; it is about the immediate measures taken to meet the government's pressing needs for cash. (See Appendix Table A4.1.)

Income tax takes a visible and large portion of the gross earnings of the majority of workers in every major Western nation today. The invention of pay-as-you-go tax deductions from weekly earnings was a precondition for the postwar growth of the welfare state. It enables government to collect large sums of money quickly, certainly, and easily. Making the income tax progressive has given government a treble dividend in an era of affluence. Firstly, when earnings rise, the revenue from income tax automatically increases; for example, a 25 percent tax on income will yield government $100 from a $400 a week income, and $125 from a $500 a week income. Secondly, the percentage of income taken in tax also increases progressively with earnings. If the extra $100 a week is taxed at a marginal rate of

30 percent, the government gains proportionately more. Thirdly, tax revenue is buoyed up by inflation; it will rise disproportionately when wages rise in money terms. For example, if the whole of a wage increase of $100 a week was simply an adjustment for a 25 percent increase in the cost of living, the person receiving it would be *worse off* in terms of real take-home pay, because of a progressive increase in marginal taxation.

An individual does not get anything in particular by paying income tax—except the reputation for being a law-abiding citizen. The revenue from this tax goes into the general coffers of government. The magnitude and visibility of income tax and the invisibility of specific benefits explain why it is so frequently an object of popular complaints. Citizens can regard income tax as money taken from their own earnings without entitling them to any particular benefits.

Social security taxes, by contrast, are earmarked as well as visible. They are visible, because the tax is levied upon a large portion of each individual's gross earnings, thus reducing take-home pay. While the individual's deduction is itemized on a pay check, the employer's contribution, which is usually larger, is not. These contributions show up in company accounts, and a firm must reckon social security contributions as a part of the cost of employing a person. This cost to a firm will in turn be reflected in higher prices of products sold to the consumer and/or less money to give workers as take-home pay. Social security taxes are earmarked, for they are paid into special government trust funds to finance social security benefits.

Social security taxes are in some ways like insurance premiums. An individual contributes money in expectation of drawing out benefits upon retirement, unemployment, or sickness. While the government retains the formal authority to repeal social security legislation, every welfare state considers itself bound to continue social security programs for which citizens have already paid contributions. The insurance principle was of crucial importance in creating acceptance of social security. Individuals were not to be given money from the public purse simply because they were in need. Instead, the state was to emulate private insurance companies, paying benefits to those entitled to them by weekly contributions from earnings. In the words of Franklin D. Roosevelt,

> We put those payroll contributions there so as to give the contributors a legal, moral and political right to collect their pensions and employment benefits. With those taxes in there, no damn politician can ever scrap my social security program.[4]

Today, social security contributions are best conceived as taxes. The contributions that individuals make are not voluntary but compulsory, backed by the force of legislation. These contributions are often described as regressive because there is a ceiling upon the total earnings liable to this tax. The ceiling is justified on the ground that individual contributions should be related to benefits, and inevitably, government must limit the amount it can pay out in pensions. As governments find it increasingly difficult to meet all the costs of social security benefits, they have raised the ceiling for tax contributions, thus making social security taxes much less regressive. For example, by 1987, the United States government intends to collect social security taxes on annual earnings up to $42,600. The deficits still remaining in social security trust funds are made up by money from general tax revenue. If social security systems were like private insurance companies and could not draw upon general tax revenues, benefits would have to be cut by up to one-third in major Western nations.

Whereas income taxes are levied as deductions from take-home pay, sales, excise, and customs taxes are levied when individuals spend their money. Every major European nation and most American states have a general sales tax under a variety of names, and with many variations. In Sweden, MOMS is not a phrase of maternal endearment, but the name of a general sales tax of 17 percent.* By European standards, United States' sales taxes of a few percent are relatively low, but Europeans are not subject, as Americans are, to as many as three income taxes—federal, state, and local. General sales and turnover taxes are usually separately itemized on bills, thus increasing visibility. But customs duties and excise taxes on such things as alcohol, tobacco, and gasoline are usually not separately itemized. Sales taxes usually flow directly into the general revenue account of government. When sales taxes are earmarked—e.g., gasoline taxes for road construction in America, and a portion of liquor taxes for antialcoholism measures in Sweden—this reflects the influence of a particularly strong pressure group rather than a departure from the broad principle of taxation for general revenue.

Sales taxes differ from income taxes in two politically important respects. First of all, every citizen pays the same sales tax regardless of his or her income. A wealthy businessman pays no more tax on cigarettes or drink than a workman with a much lower income. Low-income citizens may thus pay a higher proportion of their earnings in these taxes,[5] even though well-to-do people will pay more total sales tax because they spend more and buy more expensive goods. Secondly, sales taxes give citizens more choice about how they spend their money, or whether to spend it or save it. The ordinary individual is not better off in total purchasing power if a $50 cut in income tax is matched by a $50 increase in sales taxes. But a person does have more choice about what to do with take-home pay, and the illusion of greater prosperity, with more money to spend at the end of each week.

Property taxes, significant only in the United States and Britain, vary in visibility. Individuals who own their own homes are conscious of this tax bill each year. Even if paid monthly,

* Inevitably, changes in tax laws mean that there are year-to-year fluctuations in particular taxes. The figures cited here are normally for 1975 or 1974.

like a mortgage payment, property taxes are large enough to be noticed—especially when they are rising. Renters can let their landlord worry about the property taxes, but indirectly they will be affected, for increased property taxes put up their rent, or lead to property deteriorating. Even tenants of municipally subsidized British council houses must pay property taxes, thus contributing something to their own housing subsidy.

Taxes on corporate profits are neither visible to the ordinary citizen, nor are they earmarked for specific benefits. Few citizens are conscious of how much or how little is paid in profits tax by the companies that manufacture the products they buy. Corporation tax is levied solely on profits, and not upon gross trading revenue. In years when business is bad, automobile companies will pay no tax, or even use their losses to reclaim taxes paid on profits in previous years. In years when business is booming, profits and taxes will rise steeply. Because of this unreliability, governments do not rely heavily upon corporation tax for a large share of their total revenue. Businesses contribute more to the public coffers through sales taxes upon products sold, and the employer's contributions to social security benefits. Companies may pass the cost of taxes along to consumers in higher prices. When higher taxes reduce profits, less money is available for investment to increase the size of the national product in future. "Overtaxing" profits (however this controversial term is defined) can kill a goose that lays golden eggs.

Governments also have an effect on how money is earned and spent outside the public accounts. Through its regulatory powers, governments can compel business firms to spend corporate income to further public policy. For example, public health measures compel butchers to spend money to insure that their meat meets high sanitary standards, airline regulations compel companies to spend money to meet high air safety standards, and factory regulations compel companies to spend money to safeguard their employees. Complying with government regulations is, by definition, a necessary business expense that companies can offset against revenue. While this reduces liability to profits tax, it reduces profits too. Regulations that have been on the statute books for decades or generations may be regarded as a part of the fixed overhead costs of doing business. As long as regulations remain unchanged, these costs may even diminish as a fraction of the national pie.

The fresh concern with environmental pollution since the 1960s has everywhere increased "extra-budget" spending to promote the aims of public policy. To improve the environment, governments have passed laws regulating the companies creating pollution, e.g., chemical companies, automobile manufacturers, housing developers, etc. Higher environmental protection standards compel these companies to spend money in pursuit of public policy. The sums of money involved can be very large. The estimated ten-year cost of American air and water antipollution measures enacted in 1970 and 1972 range from $280 to $500 billion. Of this sum, about half comes directly from the taxpayer because federal legislation affects state and local authorities responsible for water and sewage treatment. The remaining portion comes from industry, which must pay for it by increasing costs to consumers or reducing profits or investment.[6]

Tax expenditures allow individuals or corporations to reduce their taxes by special or preferential deductions from earnings or profits. In 1975, tax expenditure totalled an estimated $90 billion in American federal taxes foregone, equivalent to approximately one-sixth the total cost of public policy at all levels of American government.[7] Tax expenditures are intended to promote government's purposes without the cost registering as public expenditure. For example, allowances to corporations are meant to encourage investment and help mobilize economic resources. When home-owners deduct the interest paid on mortgages from their taxable income, this encourages home ownership and construction. In Sweden, tax expenditures are important in making tolerable otherwise extremely high rates of taxation. Thanks to government investment and depreciation allowances, a company may be able to avoid paying any tax on a gross profit of up to $100 million. Swedes earning a million or more kronor a year may avoid taxes on much of that income by invoking of tax loopholes.[8] The inconsistencies of Swedish tax laws were further highlighted by a millionaire children's writer, Mrs. Astrid Lindgren, who found herself in a tax noose when she was assessed at a marginal rate of 102 percent on a multimillion kronor income. The assessment turned out to be an error, but the error created a furor about high taxation in Sweden.

Tax expenditures do not of themselves cost government revenue. If all tax expenditures were abolished, government could lower tax rates and still generate the same amount of income. For example, if a city ceased assessing houses for property tax at 33 percent of market value, and assessed property at 100 percent of market value, it would raise the same revenue if it simultaneously cut its property tax from 9 to 3 percent. If it did not do this, its increase in tax revenue could result in a real reduction in the take-home pay of many citizens.

Any move to reduce tax expenditures would invite political trouble, because it would involve repealing legislation conferring advantages upon groups accustomed to receiving them. The numbers that would be affected by abolishing all tax expenditures are great. For example, in America, 76 percent of tax expenditures go to individuals, as against 24 percent to corporations. Nearly two-thirds of all benefits, worth more than $60 billion in 1975, were distributed broadly throughout the population; for example, homeowners could deduct more than $10 billion of mortgage interest and local property taxes, and deductions for pensions were valued at more than $15 billion. Less than one-eighth of tax expenditures exclusively benefit those who are well-to-do or rich.[9] Some tax breaks given the rich are not without public purpose and advantage; e.g. deductions for contributions to hospitals, charities, and higher education. The well-to-do might claim that a maxim adduced on behalf of the poor applies equally to them: "To take less is as blessed as to give more." [10]

Patterns of taxation vary substantially among major Western nations; the differences do not reflect the amount that government takes from the national pie. High-spending Italy and low-spending France both make little use of income tax; the anti-Socialist United States makes corporations pay more than twice as much toward meeting the costs of public policy as does Socialist Sweden; and welfare-state Britain takes more revenue in supposedly regressive sales and excise taxes than does Germany (see Appendix Table A4.1).

The Anglo-Saxon tradition of taxation emphasizes taxes on income. Governments in the United States, Britain, Germany, and Sweden have confidence that their citizens will be honest when paying taxes. While tax avoidance through the ingenious use of loopholes is accepted, tax evasion is considered antisocial as well as criminal. The progressive element in income tax appeals to liberal as well as Socialist parties in Anglo-Saxon countries. Sweden, the country longest governed by Socialists, raises the highest proportion of its total revenue (46 percent) from income tax. Along with Britain, it raises relatively least from social security taxes upon income, because these taxes are not so progressive. Germany is distinctive in that the largest share of its tax revenue comes from social security rather than income tax. This reflects the high level of benefits provided by German welfare services, and a preference for taxing businesses heavily according to their number of employees. By taxing corporate profits and higher incomes relatively lightly, German tax policy is intended to encourage investment and economic growth. In Sweden companies also pay relatively more in social security contributions than in profits taxes. In all the Anglo-Saxon countries, sales taxes are relatively low. They are least in the United States, in the absence of a national sales tax, which is normal in Europe.

The Romance pattern of taxation in France and Italy is based upon mutual distrust between citizen and state. Both countries believe that individuals will deceive the government when making tax declarations, and history justifies this belief. Income taxes contribute less than one-sixth of tax revenue in France and Italy. To collect income taxes, officials estimate what they think an individual earns, and wait for the person to accept the figure or bargain for a lower tax assessment. Like buyers and sellers in a used car transaction, tax collectors try to get as much as possible, and citizens to pay as little as possible. For this reason, one-third or more of total individual income is not reported for tax purposes. A priest writing in *Osservatore Romano*, the Vatican's daily newspaper, declared that, "so long as the present system persists, no moralist can conscientiously require a rigorously and scrupulously prepared tax declaration which would inevitably result in grave loss to the declarer personally or to his business." [11]

Italy and France tax income as heavily as the United States and Britain, but they tax it differently. To generate the revenue required by the welfare state, both countries are shifting reliance from sales and excise taxes to social security taxes. Traditionally, common necessities such as salt, matches, and tobacco were made state monopolies to guarantee government a steady revenue from their sale. In France and Italy today, earmarked social security taxes on income are most important; they raise about three times the money raised by the conventional income tax. Frenchmen and Italians do not evade all taxes; they simply pay a much higher tax on employment, namely, social security levies. Employers pay the great bulk of the social security contribution. In Italy, social security taxes are equal to 54 percent of payrolls, the highest rate among major Western nations.[12] Of this total, the employer pays almost nine-tenths and the employee, one-tenth. In France, which has the second highest social security tax, the employer pays four-fifths and the worker, one-fifth. An employee pays almost nothing for social security and loses real benefits if his employer evades payment. This gives each potential social security beneficiary a vested interest in reporting an employer who deprives him of benefits by nonpayment of taxes.

At a time when government needs up to one-half of the national product to meet the costs of public policy, it must rely upon many taxes to produce so vast an amount of money. Today, taxes on earnings, whether in the form of income tax or social security taxes, account for 65 percent of the taxes paid by Germans and 65 percent of taxes paid by Swedes. The growing preference of governments for less visible taxes and taxes that earmark benefits [13] reflects the growing unpopularity of income taxes that immediately reduce take-home pay. By turning from income tax to other taxes, a government may for a short time succeed in "hiding" the costs of public policy. But the illusion cannot last, especially if taxes grow faster than the fiscal dividend of growth and cause a cut in take-home pay.

SPREADING THE BURDEN

The question of who is to pay the taxes needed by the welfare state has a short answer: *Everybody.* And each year everybody pays more. The treble affluence of the welfare state has made the average citizen a big taxpayer. For example, in 1950 the average American worker paid only 7 percent of income in tax, and the average Swede, 15 percent. As the real earnings of workers have risen, individuals need a smaller proportion for basic necessities of food, clothing, and shelter. When this happens, the logic of the progressive income tax is that the affluent average citizen should pay more tax on above minimum earnings.

From the viewpoint of government the taxing of the average worker today provides a treble bonanza. Rising wages provide more money to tax; progressive income taxes levy higher rates of tax on increased earnings; and the vast number of ordinary wage earners in aggregate yield a big contribution to the costs of public policy.

From the viewpoint of the average wage-earner, however, taxes are part of the pain of prosperity. In 1950, a British family head did not pay any income tax until his earnings reached the national average wage; by 1975, an Englishman earning less than half the average wage would start paying income tax. The average American wage-earner today is paying twice as large a share of earnings in income taxes—and paying them on income three times larger; this effectively increases his or her direct taxes by six times in current prices.

Because income tax rates are progressive, the amount that the average worker pays in tax for each extra dollar, krona, or Deutsche mark earned is significantly higher than the total share of earnings paid in direct taxes. In the extreme case of Sweden, for every extra 100 kronor that an average Swedish worker earns, whether by overtime or a wage increase, 63 percent must be paid to the government in income and personal social security tax. In Britain, the average worker has to pay 38 pence in tax for every extra pound earned in wages, and in the United States, 28 cents for every extra dollar earned.

Well-to-do citizens pay a substantially larger portion of their earnings in taxes on income than do average citizens. A Swedish head of family earning four times the average industrial wage is liable to pay 61 percent of total earnings in income and social security taxes. Elsewhere, the well-to-do pay in income tax from 46 percent in Britain to 40 percent in Italy. Nominal income tax on the well-to-do rises most steeply in

France, which asks more than five times the proportion of tax demanded from the average citizen. (These calculations assume that manual workers are proportionately as successful as middle-class workers in evading income tax.) In the United States, the tax on the well-to-do is two-and-one-half times that taken from average workers. Ironically, taxes are least progressive in Sweden, because of the high level of tax paid by ordinary workers.

Low-wage earners also contribute to the costs of public policy. In Sweden, persons earning half the average income and with normal family deductions pay as much as 31 percent of their income in tax. The proportion is lower elsewhere; in Germany, 19 percent; Britain, 18 percent; and the United States, 14 percent. In France low-paid workers are only asked to pay 8 percent of their earnings in direct taxes, and all of this is a social security contribution. In Italy nearly all of the 9 percent tax upon low-wage workers is also earmarked for social security benefits. The wide sweep of the tax net everywhere is illustrated by the fact that even old-age pensioners depending solely upon a social security payment for their income must pay a significant sum in taxes. For example, in the United States, a couple receiving social security benefits of $6,000 a year is likely to pay upwards of $1,100 annually in a variety of sales, excise, and income taxes. An abstemious pensioner, who did not use his car, drink, or smoke, and who saved a portion of the monthly pension check, would pay less tax—but might get less out of life too.

Income-tax statistics do not give a full picture of the total tax burden upon individual citizens. For example, the employer's contribution to social security is effectively a part of the tax on each individual's income, even though governments are politically shrewd enough not to allow it to be counted as a part of a worker's earnings. In France, this is equivalent to 27 percent of gross earnings; and in Italy, 41 percent. Adding this levy to income tax shows that in France 55 percent of the total labor cost of the average worker is tax, and in Italy 53 percent. Relatively low social security taxes and benefits make the proportion of income subject to these direct taxes lower in Britain, 35 percent; and in the United States, 31 percent.

Sales and excise taxes effectively reduce the value of an individual's take-home pay by adding to the cost of living. America is unique among major Western nations, for it does not have a nationwide sales tax. Nonetheless, the compound effect of state and local sales taxes adds as much as 8 percent to the total purchase price of goods in New York City. In Europe, a value-added sales tax is common, and the 8 percent sales tax, levied in Britain, is a low figure. In Germany and Italy, the rate is 12 percent, and in France and Sweden, the standard sales tax rate is 17 percent. While a few basic necessities can be exempt, common purchases such as gasoline, drink, and tobacco are normally subject to excise taxes very much greater than the standard sales tax rate.

The value of take-home pay is further reduced in America and Britain because homeowners must annually pay significant sums in property taxes, and tenants indirectly pay property tax through their rent. In every Western nation, profits taxes increase the cost of goods that people buy because companies add as much of profits tax liabilities as possible to the purchase price of their products in order to increase the net return on their investment. Even collecting taxes costs money, some of which is spent by government to maintain tax-collecting offices, and some of which is spent by taxpayers who employ accountants. Without an accountant, an individual must devote anywhere from several hours to several days of unpaid work each year to filling out tax returns.[14]

The average Swedish worker has the dubious distinction of being the most highly taxed citizen, for 46 percent of his or her gross salary goes toward tax. The 54 percent that is received as take-home pay is further reduced by the effects of sales and excise taxes, and the passing on of a portion of profits taxes.

The average German is taxed almost as highly, paying 45 percent of earnings in direct taxes. At the other extreme, Americans enjoy relatively low tax rates, for the average worker pays only 31 percent of earnings in taxes. The respective figures for other major Western nations are: France, 36 percent; Britain, 35 percent; and Italy, 33 percent. This tax take is, of course, significantly augmented by the sales and excise taxes that individuals must pay when spending their take-home pay.*

As the gap between nominal earnings and take-home pay widens, fewer people think about their gross wages. Take-home pay becomes more meaningful than gross figures that represent money never actually in a person's hands, yet employers must find the money to pay income tax and social security contributions up to 50 percent more than take-home pay. Wage negotiations are increasingly conducted in terms of take-home pay, because these are the figures that are meaningful to workers.[15] When workers talk about take-home pay as their "real" wage, they imply a claim to exemption from taxation, just as in medieval times priests claimed exemption from the authority of civil courts. To claim exemption from the government's taxing authority is a sign of civic indifference representing a big step toward political bankruptcy.

THE DUES OF CITIZENSHIP

Citizenship is the most expensive purchase that the average individual makes in a lifetime. Taxes cost the average citizen more each year than running an automobile or mortgage pay-

* The proportion of total income devoted to tax in France, Germany, Italy, and Sweden is calculated by combining income tax and employee and employer contributions to social security, and dividing by gross wages plus employer's social security contributions, as reported in OECD statistics. For America and Britain, property taxes paid by households are also included in the total income paid in taxes.

ments on a house. The average Swede works nearly half the year for the tax collector, the average Englishman more than twenty weeks, and the average American more than sixteen weeks a year to pay taxes. In the course of a working lifetime of forty-five years, the average American wage-earner "invests" about fifteen years of work to pay taxes, and the average Swede twenty-two years to pay the dues of citizenship.

In an era of treble affluence, individuals can pay higher taxes and enjoy a higher take-home pay as well, thanks to the fiscal dividend of growth. But the very ease with which increased social benefits have been financed has created little individual commitment to programs. Citizens have happily accepted more public benefits financed by the dividend of growth, but they have not endorsed the principal of cutting their own take-home pay to pay higher taxes.

Today, the squeeze on affluence focuses attention upon the costs as well as the benefits of government. Governors face the truth of the old maxim, "You can't spend it if you can't collect it." In times of fiscal stress, a government does not view taxes in terms of how much money each citizen should contribute individually, but rather, how it can collect enough money in total to meet all its commitments.

Just as world wars brought about a total mobilization of a nation's population for collective ends, the fiscal needs of the contemporary welfare state require the mobilization of a country's fiscal resources. A government heavily taxes relatively inexpensive luxuries, like cigarettes, as well as expensive luxuries like gold watches. Indirectly or directly, nearly everything that citizens buy has a multitude of taxes contributing to its cost. The impact of taxation is pervasive. The only way for an individual to escape taxation would be to live as a hermit in the woods, perhaps occasionally bartering home-grown produce for necessities from the domain of the taxed.

Government today sweeps rich and poor alike into its tax net, for it needs money from everybody. Because the distribution of income tends to be diamond-shaped, there is a middle mass of wage earners who contribute a large portion of total tax revenue. For example, in 1974, Americans earning from $10,000 to $24,999 earned 52 percent of the total gross income, paid 48 percent of federal income tax, and constituted one-third of the taxpaying population. In Germany, those earning from 25,000 to 69,999 Deutsche marks paid 55 percent of all income taxes and constituted 47 percent of the total taxpayers. In Britain, a group earning £2,000 to £3,999 in 1974 earned 50 percent of total income, paid almost half the total income tax and constituted 41 percent of taxpayers.[16] Government could not begin to finance its major policies today without a major contribution from the middle mass of taxpayers.

The well-to-do pay a larger proportion of their income in tax and pay more in total taxes than do those in the lowest income brackets. For example, in the United States, the top one percent of income earners pay approximately 20 percent of total income tax, a share more than six times as great as the contribution made by the bottom six percent, those with a taxable income of $5000 a year or less. In Britain, the top one percent of taxpayers contributes 16 percent of total income tax, whereas the bottom 14 percent of taxpayers contributes only one-tenth as much.

Yet, any scheme to finance the rising costs of public policy by a "soak the rich" taxation policy has a severe limitation: it would not provide enough money. For example, if the United States government decided to levy a confiscatory tax of 100 percent on all incomes above $63,000 a year, the top salary paid Cabinet secretaries in Washington, the total yield in taxes would be about $6 billion. But this would only be enough money to meet the growing costs of public policy for two months at the 1976 rate of increase. Such a calculation assumes, of course, that well-to-do Americans would continue to earn big salaries, notwithstanding confiscatory tax rates.

A policy of nationalizing all corporations in America could

divert to government $123 billion in company profits. But since government already collects $58 billion of this total in corporate tax and taxes on dividends and capital gains, this would only bring $65 billion in "new" revenue to government. Unless it acquired the companies by Soviet-style confiscation, government would have to deduct $52 billion paid in after-tax interest to persons given government bonds in exchange for company shares. Overall, a policy of complete nationalization would net the federal treasury only $13 billion a year, less than one percent of the total national product, and equivalent to about four months growth in the cost of public policy.[17]

A "squeeze everybody" increase in taxes promises much greater yields to hard-pressed revenue raisers. For example, a one percent increase in social security contributions in America would add approximately $12 billion a year to federal coffers, equivalent to the net receipts of nationalizing the whole of industry, and a one percent across the board increase in tax rates would yield more revenue than a 100 percent confiscatory tax on top incomes. The government's need for more revenue reduces the progressive element in income tax; those who earn less can no longer escape from contributing a share to the costs of public policy.[18] The political risk in this policy is simply stated: "Soak the rich is a great slogan. But soak the average person never won anyone an election yet." [19]

Citizens do not view taxes in terms of the revenue needs of government, but rather in terms of protecting their own take-home pay. But government does not determine the ideal tax take from the individual citizen and then ask each household to pay this. Taxes are levied in a multiplicity of ways and by a multiplicity of agencies, with no one tax providing as much as half of total revenue. Each individual must add up the total taxes at the end of the year to learn how much are the dues that he or she has paid for citizenship. Most taxpayers do not have a clear idea of the total tax taken from their gross earnings; they judge their taxes by what it leaves them in take-home pay.

While taxes are meant to be compulsory, the benefits that an individual can draw are elastic, and not strictly related to taxes paid. There is therefore an incentive for individual citizens, whether well-to-do or poor, to try to get more from the welfare state than they pay in taxes. In the centuries before the Industrial Revolution, the peasants of England were in an analogous position. They could graze their animals without charge on the common land of their parish. Each family sought to graze as many animals as possible on the common land. But the supply of pasture was not infinite. Too many animals grazing upon too little land produced "the tragedy of the commons," a preindustrial example of an overloaded economy.

Today, the welfare state risks the tragedy of the jam pot. The fact that citizens are not charged individually for each bit of "jam" they secure from government gives each an incentive to seek more. Yet the amount of jam that government can provide is limited. The more each citizen receives from government, the less that others may receive, or the more taxes that must be collected. A citizen will find that the extra jam received through public benefits is offset or exceeded by an increase in taxes. If the claims for more benefits result in a cut in take-home pay, then political bankruptcy can result.

CHAPTER 5

The Pressures for More

Frankly, I am not satisfied with the state of the
public expenditures and the rapid rate of its
growth. I trust, therefore, that we mean in a great
degree to retrace our steps.

W. S. Gladstone,
British Chancellor of the Exchequer,
1860

When asked to describe his political ideology, the
founder of the American Federation of Labor,
Samuel Gompers, replied, "More and more and
more and now."

THE VICTORIAN LEADER of the British Liberal Party and
the equally Victorian founder of the American Federation of
Labor each expressed a timeless half-truth about political economy. Gladstone gave voice to the laissez-faire belief that government should intervene as little as possible in the economy.
Gompers, by contrast, emphasized the demand of masses of
citizens for a continuing increase in material advantages from
every source.

Today, Gompers has triumphed over Gladstone. In Mr.
Gladstone's time, British public expenditure fell from 15 percent of the national product in 1830 to 8 percent in 1890.
But today, it claims 49 percent of the national product. When
the American Federation of Labor was founded in 1886, government spending equalled less than 5 percent of the national

pie; today, it is seven times as much.[1] Economizing no longer means the saving of candle ends to reduce the cost of government. In the contemporary welfare state, budgeting is about spending more rather than less of the national product. The differences between countries are less significant than the upward trend found everywhere. In the words of a contemporary Amercan sociologist, using Socialism as if it were a synonym for social welfare, "Some socialisms creep and others gallop." [2]

The desire of citizens for "more" does not have to be met by government. Living standards rose substantially in the era of Gladstone and Gompers. Most of this rise was the result of an increase in the national product rather than government policy. Labor leaders approved wholeheartedly, for they were suspicious of the powers of government being used against workers. Today, the pressures for more are directed at government, as organized labor requests more public programs for citizens, including good jobs for public employees.

Government spending grows in three different ways. First, inertia commitments lead government to do more of the same; for example, providing a standard pension costs more in total if the number of elderly increases. Second, more can mean better. To improve pensions so that the elderly share in rising living standards increases the total cost even if the number of elderly remains constant. Third, "more" can mean "new," that is, the enactment of programs providing services previously not undertaken by government. For example, the enactment of Medicare committed the American government to spend billions of dollars to care for the health of the elderly. Spending can expand under all three headings simultaneously, when more citizens demand new and better government programs.

There is nothing automatic about the upward movement of the costs of public policy. A government could repeal rather than enact or maintain laws authorizing public spending. When numbers of pupils increase, it could spend less per pupil in order to keep the total costs of education constant. But governments do not do this; they choose to follow the paths of their predecessors. In such cases, conserving past policies leads governments to spend more and more.

To understand why governments spend more and more, we turn first to the electoral cycle to comprehend how parties can bid up the costs of public policy without regard to public opinion. Inertia commitments embedded in laws of past governments are a difficult-to-resist force for more public spending. The final section of this chapter reviews the pressures of consumers, producers, and suppliers for a growth of government spendings. The pressures for more are not inexorable, but they have been predominant for more than a quarter-century.

THE BIAS IN THE ELECTORAL CYCLE

The conventional model of electoral choice assumes that individual voters determine what government does, just as consumers are expected to determine what manufacturers make.[3] This view makes no assumption about how much or how little the majority of citizens wish to pay in taxes or consume in public policies. It describes a continuing process of competition in which a majority of voters can endorse more spending at one point in time, then shift to wanting less taxes at another. Parties are expected to compete by altering their policies in accord with changing popular wishes. Electoral victory is awarded to the party that can produce the combination of programs that, in aggregate, strikes the most popular balance between the costs and benefits of government. A government cannot be said to be spending "too much" or "too little." Any party that strays (or is forced) from a course favored by the majority can expect to be promptly punished by a loss of votes.

Unfortunately, this conventional view of perfect electoral competition is no more true to reality than its counterpart depicting perfect economic competition. Elections, like markets, involve imperfect and highly restricted competition; many of the conventional assumptions about governments doing what the voters want are oversimplified and unrealistic. There is a bias in the electoral cycle favoring the determination of public policies by the producers of programs (politicians and bureaucrats) rather than by the consumers (voters).

An election gives each citizen a vote to express his or her individual preferences, but the complexities of the contemporary political economy mean that the sum of individual preferences do not always add up. In the conventional individualist model, each voter is expected to decide what combination of policies is best suited to his or her personal interest, and vote for the party that promises most nearly to match this self-interest. But it does not necessarily follow that an individual will benefit by electing a party that does what he or she wants. For example, a voter could support a party pledged to expand higher education to increase the earnings of young people, yet find that the increase in the number of graduates so reduced the scarcity value of a degree that in cash terms it was not worth the cost of getting it. A voter could vote for a party pledging to abolish wage controls, only to find that in the resulting wage explosion persons like himself were worse off in consequence of inflation. The literature of economics today highlights many paradoxes of individual and collective rationality.[4]

Although parties may offer voters a choice in terms of what they promise to do, it does not follow that they will actually achieve what they promise. In a very limited sense, every election offers a choice between the Ins and Outs. But the effect of such a choice on policy is vitiated if the Out party behaves just like the Ins, once elected to office. This happens. For example, Labour has won office in Britain pledged to reverse the economic record of its Conservative predecessors. But its performance in office has often been more in tune with Conservative economic policies than Socialist promises. In the words of a Conservative MP, "It is true the Labour government has inherited our problems. They seem also to have inherited our solutions." [5]

Electoral competition in major Western nations offers voters a very limited range of choices between parties. The United States most closely approximates the two-party ideal, but both parties are themselves coalitions of overlapping interest groups. In Europe there is usually an explicit choice between coalitions, whether between a Socialist or bourgeois coalition in Sweden, or between an Italian Christian Democratic government with a coalition that has an *apertura a destra* (opening to the right) or *apertura a sinistra* (opening to the left). But a voter has far less choice between parties than between automobiles, for even if there are only two or three home-based automobile manufacturers, foreign imports offer a wide choice between dozens of different makes. A country cannot import political parties; if this could be done, envy of the achievements of German Christian Democratic and Social Democratic governments could make these parties as popular a German export as the Volkswagen.[6]

Differences in the spending proclivities of parties do exist, but they are differences in degree or timing, and not of kind. Governments vary in the rate at which they increase spending on public policies, but the variations are limited. Germany shows the greatest movement up and down in public spending. These variations do not correlate with changes in party control in office; they primarily reflect fluctuations in growth of the national product.[7] There have been differences between parties in the timing of economic measures. A comparative study by Andrew Cowart and Anthony Blum found that governments frequently adapted Keynesian-type demand management policies affecting the balance of unemployment and inflation. But Democratic administrations in the United States and Labour governments in Britain were faster to try to reduce unemployment, and Republicans and Conservatives reacted earlier against inflation. In Germany, Social Democratic governments have been readier to intervene in the economy than their Christian Democratic predecessors. But the overall conclusion remains, "In none of these countries do we find evidence that parties of the left have fundamentally different economic goals than do parties of the right." [8]

While an election gives citizens a chance to determine who governs, it does not allow voters to determine what government does. The choice of individuals for office is very different from the choice of policies by elected officeholders. Individuals can win elections by being vague rather than specific about policies, or by stressing their personal qualities rather than an ideological or programmatic stance. Exceptionally, American state and local governments often allow citizens to vote in bond issues or referenda that directly determine a property tax for schools, sewers, or municipal improvements. But such popular votes affect only a very small proportion of the costs of public policy in the United States. Significantly, studies indicate that in bond issues and tax referenda, voters are often likely to reject tax increases recommended to them by their elected representatives.[9] For example, on June 6, 1978, voters in California voted by a two-to-one margin to reduce property tax by more than 60 percent and to limit drastically future increases in the property tax.

Parties are more important than voters in the policy process. They produce the programs offered to voters, and, after an election, they can produce decisions put into effect by government. In seeking office, party politicians differ from automobile manufacturers; they are not subject to an immediate budget constraint.[10] An automobile maker cannot promise that a car will have many desirable features without regard to cost, for the more features added to a car, the more it will cost to produce and thus, the fewer potential customers there will be for it. An automobile manufacturer must strike a balance between promising customers alot, and promising them what they can pay for. By contrast, an office-seeking politician can promise whatever the voter wants, subject to only a general constraint of credibility. A party that goes beyond the limits of credibility in "overpromising" benefits risks a landslide defeat, as Democratic Senator George McGovern unwittingly demonstrated in the United States in 1972. Equally, a politician "over promising" cuts in government spending also risks a landslide defeat, as Republican Senator Barry Goldwater unintentionally demonstrated in 1964.

Until the Keynesian revolution, most politicians believed that a balanced budget and attacks on high levels of public spending were what the voters wanted most. For example, Franklin D. Roosevelt campaigned in 1932 to cut federal spending by 25 percent and balance the budget. Today, politicians compete by promising—and often delivering—specific public policies. Politicians appear to believe that by targeting specific benefits at particular pressure groups and blocs of voters they will improve their popular standing. To identify the programs to be repealed in order to permit a tax cut would stir up intense opposition among those faced with a loss, without activating support from those who might gain a very little from the cut. Politicians may regard their promises as conferring benefits without costs. The logic is summed up by the late Senator Dennis Chavez of New Mexico, who asked an opponent of a porkbarrel public works bill, "Why is the Senator fighting this bill? There is something in it for everybody." [11]

The bias in the electoral cycle favors increased spending. Rightly or wrongly, politicians consistently calculate that vot-

ers want more, and so, they promise more. The resulting increase in taxes is not counterbalanced subsequently in time
by tax cuts. Any reaction is usually limited to the consolida-
tion of costly programs and a moratorium on tax increases.
The resistance to tax increases can apply brakes to public
spending, but does not force a change in direction. Whereas the
bread and circuses offered by the rulers in ancient Rome were
ad hoc charges upon Roman wealth, election pledges in the
contemporary welfare state become permanent charges upon
the national product. A measure pledged in efforts to win votes
at one election will not gain a party extra votes the next
election, if all parties promise to continue it. But it continues
far into the future, a mute and increasingly costly monument
of an election long past. Moreover, new spending pledges must
be made in the next campaign as past ones are buried in the
ongoing costs of government.

The politicians of the era of affluence have been taking risks:
they have assumed that however much is promised, their
promises can be made cost free, that is, paid for by the fiscal
dividend of growth. The fiscal dividend must be large enough
to pay for programs representing the ghosts of elections past,
as well as the costs of the latest victory. As long as politicians
respect the credibility barrier and growth remains substantial,
promises can be made and met up to the limit of what an
increasingly educated and sceptical electorate will believe.

The 1970s raises the prospect that the real campaign costs
of electioneering—that is, money spent from the public purse
for programs pledged to win votes—could exceed the full
value of the fiscal dividend of growth, thus threatening a fall
in take-home pay. Politicians can only continue to promise without constraint if they think that voters are both gullible enough
to believe any promises offered, and forgetful enough to give
fresh credence to politicians who have disappointed them
before.

If we start from the assumption that "voters are not

fools," [12] then the cumulative effect of politicians promising benefits could push voters in the direction of political bankruptcy. As one party succeeds another while the economy becomes increasingly overloaded, citizens will adapt their expectations. Specifically, they will expect that economic difficulties will continue, and that their governors will be increasingly ineffectual in dealing with these difficulties. In such circumstances, they can decide to look after themselves, registering indifference to politicians who have mismanaged the national economy, and leaving electoral victors wondering what to do with their eroded political authority.

INERTIA COMMITMENTS:
THE GREAT MOVING FORCE

Programs already on the statute books and embodied in government are a ghost within the machine, exerting a steady pressure to increase the costs of public policy. Established commitments do not reflect the current choices of politicians, but rather past decisions taken in the light of circumstances that may have since changed. Because they are established with the force of law, the government of the day is committed to spending hundreds of billions of dollars, Deutsche marks or kronor annually without making a single policy decision of its own. Moreover, because inertia can be a moving force, governments are typically committed to spending *more* money to provide the *same* policies from one year to the next. The best way to predict what government will spend next year is to see what it spent last year, and then add a percentage to reflect continuing pressures for more.[13]

The commitments of government are expressed in laws requiring government to pay money to individuals (e.g., pensioners), provide services to individuals (e.g., education) or to society as a whole (e.g., defense), or pay subsidies to organizations (e.g., industry, or another branch of government). The statutory presumption of costly programs continuing is reinforced by the political expectation that once benefits are provided they will not be withdrawn.

Any newly elected government, if it is to uphold the law of the land, is immediately committed to carrying out the accumulated policies that its predecessors have left behind on the statute books. This inheritance of laws can extend back for centuries. For example, the Labour government that took office in Britain in 1974 inherited laws and taxes dating from medieval times. Even though Jimmy Carter found the United States at peace upon entering the Presidency in 1977, his Administration is required to pay the debts and care for the veterans from four wars of this century: World Wars I and II, Korea, and Viet Nam. Even when a country loses a war and its regime is overthrown, the new regime continues most established legislation without change. For example, when France moved from the Fourth to the Fifth Republic in 1958, General de Gaulle produced a new Constitution, but he did not repudiate the spending commitments embodied in the social security legislation of previous French regimes.

While no government is theoretically bound to accept all the policies of its predecessors, the great bulk of spending by government today goes by on the nod. Established commitments, however large, are approved with only perfunctory examination, so that politicians can concentrate upon currently controversial policies and proposed new commitments. France has given official recognition to the acceptance of inertia commitments, dividing its budget into two categories. The *service votés*, appropriations concerning established commitments, can receive blanket approval in a single ballot. In this way, the

French Assembly gains time to scrutinize new spending commitments arising from changes in policy.[14] In its 1974 reform of budgeting, the United States Congress was not trying to cut public spending, but to establish a ceiling upon the annual increase in spending.

One reason why spending commitments continue unexamined is practical: the activities of the contemporary welfare state are so numerous that it would take the whole of a government's life to commence even a superficial scrutiny of the commitments of past generations. There is not world enough and time for politicians to scrutinize every item in a budget of 500 billion dollars or Deutsche marks. Politicians often follow Parkinson's law, scrutinizing those details small enough to be within their comprehension. For example, the German Parliament's budget committee has spent more time worrying about the employment of two typists than about spending tens of millions on agricultural subsidies.[15] Economists have tried to introduce into government new techniques to challenge established spending commitments by asking: why are we doing this at all? Whatever the label used—PPBS (Planning Program Budgeting System) in Lyndon Johnson's Washington; PAR (Program Analysis and Review) in Ted Heath's Whitehall; RCB (*Rationalisation des Choix Budgétaires*) in Georges Pompidou's Paris; or the *Gesamtplanung* of Willy Brandt's Bonn—the result has been the same. The introduction of so-called rational or scientific techniques has not reduced public spending, and a technique such as zero-based budgeting does not produce zero increase in public spending; rather it offers a new way to justify old commitments.

Another reason why spending commitments continue is political: the existing programs of the welfare state create expectations among citizens that these benefits will continue in future. A few, such as social security, are even financed by money vested in special trust funds. The majority are effectively protected by those who produce and consume the benefits; their interest in keeping what they have guarantees intense opposition to any proposal to repeal established programs. Like Gulliver, the modern welfare state is tied by a fine mesh of commitments spun around it through the years.

So strong are the commitments of government that politicians now refer to the bulk of public spending as "uncontrollable," the responsibility of their predecessors. By stressing powerlessness in the face of inertia commitments, politicians seek absolution from blame for the taxes needed to finance these policies. The uncontrollable proportion of public spending is rising, as the costs of public policy increase. Near the end of the Johnson Administration in Washington, so-called uncontrollable commitments accounted for 59 percent of federal spending; after eight years of a Republican administration, the proportion had risen to 75 to 80 percent. Brookings Institution economists go further, arguing that virtually the *whole* of the federal budget spent on nondefense programs is uncontrollable in the short run. Defense spending too is difficult to cut by more than a few percent without immediately running into major costs for such things as severance pay and military retirement pensions. Confronted with so many uncontrollable inertia commitments, President Ford complained in his first budget message, "The size and the growth of the Federal budget has taken on a life of its own." [16]

The commitments of government are dynamic, not static. Here inertia describes the tendency of a body in motion to continue in motion until arrested by a superior external force. A newly elected President or Prime Minister jumps on board an organization (some would say, an avalanche) pushing forward plans for spending. Even when a government believes it has a little money in hand because of the fiscal dividend of growth, it can find it already committed. In 1974, Republican budget officials faced their work with confidence because they had an extra $25 billion to allocate for federal spending in the coming year. But they soon learned that $25 billion doesn't go very far in Washington nowadays. The growth of uncontrollable elements in the budget left the White House with only one percent of that sum to spend for new or expanded programs.[17]

In a period of great economic growth, politicians may relax in the belief that the fiscal dividend will provide enough to meet future commitments. But the forces of inertia can easily push government in a direction that it does not want to go. For example, Richard Nixon entered the White House in 1969 with the announced intention of bringing federal spending under control. But federal spending rose by $142 billion during his period of office, and federal debt rose by $177 billion. The costs of Aid to Families with Dependent Children (AFDC), especially unpopular among Republicans, trebled during the Nixon Administration, and the number of beneficiaries almost doubled to 11.3 million. In Sweden in 1976 a bourgeois coalition took over the government after four decades of Socialist rule. Within a year of entering office, the anti-Socialist government found itself increasing government subsidies, raising taxes, and devaluing the krona; all measures inconsistent with an image of fiscal respectability, but justified on the ground that inertia commitments inherited from its Socialist predecessor allowed little alternative.

Cumulatively, even a high level of economic growth can be inadequate to meet inertia commitments after decades of new government programs. Each program may be justified and popular when introduced, and each may not cost "too much" money, at least at first. But the total costs may commit the future dividend of growth and then some, leaving no scope for any further additions without the risk of political bankruptcy. A Swedish social scientist complains that his country has now mortgaged the whole of its future as well as present growth because of planned inertia commitments. "The dilemma of preplanned society is that your future has already been determined for you. Freedom of action is decreasing all the time, since you have to pay for yesterday's good and honest ambitions, and for all the pleasant things that you already enjoy, but perhaps would not buy if you had the option now." [18]

The current status of public pensions for the elderly illustrates how inertia commitments have steadily increased the costs of public policy. When old age pensions were first introduced generations ago, the age of retirement was usually past the ordinary citizen's life expectancy. For example, when Britain introduced pensions in 1908 for needy persons age seventy and above, the average life expectancy for men was fifty-two years. When the United States introduced social security pensions for workers age sixty-five and above in 1937, the average American man could only expect to live fifty-eight years. Today, the average man can expect to live up to nine years beyond retirement in France, and at least three years in the United States, Britain, or Germany; an average woman can expect to draw a pension for up to twenty years in Italy and for twelve years or more elsewhere. The greater longevity of the population accounts for about half the rising cost of pensions policy.[19] Moreover, there are demands heard from trade unions and welfare workers to lower the age of retirement to sixty, thus increasing the cost of pensions substantially.

Everywhere in the Western world pensioners have shared in affluence; pensions have grown in real terms as the national product has increased. In the 1970s, many governments have also protected pensioners against inflation, indexing pensions so that they are automatically increased in value when the cost of living rises. In effect, pensions are now double-indexed, being guaranteed to rise when living standards are rising, and not to fall when the economy is stagnant or affected by inflation.

Can Government Go Bankrupt?

The pressures for more and more to be spent on the elderly have radically affected the financing of old age pensions. Early schemes were often ambiguous, insofar as they were promoted among fiscal conservatives on an insurance basis, and among the mass electorate as a bargain. David Lloyd George promised British workers the chance to get nine pence of benefits for every four pence that they paid in; the remainder of the money was to come from employers and from general tax revenues. General tax revenue was important in launching schemes, for elderly persons could claim benefits soon after the passage of legislation, even though they could not have paid a full insurance contribution. Today, increased pension costs resulting from inflation and higher standards of benefits mean that even those who have contributed for forty years have not paid enough into social security trust funds to provide a sound actuarial basis for a future pension. For example, in 1976, the American social security trust fund paid out $4.3 billion more than it took in as receipts; and in Germany, the deficit was 6 billion Deutsche marks. President Carter could threaten Congress with the prospect that the reserves in the Old Age and Survivors Insurance Trust Fund "will run out in 1983." [20]

To meet the mounting costs of social security, pensions are increasingly financed by present taxes rather than past contributions. Pensions have become a massive intergenerational transfer of income from those of working age to the elderly. For example, a single man retiring in 1970, after thirty-three years of paying social security contributions in the United States, would expect to have 32 percent of his pension financed by payments made into his account, and 68 percent from current payments made by generations still in work. Today's workers are not assured a pension by what they pay in, because much of their contribution is promptly spent. Present contributors depend upon tomorrow's taxpayers to guarantee payment of the pension promised them by law.[21]

CONSUMERS, PRODUCERS, AND
SUPPLIERS UNITED FOR MORE

In the contemporary welfare state, the pressures for more and more public spending come from three principal sources: (1) The consumers of welfare benefits can push up public spending by increasing in numbers or by demanding more and better public services. (2) The producers of public goods and services—from armaments manufacturers to social workers—are strategically important spending lobbies within government. (3) A growth in the supply of tax revenue, whether caused by the growth of the national product or inflation, can also lead to an increase in government spending as demand expands to consume the supply of tax revenue and then some.[22]

The programs that account for the biggest part of spending in the contemporary welfare state—education, health, and pensions—are open-ended, and have costs proportionate to the numbers consuming them. The costs of public policy inevitably grow with an increase in the number of consumers entitled by law to receive benefits. Many of the most important and expensive programs of the welfare state are open-ended commitments to give services to every citizen entitled to them. For example, laws do not state how many children shall be educated each year, but that all children of a given age must have an education. Similarly, unemployment benefits are not limited to the first 5 percent of the work force to become unemployed, but to all the unemployed who have qualified for a given benefit. If the number of children increases, government is committed to spending more money to provide extra classrooms and teachers; if the number of unemployed increases, it must pay out more in unemployment benefits. If a whole year's appropriation is spent for unemployment benefits after nine months of a fiscal year, the commitment does not lapse; it overrides budget estimates of how much money should be spent that year, and a supplementary budget appropriation is made. The costs of public policy are thus forced upward without any change in the intent of public policy.

The growth of population in every major Western nation in the past quarter-century has been a significant pressure for more. The United States has seen the biggest population explosion, both relatively (up 30 percent) and absolutely (up 65 million). Population growth has been relatively small in Britain, but the 11 percent increase is greater than the existing population of Scotland. The track record of demographers in forecasting future population trends is unreliable, but the trend is clear: a continuing increase in population. Official estimates predict that the population of Europe is likely to increase by anything from 12 to 20 percent by the year 2000 (that is, by as much as 100 million people), and of the United States by at least 30 million people.[23]

The increase in population is especially costly for government, because the fastest growing groups—the young and the old— are especially dependent upon the services of the welfare state. The young require an expensive education and a disproportionate amount of health care. It takes upwards of twenty years for government to receive taxes in return for the public services invested in nurturing a child. Even if the 1970s decline in the birth rate continues for a generation, the pressures to maintain education spending remain. Producers of education services argue that instead of cutting spending and leaving classrooms empty, a better education should be provided each child by reducing the number of pupils per teacher.

The elderly have had their numbers increase consistently throughout the past generation. Life expectancy has risen by about six years in every major Western nation; for a newborn girl it now stands at seventy-eight years in Sweden, and seventy-six in America and France. The continuing rise in the proportion of the elderly in the population more than offsets any potential saving from the decline in the number of children in school. A pensioner needs a weekly income throughout the year, and often expensive health care; by comparison, schools care for only a fraction of the needs of young people. The dependency of pensioners upon government is such that only an inhuman policy could reduce the commitments of public policy to the elderly.

The increase in the proportion of young and old in society also means a decrease in the proportion of the population of working age. It has fallen in the past quarter-century in every major Western nation; and the trend is expected to continue indefinitely. In the United States, there has been an increase of some 25 million in the number of Americans of school or pension age, and a decrease of nearly 5 percent in the population of working age. In Sweden, a seemingly small growth of 160,000 in the population not of working age leads to a decrease of 4 percent in the population of working age. The cost of caring for a growing number of dependents thus falls upon a relatively smaller number of people in work. Two additional important considerations cannot be predicted from demographic data—possible changes in the proportion of women of working age actually in paid employment, and the total number of jobs that the economies of major Western nations can provide.

The movement of population from cities to suburbs and from relatively declining industrial regions to regions where the economy is booming also generates pressures for more public spending. The pattern is the same in every major Western nation. Cities facing decline and industrial regions with rising unemployment clamor for grants to make up for lost tax revenues and to stimulate a revival of their depressed economies. Concurrently, growing suburbs and booming regions clamor for more schools, roads, and other public facilities to meet the needs of their expanding population. Whether changes result from prosperity or industrial decay, government is asked to spend more money for citizens thus affected.

Prosperity encourages citizens to want government to provide more and better public benefits. People who have more take-home pay to spend on their personal wants are also likely to want more and better public goods and services. The more educated citizenry produced by affluence is a more effective lobby for bigger and better government programs.[24] For example, a family that buys a second car will want government to spend more on roads, and a family with a rising income is likely to demand more education for its children. With affluence, the average family can afford to pay more taxes—but they will want better schools, recreation facilities, and services in return. As living standards rise, people expect government to provide higher standards of public services—as long as this can be done without cutting their take-home pay.

Producers as well as consumers of public programs exert inertia pressures for more spending. The very existence of government institutionalizes commitments to spending programs, for even if the circumstances that produce a law change, the organization remains. Like the medieval Roman Catholic Church, modern government follows the principle of *mortmain* (literally, dead hand), guaranteeing an institution existence in perpetuity independent of the wishes of its nominal superiors. Individual politicians and parties, like medieval bishops, are transients; the institutions they serve are carried on by the force of inertia.

Are Government Organizations Immortal? asks the author of a study of institutions in Washington.[25] The answer is: usually so. Any new agency that survives for more than a decade is almost invariably secure against being dismantled. The last significant cutback in government agencies in the United States was carried out by President Eisenhower in 1953. Even when agencies' names disappear in a reorganization plan, their active spending parts do not disappear but are reassigned, and the programs that they look after continue. The American experience is matched in Europe; the only notable government departments abolished in the twentieth century are those concerned with religion and colonial affairs.[26]

Civil servants are the immediate beneficiaries of the growth of government. Government maintains their income at a higher level than the earnings of many whom they serve. The producers of government goods and services have interests, just like automobile manufacturers or assembly-line workers. Public officials do not promote their interests by selling things, but by giving away goods, services, and sometimes money. The justification for their activities is not profit in the conventional sense, but the promotion of a less easily defined sense of individual and collective well-being. By virtue of professional expertise in social work, education, agriculture, medicine, or highway engineering, the average bureaucratic politician can claim to know what is best for society's needs within his or her specialist field. But while welfare officials "may believe thoroughly in what they are doing, they are nonetheless serving their private interest in seeking to extend the scope of their power, importance and influence." [27] For example, a survey of Washington public officials found that 73 percent of officials in welfare agencies favored more spending on social services, as against 33 percent of officials in other agencies.[28]

Public officials wish to promote the growth of their programs, for growth enhances their promotion prospects and the status and power of their agency by increasing the number of consumers it serves and the benefits it gives them. Because civil servants also value convenience and security, their appetite for growth is not unlimited. Because the process of growth upsets established routines, some civil servants welcome periods without change to consolidate past expansion. Moreover, growth invites controversy within government, as well as criticism from opposition parties.[29] Overall, public officials show a bias in favor of slow and steady growth, consistent with their long-term commitment to government employment.

The most obvious way in which public officials make their personal interest apparent is by bargaining for higher wages. The growth of public employment in the postwar era has increased unionization among public employees. The fact that teachers may refer to their trade union as an "association," or that doctors may use such an august title as the Royal College of Physicians and Surgeons, does not make their organization any less concerned with wages and working conditions than a union of coal miners or plumbers. For example, medical doctors have used the introduction of publicly funded health schemes to make the government guarantee them a high minimum salary, without any ceiling on the amount that they can earn. Similarly, teachers used the growth in pupil numbers in the 1960s to increase their relative earnings, and the total number of teachers on the public payroll.[30]

Government cannot reject wage demands from employees with the classic argument of the private sector, "the money isn't there." Both public officials and politicians know that the money is there, for government can always increase its revenue by raising taxes, borrowing, or printing more money. In the era of treble affluence, wage increases could be financed from the fiscal dividend of growth. But this cannot indefinitely guarantee higher wages for more public employees, because public officials contribute less than their proportionate share to measured economic growth. In a manufacturing industry, increased wage costs can often be met by increased productivity. By investing in new machinery, a manufacturer can keep labor costs relatively constant by paying higher wages to fewer workers. But with a few exceptions, such as electricity generation, government activities are labor intensive—e.g., delivering mail, health services, or education. Productivity cannot be increased rapidly by mechanization; moreover, the quality of education, health, and social services tends to be judged by how many people are employed in these services.

The fact that public officials cannot justify higher wages by dramatic increases in productivity does not prevent officials from asking for more money. The argument is voiced that teachers and firemen need to eat, just like car workers or computer technicians. Granting these claims causes a slow, steady increase in the claims of public policy relative to the national product. From 1950 to 1970 the cost of the services and goods bought by major Western governments rose by an average of 67 percent more than overall price increases, and by as much as 91 percent more in Germany. This relative price effect means that governments tend to claim at least a little more of the national product each year without providing any increase in public benefits.[31]

The wages of public officials are determined by political bargaining between representatives of public officials and government. Collectively, public sector employees constitute upwards of one-half the votes needed to win an election (see Table A3.3). In addition to this ballot-box power, many unions have a monopoly claim to expertise. A government cannot hire a doctor or teacher without a professional qualification any more easily than it can employ labor at below union rates to build its buildings. A strike by public service employees is and is meant to be a form of political pressure. Strikers seek to embarrass the government of the day by showing that it cannot offer benefits as usual. Rather than risk the political difficulties of strikes, most politicians prefer to give public officials most of what they want.

Because public goods and services are usually not sold in the market place, there is no way to decide how much is enough to be spent on the programs that public officials and their organizations provide. If education and health services were sold in the market place, producers would only be able to supply as much as the market would pay for. They are not, because political choices have determined that every citizen should receive these benefits without paying the cost of what each consumes. These merit goods are not rationed by consumer choice, but by decisions taken within government.

The producers of the major programs of the welfare state have a simple answer to the question of how much should be spent: more. The justification for expanding programs may be couched in the language of public interest (our society will benefit from more education) or client interest (the elderly need more health services). Spending more is also in their private interest. A characteristic example of how producer groups lobby for more spending is provided by OECD studies of education and income maintenance. Experts in these fields recommended that all nations move toward the "best practice" standard of the country currently providing the most benefits (that is, spending the most money on a program). In this way, every country but one is expected to increase public spending. If OECD had sought views from taxpayers, it might instead have adopted an "average practice" standard. Countries spending less than average could be encouraged to raise expenditure levels up to the international mean, and those above average could reduce what might be regarded as "too much" spending.[32]

When budget officials try to reduce spending on public policies, they are likely to find themselves isolated within government. Each spending department is ready to defend its own established claims on the national product; none will volunteer that its services should be cut, even if the overall philosophy of the government of the day favors a reduction in public spending. Rather than hoping to cut costs in absolute terms, the most that antispenders can hope to achieve is to reduce the rate at which programs grow (see infra, pp. 221ff). But government heads cannot expect their bureaucratic subordinates to cooperate happily in pursuit of budget cuts when these go against their interests. In the rueful words of a Washington budget official, agencies may sink their plans, using expert knowledge of programs and budget procedures to "bore below the waterline."

The supply of tax revenue can also be a cause of more and more public spending, according to Wagner's law, a proposition named after a nineteenth-century German economist who first developed the idea.[33] In a nutshell, it states that given a growing supply of public funds, producers of public policies will find ways to spend it. War furnishes many examples of public expenditure and public revenues rapidly expanding, then dropping with a return to peace—but not falling back to prewar levels. The peace-time rise in affluence since 1951 has similarly supplied government with greatly increased revenue, and the extra income from taxes has been used to finance the growth in government programs.

Thanks to the development of Keynesian economics, politicians have been able to make the supply of revenue exceed taxes by the simple device of producing budget deficits. In an era when balanced budgets were the ideal, politicians could not increase public spending without simultaneously increasing tax revenues and, in periods of low growth, tax rates as well. What two economists call "the old-time religion" of balanced budgets prescribed that an increase in public revenue should be used to retire a portion of the public debt inherited from past wars and depressions and to prevent debt from becoming a burden on taxpayers of future generations. For example, for twenty-three consecutive years following the American Civil War, the federal government each year produced a budget surplus. It also did this for eleven consecutive years following World War I. Then the worldwide depression and war created temporary deficits, and the triumph of Keynesian ideas installed full employment and economic growth in place of the budget rule worshipped by the old believers.[34]

The creation of budget deficits, justified technically as a means of stimulating economic growth, greatly increases the government's potential supply of money. In principle, deficits could be created by cutting taxes without any increase in spending commitments. In practice, every major Western government has increased public spending (often cutting taxes temporarily as well) to create the deficits demanded by Keynesian-type economic prescriptions. Taxpayers are immediately made better off, for they do not have to pay the full cost of public benefits when they consume them. The costs are shifted forward, being added to the public debt. The extent to which the future costs are borne by those who enjoy present benefits depends upon the age of individual beneficiaries. For example, to a person in his 20s, the present value of future repayment of debts would be almost the same as paying for a policy out of current taxes. But a taxpayer age 45, would receive the equivalent of a 15 percent discount on cost, and a taxpayer age about 60 could shift nearly 40 percent of the borrowing cost onto future generations.[35]

Governments have also taken advantage of "fiscal drag," the tendency of progressive taxes to take a larger share of the national product as money values increase through real growth and inflation. Among major Western nations, taxes have increased an average of 16 percent faster than economic growth from 1955 to 1975. Moreover, revenue from income tax has increased even more than general tax revenue.[36] The increase in government revenue resulting from inflation exerts a downward pressure upon take-home pay. Among major Western nations, only Britain has indexed income taxes to give its citizens some protection against inflation causing a disproportionate increase in income tax. This was only done in 1977, against the wishes of the Labour government of the day, through a quirk in committee procedure. Elsewhere, thanks to inflation, governments continue to increase the supply of tax revenue, even after reducing nominal tax rates.

Of course, arguments may be offered suggesting that sooner or later the demand for government programs may be saturated. A portion of the past increase in the cost of public policy reflects expanded coverage of major welfare programs: many programs cannot be expanded further, because they now cover virtually 100 percent of those in need. But there is a potentially infinite demand for the provision of more and better services. The demand comes from those who produce the services, as well as from those who consume them. A change in social conditions may simply be cited as evidence of a changing pattern of need, justifying new programs.

The minimum a government can expect to spend on public policy is 100 percent of what was spent last year *plus*. It can only contain the rate at which the costs of public policy grow. It may do this without cutting take-home pay by prudence in making spending commitments, and/or by a very high level of economic growth. But the pressures to increase spending are strong, even when the money is *not* there. For example, in low-growth Britain in 1977, the Labour minister in charge of the Department of Health and Social Security found himself confronted with a Christmas list of demands from pressure groups wishing to finance new benefits for everyone from orphans to pensioners. While a case could be made for each proposal separately, the government could only say no to these demands in aggregate, for their total estimated cost was 13 billion pounds, more than double the amount it was spending on social policies, and equivalent to an increase of almost 30 percent in income tax.[37]

The reasons for the growth of public spending are multiple. A University of California sociologist, Harold Wilensky, statistically tested the relative influence upon spending of party ideologies, national wealth, the demographic composition of the society, and inertia, as measured by the number of years a policy has been on the statute books. After analyzing evidence from a wide range of Western nations, Wilensky concluded that one of the most important determinants of how much money government spends is simply how long it has been committed to supporting a given program. Public policies are like automobiles; the older they become, the more expensive they are to maintain.[38]

CHAPTER 6

Economics Without Constraint

You've got to distinguish between a politician
using economics and using economists.
Charles L. Schultze, economist
and advisor to presidents, 1976

ECONOMISTS offer political advice in a buyer's market. Political decision-makers have no shortage of men seeking their ear, promising advice that will bring benefits to all in the future. A politician does not want to be told what to do, but how to do what he would find most congenial to do. He does not want lessons in economics; he wants help. An economist, whether motivated by professional concerns, party loyalties, or a mixture of the two, must produce help. The more help he can give, the more a political decision-maker will wish to use him. The economist is not rewarded by a salary based on corporate profits, but in the coin of politics: a reputation for influence among the powerful.

As a group, economists have advanced greatly in influence in every major Western government in the past quarter-century. Two factors have contributed the most to their success. The first is that they have been able to offer advice congenial to politicians. They offer a set of ideas that justifies politicians spending money to promote full employment and economic growth, as against the dour medicine of older doctrines of the dismal science. The adoption of a Keynesian approach to economic management occurred at different times and in different ways in each major Western nation, depending upon previous circumstances and political opposition. Different and sometimes conflicting advice may be derived from a Keynesian model. Important as these reservations are, the economic foundations of the era of treble affluence can be aptly described as Keynesian. Secondly, Keynesian economics appeared to work. It prescribed clear and potentially practical actions for governors to take to reach desired goals, and for a time at least, these goals were achieved.

The introduction of economists into prominence in government has not made government more cost-conscious; instead, it has made economists more politically conscious. Politicians have been happy to use economists as their advisors, especially when their advice has been congenial. At the height of treble affluence in the 1960s, economists were imbued with confidence that their "science" had escaped from the constraints that had led bust to follow boom in earlier generations of economic growth. This confidence led to the development of arguments and plans for spending more and more money on public policies.

Until the world recession of the 1970s, the growing affluence of Western political economies made it seem that the constraints that had worried classical economists need no longer be worries. But the benefits of affluence have not been cost-free; they only seemed so. Cumulatively, the effect of commiting a little more public money here and a little more public money there has added a lot more to the cost of public policy. Today, most politicians and many economists lack faith in promises of unending treble affluence.

The pages that follow examine four ways in which politicians have made use of economics to give political direction to

the economy. The section on one-eyed Keynesianism emphasizes that politicians can turn a blind eye to those economic
prescriptions that they do not wish to follow. The following
section shows how the absence of an all-powerful central
decision-maker in government means that there is no politician
or agency that can manage the economy in the way that economists presuppose. The ingenuity of economists in inventing
alternatives to money as it is commonly perceived enables politicians to balance their books in "unreal" terms, while citizens
must confront the reality of an increasingly overloaded political economy. Finally, when clouds of doubt and disappoint-
ment lower, they may be dispelled by happy forecasts of
future growth.

ONE-EYED KEYNESIANISM

Conveniently for those who invoke his name, John Maynard
Keynes died in 1946, before his ideas had become the conventional wisdom of economic textbooks, and his name a shibbo-
leth defining respectability in political economy. Contemporary
economists, like theologians at the time of the Reformation,
today cite selections from Keynes's twenty-seven volumes of
writings in support of contradictory policy prescriptions.[1] In
academic disputes, one *Katheder*-Keynesian might well thunder
at another, "Yes, my friend, we are both Keynesians—you
in your way, and I in Keynes's." If Keynes were alive today, his
acidulous pen would undoubtedly explode many of the prescriptions offered by exegetes invoking his name, and his fertile
mind would undoubtedly be propounding novel techniques
for coping with the distinctive configuration of economic
difficulties in the 1970s. Politicians have tended to observe
the battle from afar, following signposts pointing in desired
directions, and turning a blind eye to those pointing toward

political difficulties. The result can be characterized as one-eyed Keynesianism.

The *political* importance of Keynes derives from the fact that he suggested ways in which governments could achieve both full employment *and* a full use of a nation's economic resources for growth. In doing this, Keynes was reacting against the high level of unemployment widely prevalent during the World Depression, and also against the classical, even Puritanical, emphasis of prevailing doctrines of political economy.[2]

From this complex, logical, and mathematical analysis, a few simple (or, economists would say, "oversimple") rules have been distilled for politicians to follow.[3] By spending more money than it raised in taxes in times of economic recession, government could promote full employment and economic growth. The other side of the Keynesian coin is that in times of boom, when demand threatens to exceed supply and cause inflation, government should budget for a surplus of revenue against expenditure. The endorsement of deficit financing is conditional, rather than absolute; yet it marked a break with the doctrine of balancing the budget at all times, the orthodox wisdom of managers of the economy from William Gladstone through Herbert Hoover.[4]

The political justification for following Keynesian prescriptions has been practical rather than theoretical. Politicians who cared nothing for economics and little for political ideology could see the advantage of spending more on government programs than they raised in taxes, thus providing benefits in excess of costs. In particular, politicians in office have found it tempting to use Keynesian techniques to increase take-home pay shortly before an election—even if this required deflating the economy immediately after achieving victory. When critics of deficit spending asked, "How are we going to pay for this?" the answer could come back, "We can't afford not to."

Ideologically, Keynesianism has stood athwart the conventional battle lines of conservative and Socialist philosophies.

This is appropriate for a man who acted as advisor to British governments of every political coloration, and was himself a supporter of the middle-of-the-road Liberal Party. The Keynesian approach has appealed to Socialist politicians because it emphasizes government management of the private as well as the public sector of the economy. In the words of Hugh Dalton, a Cambridge student of Keynes and a Labour Chancellor of the Exchequer from 1945 to 1947, "We may now free ourselves from the old and narrow conception of balancing the budget no matter of what period, and move toward the new and wider conception of balancing the whole economy." [5] The approach appealed to trade unionists because it made the achievement of full employment central to government policy. Non-Socialist politicians could accept Keynesian techniques because they avoided detailed regulation of the economy, enhancing government's influence by concentrating attention upon a very few macroeconomic decisions that government would in any event have to take: decisions about the total cost of public policies and how these costs are met. Businessmen could accept Keynesian proposals to stimulate demand for their products; for high rates of economic growth promise booming profits.

While Keynesian doctrines cannot be assigned the full credit for an era of treble affluence, the political diffusion of simplified Keynesianism has gone hand-in-hand with unprecedented economic growth and sustained full employment. Moreover, thanks to high levels of growth, government debt has not become a great cumulative burden upon major Western nations. In the past quarter-century public debt as a percentage of the national product has actually fallen in twenty years in America, and in at least eleven years in every other major Western nation. In politics, correlation is as good as causation; political economists have received credit for much of the success of the 1950s and 1960s—and urged their governments to do even better.

In the 1970s something has clearly gone wrong with the promise of a virtuous cycle of growth. For example, since 1973 the British Treasury, where Keynes's ideas have been particularly strong, has had to produce *three* budgets a year on average to manage a seemingly "unmanageable" economy. With Keynes as with Marx, it is possible to go back to the master's writings and discover that contemporary interpretations are mistaken. For example, in the course of a long professional career, Keynes worried about inflation and the supply of money, as well as about unemployment and low rates of growth. To note that Keynes was concerned with many of the economic problems of today only emphasizes the extent of the difficulties; it does not resolve them. Economists today disagree among themselves about what the chief problem of the economy is, as well as how it can be resolved.

One telltale indicator of things awry can be found in the pattern of public deficits in the past quarter-century. When Keynesian prescriptions recommend a deficit to prime the pump of an economy in recession, politicians as conservative as Gerald Ford have been ready to follow in hopes of reducing unemployment with an election in the offing. But when success in stimulating the economy threatens to make demand exceed supply, orthodox Keynesianism prescribes that government should budget for a surplus by increasing taxes, cutting the costs of public policy, or by a combination of both methods. Deflating demand when inflation threatens is as important as reflating demand in a recession.

Politicians have preferred to practice one-eyed Keynesianism, managing their economies without constraint. In an era of full employment and rapid economic growth, one would expect inflation to be a risk as often as recession, with budget surpluses occurring about as often as budget deficits. In fact, no major Western country has such a record.* Italy takes the prize

---

* The deficits refer to total spending by all levels of government. As discussed infra, pp. 141ff, there are multiple budget-making centers in government.

for one-eyed Keynesianism, for in the quarter-century from 1951 through 1975, every year has shown a public deficit. In Sweden, foremost among Western nations in innovative economics, the public accounts have been in deficit for twenty-two of the twenty-five years. In the United States, deficits have been registered in twenty years; in Britain and France in eighteen years; and in Germany in seventeen years. The bias toward deficit financing cannot be explained as a simple function of recession or the absence of a risk of inflation. In the period from 1966 to 1975, when inflation, with or without recession, was a concern of governments everywhere, Italy and Sweden did not once register a budget surplus; America did so only once; and Britain and Germany twice. France is unique in the past decade, having budgeted as often for a surplus as a deficit.

Politics provides the shorthand explanation of what has gone wrong. Keynes designed a model of managing the economy that gave central importance to the decisions of government. In the abstract, Keynes was a political economist; but in practice, Keynes himself was one-eyed. He did not foresee that politicians might not follow all the prescriptions that were offered to them.

The fact of the matter is that Keynes was an elitist, raised in an English tradition of doing good for others, rather than doing what the people want. In this, if not in personal lifestyle, he resembled Fabians, such as Beatrice and Sidney Webb, and conservatives, such as Charles de Gaulle. Keynes believed in government by an educated elite, rather than by an elite of birth or social manners. He was an elitist nonetheless. In the words of his friend and biographer, Sir Roy Harrod, his economic ideas were imbued with "the idea that the government of Britain was and could continue to be in the hands of an intellectual aristocracy." [6] Keynes never tested himself in the arena of electoral politics; his role was that of an *éminence grise*. At the end of his long career, he met his comeuppance, not from an economist brighter and quicker of mind, but from

Can Government Go Bankrupt?

Fred M. Vinson, a graduate of Kentucky Normal and Center colleges, and Harry S. Truman, who never went to college at all. They taught Keynes that his assumption that the U.S. Congress would give Britain billions of dollars to finance its postwar reconstruction was a fundamental political error.[7]

Inevitably, political considerations disrupt the assumptions upon which Keynesianism is based. In the first instance, the readiness of politicians to turn a blind eye to uncomfortable Keynesian prescriptions can lead to inflation, with all the problems this causes for the predictable management of a political economy. Secondly, politicians can turn from the management of aggregate demand to the direction of specific wage and price policies, whether from a Socialist faith in national economic planning, or from an elitist corporate philosophy. Thirdly, a national government may find that its openness to the world economy leads to the importation of inflation from another land. European nations were specially threatened by this in the late 1960s, because of the international status of the dollar and the American government's use of seigniorage to finance its domestic and foreign policies.[8]

Given the predispositions of politicians and their preeminence in political decision-making, economists' prescriptions of increasingly complex and "fine-tuned" sets of policies are likely to fail. The weakest link in the political economy is the politician. In the words of Swedish political economist Assar Lindbeck, "The main obstacle for a successful stabilization policy, is the government itself." Lindbeck suggests that economists might abandon the search for complex policies and concentrate upon a search for "robust" measures "which will do some good even if they are not used in a very skilful way."[9] As an extreme example of a robust policy to avoid a politically induced catastrophe, Lindbeck cites Milton Friedman's suggestion of a fixed rate of growth in the money supply.

Bad politics can never be the basis for successful advice-giving; any economist who closes his eyes to such a fact risks pricing himself out of the political market place, or externalizing onto politicians the costs of following his advice. An economist who advances the technocratic claim that government ought to do what economic theory prescribes must be prepared to face the question, "Who elected you?" Economists are meant to advise, not supplant, elected politicians. For better or worse, politicians retain the responsibility and authority for what government does. When economists move into policy-making roles, they must accept that they are no longer engaged in a pure science. Instead, they are in the midst of political controversy, where political and not economic constraints are primary.

To criticize the political uses of Keynesian ideas is not to challenge his very considerable intellectual achievement.* It is instead to emphasize that Keynes (like Bertrand Russell, another Cambridge don) was very different as a politician than as a logician. In a world in which governments are run by elected officeholders rather than philosopher-kings, it is possible that the latter's message may in some sense be "too good" for an imperfect world.

THE CENTER FAILS TO HOLD

Managing the economy requires a manager, that is, a political figure who has in his or her hands all the powers needed to carry out decisions that will pervasively influence the economy, hopefully, for the better. It is a matter of economic in-

---

* It might also be noted that Keynes' status in part reflects attributes extrinsic to his theoretical work. Among other things, Keynes could be admired because he made money speculating in the City of London; acted as an advisor to government; wrote frequently and well for nontechnical publications; and, to cap it all, married a beautiful Russian ballerina.

difference whether the manager is an elected President or Prime Minister, a hereditary monarch or dictator, or a banking or syndicalist despot. Only insofar as there is centralized decision-making does it make political sense for economists to prescribe actions that can only be taken by such an official.

Unfortunately for economists, a centralized political economy does not exist in any Western democratic nation.[10] There is no single individual or agency within government that can cast up national accounts and strike a balance, as a professor or an OECD economist can later do after all the money has been spent. The national pie is not sliced by a single act of an all-powerful central authority. Instead, many different groups try to get their hands on individual pieces of the pie. It is not so much a question of the government's right hand not knowing what its left hand is doing, but of the chief octopus being so busy looking after his own eight hands that he cannot attend to what others are doing.

There is no single central agency within government effectively striking a collective balance between what all the institutions of government spend and what they raise in revenue. The figures cited in this book for the costs of public policy were not decided by a President, a Prime Minister or a Treasury official. Instead, they are the result of adding up the decisions taken in many different places within central government, and by local governments, nationalized industries, and other parastate institutions as well. Only if all of these separate decision-making bodies act in a similar manner will the total costs of public policy conform to any one idea of how to manage an economy.

The decisions emerging from the complex processes of political budgeting are "suboptimal," for they are not as good as they might be if government were organized according to the centralized ideal of many economic models.[11] One expert on American federal budgeting compares the process to an attempt by a crowd of 80,000 spectators at Yankee Stadium to agree with a "team" of 400-odd Congressmen on the field about how much government should spend on particular programs, as well as in aggregate. In such circumstances, it is remarkable that anything meaningful "emerges at all." [12]

The extent to which taxing powers are dispersed varies greatly between federal and unitary states. Americans pay about $2 in state and local government taxes for every $3 paid to the federal government. In Germany, about one Deutsche mark in every three paid in taxes goes to state and local government; and in Sweden more than one-quarter of taxes are raised by local government. In relatively centralized governments, such as Britain, France, and Italy, upwards of 90 percent of the taxes are determined centrally.

In every major Western country, local governments spend far more money than they raise in taxes. The disparity is greatest in highly centralized France and Italy. Local spending is more than five times the amount of local taxes in Italy, and three times the amount in France. In Britain, property taxes give local authorities more revenue, but only one-half of local spending is paid from taxes levied by locally elected politicians. Only in federal Germany and the United States, and in Sweden, which centralizes the framing of policies and decentralizes taxing and spending, does locally raised revenue begin to approach local expenditure.

There is thus a real conflict of interest between central governments responsible for raising taxes and local authorities responsible for carrying out policies financed by grants from the national treasury. When local politicians are not responsible for raising taxes, they have little incentive to restrain expenditure so as to prevent taxes from escalating. On the contrary, political incentives favor more spending, because local authorities can claim the benefits, whereas the costs are borne by politicians in the nation's capital.

Because the functional responsibilities and the tax-raising powers of state and local governments are fixed in law, they cannot easily be altered. When more burdens are placed on local authorities than they can finance, local politicians turn to their national treasury to ask for money from its greater resources. In major Western nations, there has been a slow but steady trend of local taxes contributing a decreasing share of the costs of local policies, with central government contributing an increasing share.

The jungle of financial relationships within and between central and local government (and "off" budget agencies too) creates many problems. Just as a political economist must combine data from many different spending bodies to find out what is going on, so too a politician must try to influence many more-or-less autonomous spending agencies. Because the total tax take of government does not result from a single central decision, there is a tendency for it to drift upward as different parts of government each assume that a little bit more for their own program would not be noticed, or that the costs could be blamed on somebody else. No agency gains particular credit by restraining its own spending to the general good. There is thus no way in which politicians at the center of central government can effectively control the whole of the costs of public policy.

MAKING MONEY UNREAL

In the everyday language of citizens and bookkeepers, real money is what government pays its employees, its suppliers, and the recipients of welfare checks. It is also the currency that individuals and companies use when paying taxes, and in the private sector of the economy. In spite of inflation, individuals must think of the money in their hand as real, for it is the only money they have got.

A major intellectual achievement of contemporary economics is to divorce their subject from rule by what ordinary citizens call "real money." Economists have devised a variety of theories and techniques reflecting their own ideas about what should be the measure of all things. The money that is used in everyday life is treated as if it were *unreal*. Doing this releases government from many conventional constraints upon public spending.

From the perspective of an economist, money has no value in itself, but only insofar as it can be used to command goods and services. When the amount of money needed to purchase a fixed basket of goods keeps increasing through inflation, it is misleading to concentrate upon current costs if making comparisons across the years. After all, a pound of steak that cost $1.00 at one time and $2.50 years later is still only a pound of steak, just as an hour's labor that earned $3.00 a few years ago and $6.00 today is still only an hour's worth of work. To relate prices to wages in such circumstances, economists have created notional measures of constant purchasing power to replace the actual figures used in current cash transactions.[13]

In the 1960s the British Treasury won plaudits from economists by abandoning the old-fashioned bookkeeping definition of money in favor of measuring costs in constant purchasing power. In this way, the Treasury could discount the effect of inflation when assessing policy priorities. For example, the government might decide to increase spending on education by 5 percent in terms of constant purchasing power while inflation also required a 10 percent increase in salaries to pay a given number of teachers' salaries with a constant purchasing power. In a conventional budget, this would register as a 15 percent increase in expenditure. By calculating spending in terms of constant values, it appears as an increase of only 5 percent.

Can Government Go Bankrupt?

The political attraction of using constant rather than current money values is that it makes public spending appear smaller. For example, as the British Treasury reported its figures, from 1971 to 1976 central government spending rose by 19 percent in "real" terms; this terminology masks the effect of inflation at a rate above 100 percent in the period. By contrast, in the same period Washington reported that United States federal spending rose by 58 percent in current prices. But if Washington had followed Westminster in concealing inflation's effects by definition, the American budget would have shown an increase of only 14 percent in constant dollars, less than the comparable British increase.[14]

A major American innovation making government spending deficits "unreal" is the full employment budget. This notional budget estimates what the national product and tax revenue *would have been* if the economy had been operating at full employment. For example, OECD economists estimate that government tax revenue would have been 10 percent higher if full employment had prevailed in Western nations in 1977. The full employment budget also estimates how much lower public spending would have been if a booming economy had made unnecessary spending money on unemployment benefits and other recession-related programs. After these assumptions are accepted, calculations can show that the budget would have been in surplus rather than deficit had full employment prevailed. Politicians can thus claim that their actual deficits are not the result of spendthrift policies, but result from economic difficulties over which they have no control.

In practice, there is no consensus among politicians or economists about what constitutes full employment. Yet the particular assumption made is crucial. Before the 1976 election, President Ford followed the custom of assuming full employment existed when unemployment was at 4 percent. On this notional basis, he showed an estimated $3 billion surplus in his 1977 budget: the cash budget estimated an actual deficit

of $43 billion.[15] Simultaneously, two Democrats, Senator
Hubert Humphrey and Representative Augustus F. Hawkins,
introduced a bill making 4 percent unemployment the definition of full employment, and called for massive deficit financing
to achieve this target. Yet some economists argued that
the natural rate of unemployment *at an acceptable
level of inflation* may be 6 percent or higher in contemporary
circumstances.[16]

When President Ford presented his budget proposal two
months after his election defeat, he defined the full employment budget as assuming 4.9 percent unemployment, an increase of nearly one-quarter from the level assumed before the
election. On this basis, even the notional full employment budget showed a deficit of $37 billion for 1977. The actual esti-
mated deficit of $68 billion was more than half again as much
as the pre-election figure, and $71 billion above the full em-
ployment budget produced before the election.[17] By July 1977,
Brookings economists no longer relied upon a single estimate
of full employment. They offered budget advice based upon
three different target definitions of unemployment, ranging
from 4 to 5 percent. According to which Brookings assumption
was chosen, the full employment federal budget would have
anything from a notional surplus of $9 billion to a deficit of $14
billion.[18]

Describing public policies as "investments" can also be
misleading. The capital expenditure of government is a dubious political asset, even though capital assets have an economic
value. The benefits of capital expenditure are expected to
accrue in the future, and not just within the next twelve
months. That is the justification for spending public money on
hospital buildings, roads, and hydroelectric dams. But the benefits produced by capital expenditure can involve future costs
as well. This is most obviously the case when a government
builds new hospitals or new universities. Once built, these institutions can only benefit society if government increases pub-

lic expenditure still more, to provide the doctors, nurses, teachers, and ancillary staff that are needed to produce social benefits from these physical assets.

When approving capital expenditures for nationalized industries, politicians may talk about making investments, but such spending may be differently motivated than ordinary commercial investments. For example, many so-called government investments are not intended to yield a cash return; instead, they are pork-barrel projects, intended to yield electoral support. The more a government spends without a proportionate cash return, the greater the political significance of its actions. After all, a bank will loan money to a commercially sound project, but only a government is likely to "invest" money in a commercially unsound project, as the British and French governments did for Concorde, the supersonic aircraft that cannot catch up with its money losses, no matter how fast it flies.

When a government invests money to increase the capital stock of a nationalized industry and this fails to return enough money to cover the capital cost, a government can "lose" its losses. For example, the losses of nationalized railroads do not make them bankrupt, as would be the case of a privately owned company. When accumulated losses become very large, the government simply writes them off. The losses are deleted from the accounts of the nationalized railroad, and interest on this debt is no longer a charge on the railroad's operating revenue. When losses are written off, they do not disappear; they are simply buried in the overall total of the national debt.

While each intellectual technique for making money unreal can be justified within a body of economic theory, this does not help to resolve the problems that face people who must deal with the immediate exigencies of the economy as it actually is. In the 1970s, we may not be able to afford the political luxury of treating actual cash costs as if they "really" were of no significance. As a British Treasury official responsible for introducing "constant" in place of "current" prices admitted subsequently, "When one thinks in terms of taxes, one leaves the world of GNP at constant prices and expenditures in real terms." In an English understatement, he noted that taxes belong to "the actual world of calculations in money." [19]

HAPPY FORECASTS

Forecasts about the future state of the economy cannot be said to be right or wrong when issued, because they refer to a hypothetical future time. Only time will tell whether a forecast is near the truth or misleading. But politicians do not have the time to wait to see which forecast is most accurate. Keynesian management of the economy requires politicians to act now on assumptions about the future, in order to achieve the maximum benefits of treble affluence.

Political economists face the future with "uncertain knowledge of where we are (or even where we have just been)." [20] At any given time, a government is concerned with accounts spanning at least three very different years. First of all, it is trying to determine exactly how much money it actually spent in the financial year just ended. Secondly, government tries to control accurately how much money it is spending in the current year, no easy task when inflation escalates prices at an uneven rate, recessions create urgent pressures to increase spending, and bureaucratic complexities make spending money a time-consuming and sometimes erratic exercise. Thirdly, it seeks to project future trends in the political economy from a current base of information that is not yet firm.

The seemingly technical nature of economic forecasting obscures a simple fact: at the moment a forecast is made, nobody can be certain about the state of the political economy twelve months hence. Forecasts are necessary to anticipate what is likely to happen, but the particular picture they give of the future depends upon assumptions built into them. At each point in constructing a forecast, it is possible to make more or less optimistic assumptions. The selection of economic data, the statistical methods used to analyze the data, the decision to hold certain potential influences constant, and assumptions about government policy are matters of professional judgment, not engineering science. In economics as in theology, authorities differ about what the future holds. Politicians do not need technical expertise to assess the competing claims of different economic forecasters; they can shop around among economists until they receive advice that most suits their own political needs.

The political process can convert economics from a dismal science into a happy art. The fact that the new costs are real, whereas the extra revenue is only speculative, is less immediately important than the justification that an optimistic forecast gives for doing what politicians want to do anyway. For example, in the Presidential election year 1976, even though unemployment and prices had previously been rising, President Ford's budget forecast that they would fall throughout the next four years that he wished to have in the White House. Jimmy Carter campaigned with a different scenario: if voters would elect him in 1976 and re-elect him in 1980, he pledged a balanced budget by 1981.[21]

As forecast events draw closer, there is less room for maneuver; and in periods of recession, bad news begins to break through. For example, whereas in January 1976 President Ford could forecast a federal budget of $429 billion for fiscal year 1978, twelve months later he forecast spending $440 billion in that year; and the forecast deficit of $47 billion was twice as big as that foreseen earlier. By April 1977, President Carter's advisors had revised the 1978 budget to $462 billion, with a deficit of $58 billion, up nearly one-quarter from that anticipated by President Ford three months earlier.

Sophisticated British economists have been consistently up-staged by politicians wishing to promise a Christmas tree of benefits to the electorate. In the 1950s, the British economy grew at a rate of 3.4 percent per year. But before the 1964 general election, a Conservative government promised a 4 percent annual growth rate. At the subsequent election in 1966, the Labour government raised the figure to 4.2 percent.[22] In the period of high promises, 1964 to 1970, the growth rate actually *declined* to 2.4 percent annually, leaving financial trouble for firms that had invested on the basis of government forecasts.

The apparent "mistakes" of economic forecasters are not random errors, but reflect a systematic bias in the policy proc-ess favoring news that is conveniently good. In the United States from 1960 to 1976, Presidential advisors *over*estimated the rate of growth in the national product in twelve of sixteen years, and *under*estimated the costs of public policy in four-teen of these years. Since 1970 published estimates have over-estimated growth in six of the past seven years in the United States, and in five of the past seven years in fiscally conserva-tive Germany. For the *annus horrendus* of 1975, when major economies contracted, except in the United States, official economists in major Western nations still forecast growth; one survey attributed this to a "psychological inability to forecast a classical recession" following years of continuing boom.[23]

Ironically, the world recession of the 1970s can be used to justify forecasts as happy as those of the boom years of the 1960s. The sharp decline in growth rates in the first half of the 1970s created slack in the economy. This could facilitate an equally rapid acceleration in the economy in the second half of the decade, for it is easier to expand when an economy has underutilized productive capacity. In *A Growth Scenario to 1980*, issued in July 1976, OECD economists envisaged just this, forecasting a higher growth rate—5.5 percent from 1975 to 1980—than in the boom years of 1963 to 1971.[24] In 1977, however, OECD economists concluded that recessions are not so easily reversed, forecasting an overall growth rate of 3.5 percent for 1978, a figure that was subsequently revised downward in national forecasts, as evidence of recession did not go away.[25]

When economic forecasts appear to be going wrong, a favorable gloss can be given to politically unpalatable news by lengthening its timespan. For example, the British Treasury finds it difficult to make a high level of growth appear immediately credible when the economy is stagnating, nor can it credibly forecast low growth in public spending when it is accelerating. But a five-year plan for the future can still look good, if the first two years of unfavorable news are offset by the happy forecast that in years three, four and five the economy will accelerate and public spending slow down.[26] Convenient as this practice is politically, it nonetheless has one weakness: the growth years keep on being postponed to what must inevitably be an uncertain future, while the nongrowth years belong to what is an only too certain past and a disquieting present.[27]

The standard economist's reply to criticism of forecasts is that the forecast was correct as stated, that is, that it was logically consistent and there was an empirical and theoretical justification for the resulting prognosis. As long as the forecast contains a saving *ceteris paribus* (other conditions remaining equal) clause, a misleading forecast is not wrong but inoperative, since the conditions specified in the forecast did not remain constant, making the outcome different than specified. Forecasts can be upset by what economists describe as the "avoidable" mistakes of politicians, that is, the failure of politicians to do what economists think they ought to do according to economic criteria. They can also be upset by unforeseeable political events, such as the oil crisis of 1973 or the decade-long American involvement in the Viet Nam War. There are also difficulties with unforeseen economic problems, such as the

[152

rapid and conjoint rise of wages, prices, and unemployment in the 1970s.[28]

The probative value of a forecast depends upon the realism of its assumptions. To base a forecast on the clearly stated premise, "Let us assume that only the economic conditions specified in our forecast influence the political economy," is dangerously close to an older assumption: "If wishes were horses, beggars would ride." In the real world, politicians do make mistakes, and the unforeseen happens with distressing frequency, according to the doctrine known as Murphy's law: "Anything that can go wrong will go wrong."

CHAPTER 7

Running Out of Pie: The Limits of Political Economy

Most of our people have never had it so good. Go around the country, go to the industrial towns, go to the farms, and you will see a state of prosperity such as we have never had in my lifetime— nor indeed ever in the history of this country.

What is beginning to worry some of us is, "Is it too good to be true?" or perhaps I should say, "Is it too good to last?"
Prime Minister Harold Macmillan, 1957

National governments have, like the Sorcerer's Apprentice, helped to release forces which are beyond their powers to control.
Professor Assar Lindbeck,
*The Changing Role of
The National State,* 1975

BENEFITS have their costs. For the past quarter-century economic growth has provided more and more pie for nearly everyone in society. But even the most successful political economy has its limits. If the costs of public policy rise too much, there must be a cut in take-home pay.

Past success is no proof that government will have enough pie for future needs. Twenty years ago Harold Macmillan voiced doubts about the prospects of the political economy that he had helped to create. Twenty years on, the shadow of doubt has become a pall, for the world recession of the 1970s has shown that political economies are not as easy to manage as was once believed.

A politician such as Harold Wilson may say that a week in politics is a long time, but the inertia commitments of governments continue long after individual politicians pass from the scene. Former mayors of New York City could react to the plight of Abe Beame, mayor the day that the city faced economic bankruptcy, with the thankful sigh, "There but for the grace of God go I." But seven million New Yorkers could take no pleasure from the fact that successive city administrations had allowed spending commitments to overload the city's economy. Citizens have a longer-term stake in public policies than do politicians elected to a four-year term of office. In the year 2000, pupils in school today will still be on the young side of forty, and their parents will be starting to worry about how much security their pension will provide.

Glib economists can dismiss worries about long-term financial difficulties by quoting Keynes' epigram, "In the long run we are all dead." But the statement is too clever by half. While individuals have a limited life span, societies do not. What Keynes should have said is, "In the long run, each of us is dead." The governments to which Keynes bequeathed a legacy of ideas go on and on, collectively embodying past achievements and past mistakes, to the benefit and cost of future generations.

A complex institution like the contemporary political economy cannot change abruptly. An examination of current trends in political economy thus provides a basis for understanding where we are heading in future. The depressing record of the 1970s offers a cautionary example of governments unable to manage the economy as they wish, especially those countries already overloaded before the world recession struck hard. If present trends continue, how great is the risk of any major Western nation facing political bankruptcy in the foreseeable future, or of all countries facing this fate?

DEPRESSING GROWTH: THE RECORD OF THE 1970S

The 1970s has been a decade of double disillusionment. The goals of the political economy that the Germans have aptly nicknamed the "Magic Quadrangle"—economic growth, full employment, stable prices, and a balance of payments surplus —have become increasingly difficult to achieve. Simultaneously, these four objectives have become increasingly important to governments. Failure to meet these objectives threatens to overload the political economy. Failure also raises questions about the validity of economic prescriptions meant to assure continued economic well-being.

Politicians and economists looking for a scapegoat cannot blame OPEC for abruptly quadrupling oil prices following the Middle East War of 1973. The oil crisis did upset world trade and create balance of payments problems. but signs of trouble were evident before the oil crisis commenced. The oil crisis intensified the economic problems of government; it did not cause them.

Throughout the Western world, the escalator of economic growth has slowed down in the 1970s. Economies have con-tinued to grow, but at a depressed rate. In the 1950s and 1960s, the national product of major Western nations grew on average 4.8 percent a year. From 1970 to 1976 the national product has been growing at half that rate. Growth has kept up best in France; the national product has grown 3.7 percent annually in the 1970s, one-quarter below the figure for the preceding two decades. The German economy has slowed down most in absolute and relative terms; from 1951 to 1970 it grew at an annual rate of 6.4 percent; in the first six years of the 1970s it has grown at an annual rate of only 2.5 percent. Growth in the Gross Domestic Product, 1970 to 1976, averaged 2.3 percent in the United States, 1.9 percent in Britain, 3.7 percent in France, 2.5 percent in Germany, 2.7 percent in Italy, and 2.2 percent in Sweden.

In 1975 there was a pointed reminder that while growth is usual, it is not automatic. The Gross Domestic Product actually *fell* in most major Western nations. The national pie contracted by as much as 3.7 percent in Italy and 3.2 percent in Germany. In the United States it fell by "only" 1.3 percent, equivalent to a loss of $23 billion in national product (that is, more than $400 for every American family). Among the major Western nations, only Sweden could show a positive rate of growth, a meager eight-tenths of one percent. Sweden has since shown that it is not immune to economic difficulties, suffering two devaluations of the krona in the first half of 1977.

The performance of major Western economies today indicates that recovery from recession is not as easy as Keynesians once assumed. The relatively optimistic McCracken Report to the Organization for Economic Cooperation and Development in mid-1977 said that "compared with what was achieved during the 1960s, *potential* growth rates will probably be somewhat lower." It further lowered expectations by adding, "The fact that growth rates should be technically feasible does *not necessarily mean* they will be achieved." [1] In other words, the best that the governors of major Western nations can hope for in the foreseeable future is a pie growing slower than in the past—

provided that governors do not once again make "avoidable" mistakes.

The dismal science of economics can produce reasons why economic growth should be lower in the near future than in the decades of affluence. One reason is the changing composition of the economy. An increasing proportion of the labor force in every major Western nation is today employed in service industries, both in the public sector (teaching or health care) or the private sector (e.g., leisure and holiday trades). The productivity of service workers cannot be increased as rapidly as that of factory workers by substituting machines for human labor. From 1960 to 1973, the productivity of labor in industry grew on average 4.5 percent a year; in the service sector, it grew by only 2.4 percent a year.[2] As the proportion of a country's labor-force in "slow growth" jobs increases, the more difficult is the return to rapid growth.

A second reason for slow growth is a squeeze on the profits that finance the investment necessary to increase the national product.* In contemporary mixed economies, companies finance a significant proportion of investment from retained profits, and the prospect of profit is usually a precondition for a company to invest in growth. In an overloaded economy, one way to sustain wages and salaries is to reduce profits. While this policy has short-term political advantages, it is dangerous, insofar as reduced profits lead to reduced investment and a lower rate of future economic growth. In every major Western nation there has been a long-term squeeze on profits since the 1960s.[3]

Thirdly, government has increasingly become responsible for investment decisions in industry. Government encouragement of investment starts with the best of intentions: to promote a

---

* Recall that our measure of take-home pay includes net profits and rents with wages and salaries, as all are forms of post-tax non-governmental receipts.

higher rate of economic growth. But the long-term effects may be different, for the criteria of government investment are ultimately political. A government does not require that the industry in which it invests make a profit contributing to economic growth. In the last resort, tax revenues rather than profits can meet their costs. The more money that government invests on "nonprofit" or loss-making political criteria, the greater the probability that its activities may depress rather than stimulate economic growth. In Britain, Labour and Conservative governments subsidize firms making everything from Rolls-Royce airplane engines and ICL computers to ships built for foreign customers. Firms receiving so-called investment subsidies are to an extent social services, providing jobs for workers, rather than a source of economic growth.[4]

From a conventional Keynesian perspective, it can be argued that the growing costs of public policy have been desirable in the world recession of the 1970s. Had governments not spent more money for such countercyclical policies as unemployment benefits, the slump might have been intensified. When economic growth accelerates once again, the costs of unemployment should fall, and tax revenues should increase in a virtuous cycle that complements the current vicious cycle of rising costs and a loss of tax revenue from those out of work. But such an argument presupposes that it is not difficult to finance increasing public deficits; this assumption is falsified dramatically by the experience of Britain and Italy. It also assumes that the depressing record of the 1970s is part of a normal business cycle, to be followed by an equal number of boom years in the 1980s, rather than a stage in a longer-term decline in the rate of economic growth.

From the viewpoint of the ordinary citizen, depressing growth first becomes evident through an increase in unemployment. Crossnational differences in defining unemployment make comparison difficult, but within every major nation the record is the same: unemployment has risen substantially since 1970. Unemployment in 1977 was up more than five times in Germany, and nearly twice as high in Britain. It was up by "only" two-thirds in the United States, because the U.S. has long had relatively high rates of unemployment by European standards. In France and Italy, unemployment was up by half from the start of the decade. Sweden has managed to keep unemployment from rising, but only by subsidizing labor. In 1977, this created a new problem: how to meet the cost of subsidizing Swedish workers when the goods they were making could not be sold abroad at a profit.

Consistent with Keynesian prescriptions, governments have reacted by spending more on countercyclical public policies and increasing public deficits. This has not been followed by lower unemployment, but by increased inflation. A small amount of inflation has been commonplace in every major Western nation since World War II. Since 1970, however, inflation has been rising, approaching or exceeding double digit figures each year. This is especially evident in Italy and Britain. The cost of living index, standing at 100 in 1970, reached 249 in Britain by the end of 1977, and 234 in Italy.

Stagflation is the shorthand name given to the unexpected conjunction of rising unemployment and inflation that has characterized the 1970s. Stagflation poses a double threat: a rising standard of living can no longer be taken for granted, and the value of money may itself become illusory. Stagflation is also evidence of a crack in the foundations on which economists have built their expectations of future growth. At all times managers of a Keynesian economy expect problems of unemployment and inflation to arise, but only one at a time. In a sense, the remedy for each problem is the cause of the other. When unemployment was regarded as the greatest difficulty, a government could stimulate demand through deficit financing. When excess demand made inflation the problem, it could reverse its policies, incidentally increasing unemployment. If all went well, politicians would be in the boom phase of a cycle before an election, and in the deflationary phase after victory was won. So precise and regular did the trade-offs between unemployment and inflation appear, that social scientists could graph how much unemployment was required to reduce inflation by a given rate, how much inflation was needed to reduce unemployment, and what effect either mix of policies could have on electoral support. The 1960s saw the rise of this technique for the political management of the economy; the 1970s have seen its collapse.[5]

In the uncertain and novel circumstances of the 1970s, measures that once produced good news now produce bad effects or, even more puzzling, none at all. Economists debate the causes of stagflation with the fervor of Reformation and Counter-Reformation theologians. The sum of brilliant analyses leads to inconclusive or contradictory prescriptions for public policy. Meanwhile, politicians must steer the economy through the torrents, wondering whether the charts they are using are leading them away from or toward the rocks.

HOW CLOSE TO POLITICAL BANKRUPTCY?

If politicians reacted instantly to every prophecy of doom, political disaster could result as efforts to forestall nonexistent problems created even worse difficulties than were foreseen. Yet history reminds us that there are moments when bad things *can* happen here. From our great distance in time, we smile at descriptions of Nero indulging himself at the expense of the Empire he was meant to be governing.[6] It would be ironic if the Age of Democracy simply substituted a picture of Every-man doing his own thing while the government of his choice approached political bankruptcy.

Political bankruptcy is not the result of a sudden slump in the economy. Instead, it is the cumulative consequence of a nation year after year seeking to consume more than it produces. The more immediate and severe the consequences of mistakes, the greater the need for politicians to guard against risks. We do not expect (though some might wish) a government to act today to deal with hypothetical shortages of raw materials at some point in the twenty-first century. But we do expect government to act promptly to deal with immediate problems of the political economy. The crucial question is: how close are we to political bankruptcy?

The 1970s have demonstrated that continued affluence is not enough to secure citizens from the risk of a cut in take-home pay. In every major Western nation, the national product has continued to expand. From 1970 to 1976 it has grown at an average annual rate of 2.5 percent. In France, it has grown cumulatively by as much as 24 percent, and in the United States by 18 percent. Even in Britain, where growth has been slowest, the national product has increased by 10 percent in this period.

But the costs of public policy have been rising in the 1970s at a much faster annual rate (6.1 percent) than the national product. From 1970 to 1976, even after allowing for the effects of inflation, total costs have increased by 49 percent in Sweden, and by 48 percent in Italy. In the United States, the costs of public policy have risen least, 25 percent, thanks in part to the slowing down in defense spending at the end of the Viet Nam War.

The take-home pay of the average citizen has risen in the 1970s, but the annual average increase of 1.3 percent is less than that of the national product, and much less than the costs of public policy (see Table 7.1). The optimistic view of take-

TABLE 7.1

The Trajectory of Take-Home Pay since 1970

	1970	1971	1972	1973	1974	1975	1976	1976 Pay
		(Percentage of change from the previous year)						(1970 = 100)
America	100	+3	+5	+5	−7	−3	+6	109
Britain	100	+2	+2	+6	+1	−4	−2	106
France	100	+5	+6	+6	+3	−2	+0.2	118
Germany	100	+2	+2	+2	−0.6	−4	+2	104
Italy	100	+1	+4	+7	−2	−4	−1	105
Sweden	100	−3	+1	+6	+1	−3	−5	97

Sources: See Tables A2.1–3.

home pay emphasizes that it has continued to increase from 1970 to 1976. Notwithstanding the many difficulties of the period, individual take-home pay has risen by as much as 18 percent in France. The pessimistic view emphasizes that take-home pay has fallen at least once in every major Western nation, in 2 years in the United States, Britain, and Germany; and in 3 out of 6 years in Italy and Sweden. On average, citizens were 6 percent better off in take-home pay in 1976 than in 1970. In Sweden, the take-home pay of the average citizen was 3 percent less than in 1970.

It is of crucial importance to political authority whether the decline in take-home pay is temporary, or the start of a trend. Unfortunately, there is no agreement among social scientists about what constitutes a trend. A professional pollyanna may dismiss a few years of falling take-home pay as no more than one phase in an up-and-down cycle leading to continued growth. A congenital doom-monger may infer collapse from the events of one unfavorable year.

The conventional economic view is to expect economic growth to improve take-home pay. In 1976, the national economy in every major Western nation grew and did so by an average of 4 percent. Moreover, in every major Western nation but Sweden, the costs of public policy increased by less than the average rate for the decade. Notwithstanding these relatively favorable circumstances, take-home pay continued to fall in Britain, Italy, and Sweden. The benefits of greater growth went first of all to the taxman, and also to government's domestic and foreign creditors.

The 1970s have demonstrated three different ways in which take-home pay can be cut: by a rapid increase in the costs of public policy, by a decline in the growth rate of the national product, and by a scissors squeeze of accelerating costs of public policy and a decelerating growth of the national product. Whether a nation runs into political bankruptcy by overspending, or backs into bankruptcy by inadequate economic growth, the risks to its political authority are real.

What will happen to take-home pay if past trends persist into the future? Insofar as the growth of the national product and the costs of public policy reflect inertia forces, then the past is truly a prologue to the future. We need not assume an unprecedented decline in the national product, or an unprecedented rise in the cost of public policy to make future projections.

In the strictest sense, there is no certainty about the future.[7] Many unexpected things can happen, some making the threat of political bankruptcy less likely, and others making it more likely. Keeping an eye out for the unexpected should not, however, mean shutting our eyes to trends already underway. The closer the distance in time between what has happened and what is projected, the more confident one can be about the importance of inertia trends. We therefore concentrate attention upon the possible trajectory of take-home pay in the decade up to 1985, one year after the date that George Orwell chose to signify a new political era.

In the pages that follow, we consider three different assumptions about trends in the political economy. The first is that the patterns of the quarter-century of treble affluence will continue into the future. The second is that the years ahead will continue along the more recent short-term lines of 1970 through 1976. Thirdly, we assume that future growth may involve changes in the economy, rather than the persistence of short-term or long-term trends.

To see whether different assumptions or different techniques yield very different answers, the results of six different projections are reviewed here. (In fact, we tested many more projections than the six discussed; all produced substantially the same results.) Insofar as different projections all point to the same conclusion, the greater the weight that can be placed upon it. To avoid taking any single projection out of context, we have not summarized results in a falsely precise table or graph. In any event, dates can only be approximate; a turn down in take-home pay could start a few years later or earlier than the year spotlighted by these projections.

The simplest way to project inertia trends for the quarter-century since 1951 is to assume that the national product will grow in future at the same rate as in the past, and that the costs of public policy will grow likewise. On the basis of such a straight-line trend (in statistical terms, a least squares regression line), the difficulties of Sweden today are not a temporary problem, but threaten the start of a long-term decline in take-home pay. In Britain and Italy, full recovery from the difficulties of the first part of the 1970s would still face both governments with the prospect of take-home pay falling by 1982, if long-term trends continue. In the United States, the threat of a fall in take-home pay is a decade away, if long-term trends continue. In Germany, long-term trends indicate security until the early 1990s, and in France until the twenty-first century.*

If the economic difficulties arising from the world recession

* All projections given in this and subsequent paragraphs are based upon a ceteris paribus assumption, that is, that all other conditions remain equal. The hasty reader ignores this qualification at his individual peril. But the politician who uses uncertainty about the future to dismiss the risks highlighted here does so at his country's peril.

of the 1970s are taken as the harbinger of the years ahead, then the prospects immediately become much bleaker. If politicians in Sweden, Italy and Britain cannot reverse the straight-line trend from 1970 through 1976, then the decline in take-home pay shown in Table 7.1 will not be a temporary phenomenon, but the start of a long-term decline. In the United States and Germany, take-home pay could start falling at the beginning of the 1980s, and in France, at the beginning of the 1990s, if the trend of this decade continues indefinitely. If recent trends continue, then by 1985 Swedes, Italians, Britons, and Americans could even find their take-home pay purchasing less than it bought in 1970.

A simple straight-line projection does not allow for the fact that the absolute value of a 5 percent change in the national product or in the cost of public policy is very different if it refers to a trillion dollars rather than 250 billion dollars. The transformation of these figures into logarithms controls for the difference between the size of political economies in the 1950s and in the 1970s. This logarithmic projection of trends from the past quarter-century signals greater risks. On this basis, Sweden, Italy, and Britain are already at the start of a down trend in take-home pay, and Germany faces this risk by the 1980s. Moreover, this projection suggests take-home pay could be lower in 1985 than it was in 1970 in Sweden, Italy, and Britain. Only the United States and France are secure for a decade ahead.

In real life, many trends do not follow a straight line; take-home pay may curve up, flatten off, or even turn downward. Our model of the changing characteristics of the three faces of growth implies a curving trajectory of take-home pay. Fitting a non-linear regression equation to the path of take-home pay provides a means of projecting future movements that may follow a curving trajectory. On this basis, the curve down in take-home pay has already started in Sweden, Italy, and Britain, and in Germany this trend could appear by 1982. A curve down in take-home pay would be likely in the United States and France by the second half of the 1980s, if the trajectory of the past continued.

Since the future never repeats the past exactly, it is desirable to examine forecasts of economic growth that explicitly take into account the future implications of changes in the world economy of the 1970s. Expert economists of the Organization for Economic Cooperation and Development (OECD) do just this at their Paris headquarters. Multinational teams of economists there monitor the performance of all Western economies, in consultation with representatives of national governments. OECD forecasts are thus likely to be relatively optimistic, given the semiofficial status of the agency and the sensitivity of national governments to forecasts suggesting trouble ahead.

When Paul McCracken's multinational group assembled to prepare their report to OECD, *Towards Full Employment and Price Stability*,[8] they based their relative optimism upon OECD forecasts published in July 1976. This set of forecasts assumed that the second half of the 1970s would show a faster rate of economic growth to compensate for what had been lost in the first half of the decade. But when OECD economists again reviewed the evidence at the end of 1977, they concluded that their earlier optimism was not justified.[9] Projections based on the 1977 OECD figures indicate that a down trend in take-home pay is already starting in Sweden, Italy, and Britain. Moreover, there is a risk that this will also happen in Germany and the United States in about a decade, and in France around the end of the century. The picture is virtually the same whether the OECD forecasts of the economy are related to costs of public policy which are projected to grow at the rate of the past quarter-century or at the rate of the 1970s. If the earlier July 1976 OECD forecasts are used, the projected date for take-home pay trending down is moved backward by about four years for each country.*

The biggest differences between projections are not caused by the techniques used, but by the assumptions fed into them. If the first part of the 1970s is assumed to set the pattern for the ten years to follow, then the risks to public policy are widespread, affecting Sweden, Italy, and Britain immediately; and Germany and the United States by 1985 as well. Only France appears relatively secure from the logic of compounding commitments. The picture changes somewhat if one assumes that the growth of public policy in the Thrifty Fifties and in the national product in the Golden Sixties will characterize the foreseeable future. On such a basis, the United States, Germany, and France are relatively secure. But the continuance of the past quarter-century's pattern of growth still faces Sweden, Italy, and Britain with big and immediate problems.

The growth statistics for 1977, available from OECD only after these projections were prepared, call attention to yet another possibility: the next five years may be *even worse* than the first half of the 1970s. In 1977, the economy of every major European nation grew at a slower rate than its average annual growth from 1970 to 1976. In two countries—Britain and Sweden—the national product actually contracted. Only in America was the year's growth rate (4.9 percent) above its historic average.† Official and semiofficial forecasts for 1978

---

* Additional projections based upon the forecasts of economic growth contained in the LINK World Trade Model, which reconcile and integrate different national economic forecasts made within major Western nations, show similar results to those reported in the above paragraphs. The data were kindly made available by Professor Laurence R. Klein of the University of Pennsylvania.

† The preliminary 1977 figures for growth in the gross domestic product are: America, 4.9 percent; Britain, −0.3 percent; France, 2.9 percent; Germany, 2.4 percent; Italy, 1.7 percent; and Sweden −2.4 percent. From *Main Economic Indicators* (Paris: OECD, 1978), p. 156. Cf. 1970–76 average growth rates, cited above at p. 49 and 1951–76 averages, cited in Table A2.1.

reinforce the prospect of gloom; except in the United States, they predict the continuation of the depressing pattern of 1977.

The projections are most consistent for the three countries facing the most immediate risks—Sweden, Italy, and Britain. In the extreme case of Sweden, all projections from past trends indicate that the fall in real take-home pay, already recorded in 1975 and 1976, can continue indefinitely. For Italy there is a leeway of four years from 1978 in estimates of the start of a long-term down trend in take-home pay; in Britain, a down trend is threatened at any time from the present to 1984. The small differences between projections for these three countries are less significant than the recurring indication of big troubles by 1980. The most optimistic interpretation is that the worst has already happened in Italy, Britain, and Sweden. The fall in take-home pay experienced in the mid-1970s could be a sharp enough warning to make governors reverse past spending policies in order to prevent a continuing fall in take-home pay.

The immediate future is less clear for Germany and the United States. If the trends of 1970–1976 continue, Germans could face a fall in take-home pay by the early 1980s, and Americans could face it by about the middle of the decade. But long-term trends imply that both countries could be secure until the 1990s. The forecasts about France are unreliable, yet highly favorable. Depending upon the assumptions and methods used, treble affluence in France could continue for anything from a decade to a generation or more. While the results are widely scattered, the overall pattern is reassuring to Frenchmen; three projections indicate no trouble until the twenty-first century, and none warns of trouble in the next decade.

Politically, the most important point is not whether any of these projections is accurate, but rather, whether governors wish them to be true. Like navigation signals of danger, warnings of economic trouble ahead are intended to be falsified. A ship's captain does not wait until his boat is on the rocks before deciding to alter course. Nor need politicians wait until a fall in take-home pay has already occurred for three, five, or seven years before deciding that something must be done. The projections given here are signals of trouble ahead *if* the present course is not changed. But inertia forces can be redirected if, and only if, governments have the will and the knowledge to do so.

There is more than one road to ruin in a political economy, and more than one way in which nations can maintain treble affluence. Major Western nations demonstrate this point.

BIG TROUBLE NOW

The high growth rate of the Italian economy has long been admired by foreign economists, just as the byzantine structure of the Italian government has long been the bane of Italian citizens, and sporadic antiregime violence has shown how vulnerable is Rome's hope to govern by consent. In an era of treble affluence, the ruling Christian Democratic party could spend the fiscal dividend of economic growth lavishly, providing patronage benefits for its supporters, as well as introducing and expanding modern welfare state services. The rapid growth in the costs of public policy was obscured for a time, because the national budget accounted for relatively little of the national product in 1951. But inertia commitments have grown at a rate that cannot be financed indefinitely by any economy, even one as buoyant as that in Italy. If Italy's government is to avoid cutting the take-home pay of its citizens, it must find a way to control its own spending proclivities. In 1977 the International Monetary Fund gave it a push in that direction, after the political economy had already reached a perilous state. Today, the old claim that there are more Italians in New

York City than in any city outside Rome might be supplemented by the statement, "The Minister of Finance in Rome is in worse shape than any other financial official outside New York City."

In Britain, Her Majesty's Treasury has been singularly successful in controlling the growth of government spending. Conservative and Labour Cabinet ministers might find such a statement surprising, for they perennially face the problem of raising money to meet the growing costs of public policy. But the cause of their trouble is not lavish spending. By European standards, welfare benefits are relatively low in Britain, and so are the cash costs of public programs. Britain's difficulty is that it has the lowest rate of economic growth in Europe. This is not something that can be controlled exclusively by government. Since the Second World War, some of the world's most renowned economists have advised the British government about how to stimulate growth. But growth has not occurred. The most optimistic feature of the economy today—prospective short-term tax revenue of upwards of £5 billion a year from North Sea oil—is not the result of Treasury policy, but of an act of God and good fortune. Moreover, a country with sixty-four times the population of Kuwait may find that oil enough to light the lamps of a modern Aladdin may not be enough to resolve the underlying difficulties of its political economy. The less successful the British government is in increasing the national product, the more successful it must be in limiting the growing costs of the country's once vaunted welfare services.

For two generations Sweden has been a byword for the sophisticated management of its political economy, as well as for the scale and imaginativeness of its welfare benefits. Socialists and social scientists (sometimes, the same person) have written glowing reports about the achievements of the Swedish welfare state. Often, welfare benefits have been praised without thought of cost. It was assumed that the sophisticated managers of the Swedish economy would inevitably be able to meet these costs from the fiscal dividend of growth. By comparison with Britain, Sweden has maintained a respectable rate of economic growth, and avoided as rapid a growth in the costs of public policy as Italy. But the steady compounding of historically high costs of public policy today confronts Swedes with a question they have heretofore avoided. If forced to choose by economic constraints, should take-home pay be cut or new welfare programs foregone when the national pie no longer provides enough for both?

TROUBLE AHEAD

Comparison with Europe emphasizes how successful the United States government has been in limiting the growth of public spending. Defense spending, historically large, may level off in the coming years if there is no return to the Cold War or a shooting war like Viet Nam. But because America did not adopt a national health service when European nations did, the costs of public policy could be subject to a major tilt upwards, if government decided to meet the health costs of more than 200 million Americans. The transfer of health costs to the federal budget from third-party insurors would involve public political responsibility replacing that of private insurance companies, even if costs were unchanged. The argument of this book suggests that health spending would in fact escalate because costs would inflate without a proportionate increase in health services. If inertia policies remain unaltered, the chief threat to take-home pay in the 1980s will not come from prodigal spending, but from a rate of American economic growth that is lower than that of any other major Western nation except Britain.

The performance of the German economy since 1950 has been the envy of every other European nation. Not only has the economy grown greatly, but spending on social policies has also grown greatly. The German government spends about the same share of the national product as the British or Italian government, but it provides bigger per capita benefits because Germany's national product is so much greater. If trends of the past quarter-century continue, the German political economy appears secure into the 1990s. But such a calculation reflects "hypergrowth" induced by postwar reconstruction in the early 1950s. Since then, public spending has been accelerating in Germany while economic growth has been slowing down. There is thus a bigger risk in Germany than in the United States of a continuing decline in take-home pay occurring by 1985.

France, long a byword for peasant conservatism, is relatively secure today because it has combined a conservative fiscal policy with a dynamic economy. The achievement of a high rate of economic growth is perhaps more remarkable than in Germany, because the French did not start from the imperative need to rebuild a war-ravaged society. Instead, in the 1950s French governments faced a society in which immobility was the greater problem. The use of the positive powers of the state to encourage growth was matched by growth in the costs of public policy, but not to the extent of jeopardizing the take-home pay of Frenchmen. Moreover, official statistics underestimate the increase in take-home pay because they ignore earnings that Frenchmen do not report for tax purposes. The challenge to political authority in France today does not come from inertia trends in the political economy, but rather from stagnation in party politics. Since 1958 government has been controlled by Gaullist-type leaders, and Socialists as well as Communists have been excluded from office. Spreading economic benefits is important, but cannot guarantee political authority against all forms of political challenge.

CHAPTER 8

The Costs of Buying Time

If you see ten troubles coming down the road,
you can be sure that nine will run into the ditch
before they reach you, and you have to battle with
only one.

President Calvin Coolidge, 1924

Ministers should not remain unwarned that they
are going down the drain at a great pace. Nothing
but waste and humiliation can result from not
looking ahead and keeping within our long-run
capacity. For there is not the faintest prospect,
on any hypothesis, of our being able to carry on
our present practices.

Lord Keynes, Memorandum to
the British Cabinet, 1946

HOWEVER GREAT the difficulties facing a country, there is
always one policy that harassed governors can adopt, temporarily at least: They can do nothing. There is always a chance
that a threatened difficulty will turn out to be harmless, if only
a politician stands still until it evaporates. In the 1920s Calvin
Coolidge practiced what he preached, setting a modern record
for the amount of time a president spent sleeping; he passed
on the cost of doing nothing to Herbert Hoover. Today, some

citizens might wish that their hyperthyroid governors would follow Coolidge's example, sleeping more and governing less.

Doing nothing is always an attractive policy to a politician in office. The government of the moment wants to assure its citizens that everything is going well. By virtue of holding office, politicians themselves have a lot to be satisfied with. They see no need to react immediately to a change of a few percentage points in a trend line on a graph. But doing nothing risks making things worse. For example, within a year of Keynes' memorandum warning that Britain was "going down the drain at a great pace," the convertibility of the pound was suspended, and the first of three decades of emergency budgets launched.[1]

Governments have exhibited a notable resilience in the face of problems in the political economy. But they have often responded with measures that simply buy time, tiding their country over difficulties in hopes that things will turn up for the better. But buying time is costly; it not only involves money, but also political risks.

This chapter reviews a variety of ways in which politicians can buy time. A do-nothing policy depends upon nothing untoward happening meanwhile. As and when events force action, a government can try to sustain the illusion of affluence by inflation. In reaction against inflation, a government can organize agreements with business and labor leaders in an effort to control the wage and price rises that disturb its citizens, or it can turn to international banks for loans that temporarily provide money that a country cannot earn for itself. However, these policies do not provide long-term security. A government pursuing any of them or all in turn may find, in the vivid metaphor of Peter Jay, "The threatening tidal wave has grown steeper and higher, as it has been pushed back."[2]

MR. MICAWBER'S POLICY

The fiscal policy of Charles Dickens' Mr. Micawber, the impecunious friend of David Copperfield, can be stated in two sentences, "Annual income, £20, annual expenditure £19.19.6d: result, happiness. Annual income, £20, annual expenditure £20.0.6d: result, misery." A public official today might envy Mr. Micawber the certainty of identifying exactly the line separating fiscal happiness and misery, while sharing his anxiety about being on the right side of the line. A politician advised to adopt unpalatable measures to return the economy to happiness might take comfort in Mr. Micawber's justification for continued spending, even when bankruptcy threatened: "a hope of something turning up." After all, if only the rate of economic growth would turn up, the immediate fiscal pressures upon politicians might relax or go away.

Politicians may justify a refusal to worry by pointing out that many doom-sayers turn out to be Cassandras of the nonevent. Gloomy forecasts can be discounted by invoking relatively optimistic forecasts indicating that the political economy is about to take a turn for the better. Tomorrow's growth may be invoked to pay for yesterday's commitments and today's debts. The difference between the Victorian Mr. Micawber and the modern-day optimist is that the former risked imprisonment for debt if his optimism was not justified, whereas latter-day economists can externalize (that is, dump) the costs of their forecasting errors upon politicians who believe them.

The problem of the 1970s is that time after time political economists have forecast turning points—but the political economy does not turn. Some politicians believe that the risk engendered is acceptable. If a crisis does result, then the very conditions of crisis make it *easier* to secure acceptance of politically unpalatable but necessary measures. For example,

President Nixon secured acceptance for anti-inflationary policies in 1971 that would not have proven acceptable, except for the emergency devaluation of the dollar. Similarly, the Italian Christian Democratic government has used the weakness of its economy as an argument for Italian Communists tacitly supporting unpopular policies. While politicians are correct that crisis greatly expands the room for political maneuver, the cost of waiting for a crisis to emerge greatly reduces the choice between unpalatable policies.

Another reason for doing nothing is that all the alternative courses of action appear, for the moment at least, politically unacceptable. Politicians responsible for controlling public spending may find that colleagues responsible for public benefits are unwilling to sacrifice their departmental interests to assuage a colleague's fiscal worries. Leaders of unions and businesses may be loath to accept cuts in real wages or to make potentially unprofitable investments in order to solve the problems of politicians. Nor is the prospect of seeking an international loan attractive, when bankers wish answers to awkward questions about whether the loan can be paid back promptly in a hard currency. When there are real objections to policies intended to avoid hypothetical risks, a politician may prefer to do nothing. As a British Chancellor of the Exchequer, Denis Healey, confessed in a harried moment, "If I worried about all the problems I have to face, I would have died within a month of taking office." [3]

Mr. Micawber's readiness to trust to luck is unsatisfying in a rational age, for he had no theory to explain why conditions should get better. To justify optimism with the statement "Things may turn out for the best," is to invite the retort "Or, they may turn out for the worst." Americans can take no comfort in being reminded of what the Prussian Chancellor Bismarck offered: "There must be a special Providence looking after fools, drunkards, and the United States of America." Nor can citizens of the country of Adam Smith and Keynes take comfort in a judgment by Parliament that there is no point in making plans to improve the British economy since it would take "almost an economic miracle" to achieve them.[4]

A Micawberish economic policy is an expression of despair. It recommends doing nothing because it is assumed that conscious action by government is more likely to make things worse than better. It trusts to luck to get the economy right. Yet to rely solely on luck, without understanding the causes of good fortune, is to run the risk that sooner or later luck will run out.

Mr. Micawber's policy for managing the economy is a waiting game. The amount of risk involved in waiting depends upon how much time a country has before take-home pay turns down. Italy, Britain, and Sweden can no longer afford the luxury of doing nothing. The United States, Germany, and France may still pursue a Micawberish policy—but this only increases the costs of buying time, if their faith in the future is ill-founded.

MONEY ILLUSION AND DISILLUSION

Everywhere in the Western world, politicians have reacted to the predicament of their political economy by invoking the money illusion of inflation. Inflation increases the take-home pay of citizens, and it also makes it easier to meet the costs of public policy. Momentarily, inflation has replaced economic growth as the chief political solvent of potentially overloaded governments. In the words of Peter Jay, "Inflation has in a true sense been the safety valve of political stability, the unseen hand which temporarily accommodated the imperatives of political survival to the imperatives of economic supply by debasing the coin in which unfillable political pledges were made." [5]

Inflation is a consequence and not a cause of the overloading of the contemporary political economy.[6] The monetarist theory of inflation emphasizes the active role of government in stimulating inflation by increasing the supply of money much faster than the increase in the things that money can buy. From 1970 through 1977, the money supply increased by one and a half times the growth rate of the economy in the United States; and by four times in France and Germany. In Sweden the money supply rose by more than six times the growth of the national product, in Britain by eight times, and in Italy by more than ten times.[7]

The cost-push theory of inflation emphasizes that the determination of wages and prices is subject to organized pressure. The market price of organized labor is affected by the power of unions to prevent wages falling and to push for increases in money terms. In every major Western nation since 1970, wages have been rising much faster than the real growth of the national product. In the United States, wages have "only" gone up three times as much as the real increase in the national product; in Germany by four times; and France by five times. In Sweden, the percentage increase in wages is eight times the real increase of the national product; in Italy eleven times; and in Britain, twelve times.[8]

The 1970s have seen inflation on a scale unprecedented in the Western world since the resolution of World War II (see Table 8.1). The average annual rate of inflation is 6.1 percent, more than twice the rate of the 1960s.[9] Double-digit inflation has occurred in every major Western nation except Germany at least once since 1970, and Britain and Italy have had prices rising by more than 10 percent annually since 1973. On average, in major nations prices have almost doubled from 1970 to 1977; prices have risen by as much as 149 percent in Britain. German inflation has been the lowest by comparative standards, but a 46 percent increase in price is still regarded as excessive in Germany.

TABLE 8.1

The Accelerating Pace of Inflation

	1950	1960	1970	1977
Consumer Price Index (1970 = 100)				
America	62	77	100	156
Britain	44	66	100	249
France	38	65	100	183
Germany	55	71	100	146
Italy	48	64	100	234
Sweden	42	66	100	180

Source: International Monetary Fund, *International Financial Statistics* 31 (May 1978) national tables; 24 (June 1971); and 14 (June 1961).

Cumulatively, single-digit and double-digit annual inflation result in treble-digit inflation. If 1950 prices are taken as the base, then the price of a standard basket of goods is now more than 500 percent higher in Britain, France, and Italy, and up by more than 400 percent in Sweden. Whereas from 1950 it took twenty years for the cost of living to double in Italy, and nineteen years in Britain, the cost of living doubled again in both countries in a four-year period which began in 1973. In France, the cost of living has doubled in an eight-year period which began in 1969, and in Sweden it has doubled in nine years. Only the United States and Germany have escaped a doubling of prices in the past decade. In the United States the doubling of prices occurred over a fourteen-year period which began in 1963; in Germany it occurred over a sixteen-year period which began in 1961.

Politicians have tried to disguise the escalation in prices by quoting inflation rates on an annual basis. For example, to say that 1977 prices have risen 10 percent by comparison with the year before sounds better than saying that a basket of goods that cost 100 units in 1970 and 160 in 1976 now costs 176 units of a nation's currency. The two statements are in fact identical. If inflation figures are quoted on a three-month basis, a quarterly rise of 2.5 percent appears much smaller than its annual equivalent of 10.4 percent. A politician may even announce that inflation has "fallen," if the preceding quarter registered a price rise of 3 percent. Inflation has a pervasive and continuing effect upon everyone in society. People are affected by inflation whenever they go to a store to buy something, and find out the price has gone up since a year or a month ago. They are also affected by inflation every time they sit down to figure out why a raise in pay does not necessarily make it easier to cope with a rising cost of living. By contrast, unemployment affects only a fraction of society: those who are currently or recently unemployed, their dependents, and those who fear that they may soon be unemployed if unfavorable economic trends continue.

Inflation redistributes income, increasing the purchasing power of those whose earnings can be adjusted rapidly, whether they are farmers selling produce, hourly wage workers with cost-of-living escalator clauses in their contract, or middle-class professionals charging fees for services. Inflation decreases the purchasing power of others within society, whether hourly wage workers without automatic cost- of- living increases, middle-class employees with fixed annual wages, or self-employed workers and farmers who find that their costs of doing business rise even faster than their income.[10] In the Alice-in-Wonderland world of inflation, individuals may find that a 20 percent wage increase leaves them worse off than before. In such circumstances, a demand for a 25 percent wage increase may be regarded as "conservative," that is, an attempt to prevent take-home pay from falling in purchasing power.

Inflation makes it difficult for individuals to figure out whether they are gaining or losing from a rapid rise in prices and wages. Economists calculate inflation's effects on average, but individuals are only interested in its effects in particular. Very few citizens compare their weekly or monthly pay with a cost of living index to see where they stand. Rapid rises in prices can bring about a negative reaction, whether or not wages have risen equally fast. People complain about how expensive everything has become, even if their earnings have kept pace with a rising cost of living. The rapid change in the prices of goods is upsetting to ordinary individuals accustomed to thinking of money as having a "real" (that is, fixed) value.

The erroneous assumption that money has a relatively constant value is today a major bulwark against institutionalizing double-digit inflation. If individuals expect inflation continuously to erode the value of money, they will adapt their behavior, with important economic and political consequences. Saving is likely to decline, borrowing to increase, and spending to take the form of hedging against inflation. For example, in Britain or Italy in the 1970s, putting money in an automobile has been a better hedge against inflation than buying government bonds, for a secondhand car has depreciated less in value than a government bond. Of course, what an individual may gain from the appreciation of a used car is only relative to fixed interest securities; the motorist is a loser when trading in the car for another, since inflation will increase the cost of a replacement new car more than it protects the nominal money value of a used car.

Government is immediately and uniquely a beneficiary of inflation. It can print money as and when it needs it. As a German economist caustically explains, "This power is denied to all those who do not have a central bank." [11] The money it creates can be used to provide more collectively determined benefits of public policies, or to put more money in the hands of citizens, in the belief that this will be both good for the economy and good for the government's political fortunes as well. This assumes that public deficits will stimulate employment and economic growth, as well as inflation. Some economists now argue that Keynesian-type policies will not decrease the "natural" rate of employment and through inflation, may even increase it.[12]

Inflation benefits debtors. As government is the biggest debtor in every society, in inflationary times it enjoys the classic debtor's advantage of paying back its debts in a currency that is worth less in purchasing power. Government debts are fixed in money terms, whereas its current revenue from an inflated national product tends to rise. Thus, it is possible for government debts to grow substantially while declining in relation to the total national product. For example, in the United States the federal debt more than doubled from 1957 to 1977, reaching a total of $709 billion. Simultaneously, it fell as a proportion of an inflated national product from 63 to 39 percent.

Inflation hurts creditors, and individuals tend to be the biggest creditors in society. They are the source of the savings loaned to government to finance its activities, and to banks and industry as well. Of the total federal United States debt, 78 percent is held by the public.[13] In the 1970s, individuals who have loaned money to government have enjoyed the dubious certainty of knowing that what they receive in return is worth less than the money loaned. The purchasing power of a government bond can depreciate to half or less its face value in a five- or ten-year period, and annual interest can be *negative* interest, that is, less than the annual rate of inflation. For example, in 1976 the British government was paying an average gross interest of 14.4 percent on government bonds, but the cost of living was rising at an annual rate of 17 percent.[14] Among major Western nations, only Germany was paying a gross rate of interest higher than the penalty of inflation. After paying tax on interest income, an individual will be even worse off than if the money had been spent rather than saved.

Inflation helps tax collectors and squeezes taxpayers, because rates of tax increase progressively with income. In an inflationary era, a citizen can see gross earnings rise by 50 percent, but not gain a penny in real purchasing power. Simultaneously, the taxes on that income will rise by more than 50 percent, because the progressive income tax takes a higher proportion of income as it rises in current money values. Citizens trying to hedge against inflation by buying stocks also face tax problems, for capital gains are levied on increases in the money value of a stock, and not on its purchasing power. The tendency of taxes to rise *faster* than the cost of living means that individual earnings must run ahead of inflation to protect post-tax take-home pay.[15]

In the midst of a sudden burst of inflation, many people make the false assumption, "It can't go on like this." But the evidence is that it can. The rising rate of inflation in the 1970s does not of itself threaten hyperinflation, like that of Germany in 1923, when prices rose by more than 100 billion times in fifteen months. More worrisome is the evidence of Latin America. It shows that meso-inflation—that is, annual inflation at double-digit rates from 10 to 99 percent—can persist for decades without skyrocketing as once happened in Germany. Argentina, Brazil, Chile and Uruguay have experienced steady double-digit inflation since the 1950s.[16] These countries have had rates of economic growth comparing satisfactorily with major Western nations, but they have also had political experiences that do not compare favorably.

Double-digit inflation is disturbing politically, because it implies the loss of government's credibility. A government's economic credit is derived from the belief that its money commands goods and services in national and international markets. The credit of government is not based upon the intrinsic value of its currency. Elephantine Italian notes for 10,000 or 50,000 lire are not valued for their compactness or crispness, nor are American big bills valued for the beauty of the engraved features of Salmon P. Chase or Grover Cleveland. A nation's currency is valued only insofar as people believe that they can exchange it for goods and services. If the money that government prints loses credibility, then individuals may turn to cigarettes or foreign coins as the chief medium of exchange, as occurred in many occupied European countries in World War II. In the extreme case of Italy today, the government is itself no longer able to print enough money to meet the nation's needs. Government agencies use postage stamps, bus tickets, and chewing gum as small change, and banks print 50 and 100 lire notes on their own authority, and to their own profit. The government's monopoly of money has been abandoned.

The greatest threat that inflation poses is the threat of success. Inflation works (sic) by disguising real shifts in resources behind the money illusion of constantly and unequally changing prices and wages. Inflation does not increase the size of the national pie; it only redistributes it. By means of inflation, politicians can meet the rising costs of public policy, but this cuts take-home pay and risks political bankruptcy. At this juncture, inflation is no longer a solution to the problem of running an overloaded economy; it becomes a problem in its own right, and a problem that politicians must urgently do something about.

GETTING ORGANIZED

Confronted with a political economy that appears increasingly unmanageable, the managers of mixed-economy welfare states have voiced a common response: "We must get organized." Organizations are a resource that government can command; whereas market forces, as the events of the 1970s make clear, cannot easily be manipulated.

Can Government Go Bankrupt?

Corporatism is the generic label given to institutions bring-ing government, business, and labor together to share the burden of managing the economy. The concept is an old one; corporate institutions antedate the world recession, treble afflu-ence, and democracy, as well.[17] Corporatism is based upon the assumption that if the leaders of the major organizations in society agree on a policy, then their followers have no choice but to accept this, as there is no other channel of political representation open. In the contemporary Western world, cor-poratism assumes that government by itself cannot control the whole of the economy, for labor unions and businessmen also make decisions in the marketplace. In law, a government is sovereign, but in practice it must bargain on a tripartite basis with business and union leaders. "Votes count, resources decide." [18]

Corporate institutions differ from conventional Socialist and free enterprise ideas. Socialists assume that the ownership of economic resources is crucial, and that a Socialist state can effectively command the economy. Free enterprise doctrines assume that private ownership can minimize government's in-fluence in the market place. Corporatism emphasizes the in-terdependence of resources dispersed in the hands of business, labor, and government. It has a roundtable model of managing the economy. Leaders of business, labor, and government are meant to sit together and bargain in order to arrive at a con-sensus about policies in the collective interest of society.

The object of creating formal or informal corporate institu-tions is everywhere the same: to get the nation's economy right or at least to deal with the worst problems of stagflation. Insofar as rising prices are the problem, then something must be done about rising prices. Insofar as wage claims are reckoned to push up costs and prices, then something must be done about wage claims too.

In efforts to control the inflationary drift of wages and prices, major Western governments have relied upon three distinctive mechanisms.[19] At one extreme, Germany and Sweden have encouraged highly centralized labor unions and business groups to bargain with each other; government tends to act as a mediator, but the results of these decisions are not enacted and enforced by the government. Until the mid-1970s the German deliberations appeared to work better in times of economic recession; wages have rushed upwards in times of prosperity. The Swedish system, by contrast, has worked better in periods of affluence; it broke down in the midst of the nation's economic difficulties and change of government in 1976. France has followed a second alternative, indicative policy-making, in which the French government sets desirable goals for the growth of wages and prices, but does not attempt to enforce its views in all the settlements made by the ideologically fragmented institutions of labor and management in France. In the public sector, which includes a substantial portion of large employers, the government directly intervenes. Thirdly, the United States, Britain, and Italy have each attempted statutory periods of wage and price controls; in each country the measures have been temporary rather than permanent. In the case of Italy, the *scala mobile* law has been popular with those covered by it; the law has automatically indexed wages so that cost of living increases are paid every three months. In the face of recurring economic crises Britain has attempted at least five major programs backed by statutory authority. The United States has tried at least four different types of wage and price policy, including statutory measures during the Korean and Viet Nam Wars. In the words of a former White House advisor, Arnold R. Weber, the thirty years of American trial-and-error experimentation shows that "there has been as much of the latter as the former." [20]

Wage and price policies, whether sanctioned by law or informal jawboning, can have desired short-time effects. Gradually the effectiveness of these policies is eroded, however, because of inherent problems. Freezing wages is discriminatory, insofar as there is not simultaneous control over rents and dividends. Allowing a limited flat-rate increase in wages benefits relatively lower-paid workers and erodes trade union differentials in wages between skilled and unskilled workers. Wages tend to drift upwards, notwithstanding controls, as managements upgrade workers to higher pay classifications, grant overtime payments and bonuses, or otherwise supplement take-home pay outside the norms of wages policy. Government and its business and labor partners find it increasingly difficult to monitor and adjudicate all the wage and price increases sought in a complex modern economy.

The fundamental weakness of corporate wage and price policies is in their political assumptions. Corporatism assumes a consensus where none can be agreed. Since the Middle Ages, philosophers have debated the theory of the "just" wage and "just" profits. The growth of free market industrialism side-stepped rather than resolved the issue. Economists searching for a scientific basis for wages, prices, and profits are pursuing a chimera. There is a real conflict of interest between business and labor about the relative share of the national pie that each gains. Moreover, there are conflicts among unionized workers about the "just" differential in the wages of a plumber, a truck driver, and an unskilled factory worker; and within the middle class about the earnings of an executive, a farmer, and a teacher. To assume that any machinery for consultation can remove these differences is to assume the end of politics, that is, an end to the conflicts of interest that are a persisting and pervasive feature of the political economy that we know today.[21]

Contemporary corporatism also assumes that the leaders of business, labor, and government can make effective agreements. The bargains of corporatism are not determined by votes or by market-place decisions, but by negotiations between a few top leaders in each organization. The agreement of elites may derive from a preference for winning part of a loaf by negotiation, rather than going for an all-or-nothing strike. But calling groups "corporations" does not mean that each can move as a single body. Within the world of business there are many different types of institutions, with interests that can differ greatly: banks and insurance companies that specialize in the management of money; industrial firms that produce goods; and retail firms that must sell them. Equally, trade unions embrace everything from manual workers paid on an hourly rate, through routine white collar workers, to professional associations of doctors and lawyers. Within government, there is no unity of interest between spending departments and agencies trying to find the money to meet the rising costs of public policy.

Another politically crucial assumption is that the national product is growing sufficiently to provide something for almost everybody in the bargains that are struck. In the era of treble affluence, this was the case. But in the 1970s, there may *not* be something for everybody. In an overloaded political economy, no amount of goodwill or talk can hide the fact that either the real level of spending on public policy or the real value of take-home pay (or both) must be limited.

The goals of corporate institutions are easy to state, but difficult to achieve. Legislation can be enacted to control wages, prices, or both, in hopes that laws will prevent inflation from intensifying. But any measure that controls wages when prices are rising in an international as well as a national economy implies that workers will suffer a cut in their standard of living. Any measure that controls prices when money wages are rising puts a squeeze on profits that will sooner or later drive firms toward bankruptcy. To try to control both wages and prices, when one-quarter to two-fifths of a nation's trade is with foreign countries, is to aspire to an isolated siege economy from a position of weakness, rather than strength.

Corporate institutions are an exercise in blame-sharing. Politicians have found that they cannot control an economy influenced by powers that are shared domestically and dispersed internationally. Blame-sharing does not solve the problems of stagflation; but it does solve the politician's first problem, which is how to make clear to the electorate that the economy that government is meant to manage is temporarily unmanageable by those responsible for it.

In political terms, the costs of successful corporatism may be greater than the costs of failure. If corporate agreements are to become fully effective, they require the transformation of many established social relationships. Government would require powers to control both labor and capital, imposing real cuts in living standards, even if only temporarily, as the price of achieving larger economic goals. It would also require the power to direct the market activities of businessmen, whether through official agencies or the more or less willing cooperation of institutions nominally formed to represent the interests of business. A command economy directed by official or quasi-official bureaucracy would dominate market decisions.

The effectiveness of corporatism is limited in society as we know it today. Workers and businesses enjoy the right of freedom of contract. Unions can strike if they do not like the wages offered, and businesses can refuse to invest in the absence of profits. Unions are not meant to provide benefits for the whole of society, but for their members, just as companies seek profits for their directors and owners. Corporate agreements can only proceed at the speed of the most recalcitrant partner, for each has a *liberum veto*. Success is contingent upon the mutual conjunction of the interests of business, labor, and politicians, and not upon the abdication of these interests in the name of a global public interest. A rapid and intense inflation, such as Italy and Britain have experienced in the 1970s, can temporarily create a mutual agreement among corporate leaders that any form of controls may be better than accelerating inflation. But this agreement will last only as long as each side continues to believe that the particulars of the agreement are in its specific interest. While it can be argued that it is in the collective interest of all citizens to avoid inflation and maximize growth, it does not follow that it is in the individual interest of each citizen to take the measures necessary to achieve these collective ends.[22]

To demand too much from corporate institutions is to jeopardize the political authority of government. As long as corporate policies are voluntary, there is no question of laws being broken if groups act in their market interest. As long as wage and price regulations have loopholes—such as provisions for productivity increases or other forms of wage drift, or for price increases reflecting rising import costs—then groups can avoid control when the pressures of a successful policy become uncomfortably strong. Governments too may wish to slip from the constraints of such policies to appease their own supporters or to court electoral favor. As long as wage and price controls are temporary, business and labor groups may accept them in the hope that some general good may be accomplished, and that any advantages temporarily foregone can be won back as soon as controls are relaxed.

If a government were to insist upon trying to control wages and prices indefinitely, it would put its political authority at risk. Trade union leaders might refuse cooperation with an elected government and publicly press for higher wages in defiance of government norms, as the British miners did in the autumn of 1973, leading to the downfall of the Conservative government of Edward Heath. Alternatively, business leaders might announce that without hope of maintaining profits, business firms would refuse to invest as their government planned.

If politicians convinced business and union leaders to accept measures immediately against the interests of their members, those who felt misrepresented by their leaders would demonstrate that corporations are truly "artificial persons." [23] Individuals can turn their backs on organizations for freedom of action in the interstices between organizations. Investors who trusted in corporate managers to provide dividends and capital gains could withdraw their money and put it into real assets that they could see and touch, whether a home, a car, or gold. Workers disenchanted with the ability of unions to protect their living standards could bargain directly with employers, trying to protect their earnings within the law, or by wildcat strikes. The failure of corporate institutions to do the difficult (restore treble affluence) as well as the impossible (take the conflict out of politics) would unite followers against leaders. The flight of indifferent individuals from corporations that misrepresent them would generate organizational incompetence.

INTERNATIONAL INCREDIBILITY

Historically, governments have viewed international trade in political terms. The events of World War II made clear that no Western nation, however strong, could be an island, entire of itself. The rapid growth of international trade in the era of treble affluence was evidence that cooperation rather than conflict could make international relationships mutually profitable to every nation. While national economies have become more closely integrated, no political community has grown up coterminous with international trade. The European Community divides Western Europe into nine member and eight nonmember states; it also divides major European nations from the major economies of North America and Japan. NATO military defense bridges the Atlantic, but it is conspicuously not a free trade area; its membership reflects military, not economic, considerations. The 1973 oil crisis and its aftermath have demonstrated palpably and publicly that economic interdependence does not lead to political community. The tie that binds importers and exporters is the cash nexus.

Today, every national government must maintain the international credibility of its political economy if it is to manage its domestic economy effectively. Whereas a government need only seek popular endorsement from its electorate every four years or so, it must maintain continuous endorsement of its currency in the market places of the world. The free movement of goods and money within the Western world subjects nations to international market pressures. Major European nations export upwards of one-quarter of their national product; and the United States exports about one-tenth of its vast national product. Foreigners will not buy these goods if inflated costs make a country's exports more expensive than the goods of its competitors. Every major Western nation needs to export goods in order to earn foreign currency to pay for its imports of raw materials and consumer goods. But no country is required to import the goods of any one particular country, or to take its currency for their exports.

When a government turns to inflation to buy time domestically, the resulting rise in prices initially makes the goods it exports more expensive, and foreigners may therefore reduce their purchases. Simultaneously, foreign imports become relatively cheaper, by comparison with inflated domestic products. But the national currency paid foreigners in exchange for these imports no longer buys as much as before. Foreigners are not subject to a money illusion, as citizens of a country may be. Nor do they have to hold a given nation's currency. Their refusal to accept or hold a nation's currency further destabilizes a nation's domestic economy. With free movement of currencies and floating exchange rates, pressures can be felt with great swiftness. For example, the German Bundesbank is able to take in the equivalent of up to $1 billion *an hour* from "hot money" speculators who prefer to hold Deutsche marks rather than dollars.

If all countries in the Western world experienced the same rate of inflation at the same time, then no country need be subject to the pressures of a rapid devaluation of its currency. But this has not been the case (see Table 8.1). Inflation has been twice as great in Britain and Italy as in the United States and Germany. In turn, this has a major effect upon the value of national currencies in relation to each other. Relative inflation is not the only influence upon currency exchange rates; they are also affected by such things as tangible fluctuations in terms of trade and balance of payments, and by intangibles such as foreign "confidence" in a currency (see Appendix, Table 8.1). From 1970 to the end of 1977, the British pound and the Italian lira have each lost more than one-third of their value when compared with a basket of world currencies, that is, monies averaged together in proportion to their share of world trade.[24] Simultaneously, the German Deutsche mark has risen by 53 percent overall on foreign exchange markets, making it worth twice as much as the pound or the lira by comparison with 1970. The Swedish krona and the French franc have generally held their own. The dollar has fallen on average by 18 percent on world markets. It has risen by as much as 28 percent against the lira, but dropped by 77 percent against the Deutsche mark.

Travellers immediately notice the effect of changes in currency values. For example, in Frankfurt, an American finds that a dollar that bought 3.6 Deutsche marks in 1970 would only buy 2.1 Deutsche marks in 1978. What was once a $10 meal at 36 DM, through a modicum of German inflation and even bigger changes in exchange rates, becomes a $23 meal. By contrast, in London a $10 bill that bought £4.17 in 1970 would be worth anything between £5.00 and £6.00 in 1978, depending upon the fluctuations of the British currency. Yet even a favorable increase in exchange rates does not compensate for the effects of British inflation, for a restaurant meal costing $10 in London in 1970 would cost about $18 in 1977.

Stay-at-home citizens do not escape the effects of changes in the value of their national currency. When a substantial fraction of a country's consumption consists of imported goods, a fall in the value of its currency pushes up the cost of living. The decline of the British pound and the Italian lira has boosted the cost of their imported goods by about 50 percent in five years, increasing the cost of living as much as a year's double-digit inflation. A boost in the cost of imported goods is much the same as a cut in the real purchasing power of take-home pay. If citizens react by claiming higher wages, thus pushing up domestic costs, this can set off another round of international devaluation and domestic inflation.

Within the boundaries of a national political community, the burdens of an overloaded economy are shared; in the name of a common citizenship, prosperous regions pay more taxes to subsidize citizens in poorer regions. No such community exists at the international level. The richest nations are not prepared to tax their citizens heavily for the benefit of poorer neighbors within the Western world, let alone in the Third World.[25] The European Economic Community, while a common market for trade, is not a single community sharing taxes and welfare benefits equally from Southern Italy to Northern Germany, or from Paris to the Scottish Highlands.

President Richard Nixon expressed the characteristic reaction of a harried national leader to economic difficulties abroad. According to a Watergate tape, when asked by aide H. R. Haldeman whether he had heard that the British had floated the pound, he replied, "I don't care about it. Nothing we can do about it. It's too complicated for me to get into." When told that the Federal Reserve Board was concerned about speculation against the Italian lira, he commented, "Well, I don't give a (expletive deleted) about the lira." [26] President Carter has shown a more polite but equally clear recognition of the primacy of political independence. In an interview with European journalists before the London international economic summit of May 1977, the following exchange took place:

REPORTER: The meeting of the heads of states shows clearly how interdependent the economies are, and that this interdependence is rapidly growing. How much sovereignty is the United States willing to give up in the decision-making process?

PRESIDENT CARTER: None.[27]

The overloaded governments of Britain and Italy have learned the hard way, by unsuccessful efforts to make the United States, German, and Japanese governments stimulate world trade, that there is no community of burden-sharing. British and Italian politicians regard increased consumption by their richer trading partners as desirable for their export industries. But politicians in Washington, Bonn, and Tokyo reason that taking measures to stimulate world trade would increase inflation within their own countries. They have no wish to import inflation. National governments remain responsible for national economic difficulties. In the words of the German co-author of the McCracken Report, "If a country suffers from unemployment and inflation it cannot be helped by other countries." [28]

Overloaded governments can turn to the International Monetary Fund (IMF) for a loan to buy time to resolve their economic difficulties.[29] But borrowing money from foreigners is not as congenial a way to buy time as printing money oneself. British and Italian governments, which have had to resort to the IMF for loans in 1976 and 1977, respectively, can testify to this.

As an international organization whose 130 member-states represent all corners of the earth, the IMF is unconcerned with many of the problems that worry politicians accountable to a national electorate. Whereas politicans may concentrate attention upon the benefits of policies, IMF officials are primarily concerned with their costs. While neutral as between political parties, the IMF is highly partisan in defense of the proposition that a nation cannot continue to consume more than it produces.

A country that comes to the IMF for a loan by definition has problems with its political economy. The IMF is not interested in loaning money to governments that will simply persist in the policies that have overloaded it. Nor are representatives of the major countries supplying its loan capital, such as the United States and Germany, anxious to finance elsewhere measures that their own national electorate would not pay for at home.

Like the character with a broken leg in *Games People Play*, politicians may try to use their weakness to claim special international treatment. For example, some British politicians assert that other countries would not wish the British economy to collapse, because of Britain's major role in world trade. Italian Christian Democrats can threaten Washington with the prospect of a Communist government in Rome, if their own policies are not funded. But such threats are double-edged. If London were to collapse as an international financial center, this would hurt Britain more than any other single nation, and a Communist takeover in Italy would be a far greater blow to Christian Democrats than to politicians in other countries.

A country applying to the IMF for a loan seeks an international "Good Housekeeping Seal of Approval" for the management of its economy. The sums involved in IMF loans are small in relation to a recipient's national product, and trivial by comparison with the volume of international trade. Nor does the IMF have to worry about the repayment of a loan. No member state has ever publicly defaulted on a loan. To do so would face it with an international vote of no confidence in the market place of world trade. An IMF loan gives a country fiscal respectability, enabling it to augment this loan with substantial international borrowing from other public and private sources.

The negotiations for an IMF loan concern the measures that a government will adopt to reduce the causes of its economic troubles. Until a government gives evidence that it will improve its domestic economy, the IMF will hesitate to provide the money that the borrowing country badly needs. Within a national government, politicians and central bankers anxious to reduce the overloading of the economy can use negotiations with the IMF to force reluctant colleagues to accept measures that would otherwise be rejected. For example, when Britain formally requested an IMF loan in 1976, its letter of intent listed many things it had done to improve its political economy. It also enumerated the stringent measures it proposed to take in the forthcoming months to avoid yet another international "bailing out" of the pound. Many of the measures promised to the IMF contradicted what the government's domestic supporters wanted it to do.

At first sight, the IMF appears as a potentially dictatorial and alien ruler of an overloaded nation's political economy. But dictating domestic economic policies would change the Fund from a lending institution into a surrogate national department of finance. Since the political economies seeking loans from the Fund are, by definition, difficult to manage, the Fund has no incentive to become deeply involved in national politics. Nor does it have the staff or legal authority to do this. The IMF is more concerned with a country's financial targets than with the means that it chooses to reach its targets.

The IMF is a buffer institution, seeking to prevent national mismanagement of an economy from damaging the international trading system of which it is a part. It is concerned with seeing that inevitable fluctuations in world trade occur within a context favorable to continuing growth. It is opposed to abrupt or extreme changes in international exchange rates or world patterns of trade. It is not opposed to gradual changes in the international status of a particular country, whether up or down. By definition, if one country's currency goes down in international value, others must go up. The gainers as well as the losers are members of the IMF.

As an intergovernmental international agency, the policies and procedures of the IMF tend to be cautious and consensus-seeking. The simplest thing for it to do when a country first asks for aid is to provide, on more or less commercial terms, short-term credits to finance deficits in the country's current balance of payments. If this is insufficient, longer-term loans can be granted with increasingly stringent conditions. The IMF has no wish to bear the onus of causing the collapse of a nation's currency in foreign exchange markets. At the margin, the IMF is ready to give a national government the benefit of the doubt, if it can plausibly claim that something may turn up to alleviate its difficulties. At times, it is prepared to pull its punches in negotiations, imposing easier conditions upon a borrowing country than some within it think necessary.

The strength of the IMF is primarily negative. Its leadership is not dependent upon any national electorate for its political future, and Fund staff must attend to the views of well managed, prosperous countries as well as to the requests of governments seeking loans. A government cannot expect the IMF to give it money to buy time, if it proposes to continue overloading its political economy. An IMF loan gives a government the time (and, often the necessary prod) to reverse policies that have landed it in international financial trouble. International civil servants sitting in the air-conditioned elegance of the downtown Washington office of the IMF have no wish to become caught up in the domestic political difficulties of an overloaded political economy. If a government cannot promise to set its own political economy in order, the IMF cannot do this for them. It can only leave those who have overloaded a nation's economy to face the consequences.

CHAPTER 9

Forced Choice

The party is now over. In the rest of this decade world statesmen must either persuade the world's population to live within the world's means, or be overwhelmed when a furious citizenry discovers the hard way that a broken pint pot not only does not contain a quart, but does not even contain a pint.

Peter Jay,
The International Scene, 1975

THE MANAGERS of an overloaded political economy can only buy time for so long; there then comes a moment "when the kissing has to stop." [1] The money illusion fails to deceive, the chief corporate institutions of society cannot deliver what they promise, and foreigners are no longer willing to lend money to fill the gap between what a nation produces and what it consumes. Governors are forced to make major strategic choices. Doing nothing is the worst choice of all, for government then backs into political bankruptcy.

When the take-home pay of a nation registers a steady trend downwards, there is no abrupt challenge to authority, as in Peter Jay's image of a broken pint pot; but the gradual erosion of government's reputation for effectiveness makes it harder to change course abruptly. The longer the trend continues, the more widespread popular disaffection becomes, as the consequences of overloading the national economy become increasingly apparent in household accounts.

In reviewing strategic alternatives, the first step is to dismiss choices that offer solace without solution. There are many placebos at hand, but none can immediately resolve the problems that arise when the costs of public policy force a steady cut in take-home pay. Planning is a symbol of power to the tidy-minded, but planning of itself does not create more resources for a country to consume. German growth has been much greater than British growth, notwithstanding the fact that the British have often tried to plan and the Germans eschewed it. In France, often cited as the best example of economic planning, experts now suggest that economic growth was necessary for the success of planning, rather than the opposite.[2] Increasing efficiency is a perennial money-saving nostrum. But when President Carter asked Congress for authority to reorganize the federal government in 1977 he also asked that it not require him to estimate how much money would be saved, "for detailed savings estimates are very difficult to make accurately" in dollars and cents terms.[3] The more often management reforms fail to make any difference to the costs of public policy, the more this emphasizes the resistance of institutions to reform. Another structural change—altering the party in control of government—does not give a new government more resources to spend; it punishes new governors by willing them a legacy of spending commitments from their predecessors. In the extreme case of Sweden, the anti-Socialist government elected in 1976 found that its predecessors had overloaded it with a generation of spending commitments. Even changing the ownership of the means of production, the favorite Marxist panacea, does not increase the national product. But a Marxist government still needs to make fundamental choices about the distribution of a finite national product among claims for public spending, take-home pay, and investment. Placebo policies offer reform without change. While those administering placebos wait for some effects to register, government drifts closer to political bankruptcy.

When a government has no more time, as well as no more pie, it has three broad strategic alternatives. It can continue on a business as usual basis, consciously or unintentionally discovering for itself what the consequences are of going into political bankruptcy. It can make public policy sacrosanct, promoting the further growth of public policy by making cuts in take-home pay on the ground that collectively provided benefits are better than what individuals would otherwise buy. Or, a government can decide that the time has come to give first priority to protecting the take-home pay of individual citizens, limiting the growth in the cost of public policy to the growth of the national product.

BACKING INTO BANKRUPTCY

Neither governors nor governed vote for political bankruptcy; it is something that happens in spite of themselves. It is the unintended result of a sequence of actions in which everyone does what each thinks best, but which cumulatively produces results far worse than anyone intended. Citizens do not choose political bankruptcy; they back into it while trying to avoid seemingly worse difficulties.

Politicians encourage political bankruptcy when they try to paper over the gap between national commitments and the national product. Loading more commitments onto an increasingly overloaded political economy reduces the efficiency and effectiveness of government, for the shortage of resources makes it increasingly hard to carry out established and new programs. When government expands its commitments, the costs of coordination and the risks of contradiction increase, thus further increasing the overhead costs of government. The resulting decline in effectiveness is demoralizing for those who provide public services, as well as for the citizens meant to receive the benefits.

As consumers of government benefits, individuals cannot help but notice when public services do not work as well as they used to, and inefficiency results in higher costs as well. In times of treble affluence, individuals can adjust, by relying more upon goods and services bought privately and paid for from their own take-home pay. But the 1970s raises the prospect that individuals may not be able to buy substitutes for inadequate public services in future. Simultaneously, they may object if government increases taxes for poor services provided on their behalf.

The unexpectedness and novelty of political bankruptcy makes it difficult to visualize what can happen until it is too late. What we can do here is to explore consequences of a government persistently reducing take-home pay even though the national product continues to rise. One possibility is political conflict about the distribution of cuts in take-home pay. But a more likely possibility is the undermining of political authority by citizen indifference. Government will only become the focal point of conflict if citizens demand that it do something about falling take-home pay. But individuals may not do this, because they lack confidence in a government that has palpably failed in its tasks.

Individuals are concerned with particular, not general, effects of public policy: *whose* take-home pay will be reduced and *whose* protected? Government cannot deny its responsibility for sorting citizens into those who are protected and the larger number who lose, when it is the taxman's take that is the immediate cause of the fall in take-home pay.

One way in which a government might try to avoid dividing

society is to treat every citizen alike. It could declare a national emergency, and ask everyone to make a sacrifice in the name of a common citizenship. But doing this does not dispose of the problem; instead, the distribution of cuts becomes the immediate political issue. To ask the same sacrifice from everyone would not mean an equal sacrifice from each. The elderly, the unemployed, and low-paid workers would lose a much larger proportion of their income than the middle-aged, the active, and the well-paid. To reduce every income by the same percentage each year would still not produce an equality of sacrifice, for a bank janitor needs that last few percent of income much more than a bank president.

If a government starts to exempt some citizens from cuts in take-home pay, whatever the social merits of its decision it faces political dangers. Discriminating among citizens by guaranteeing the earnings of some at the expense of others invites a host of demands from groups arguing that it is in the national interest (or at least, in their own interest) to be exempt from cuts in take-home pay. The fact that government is prepared to exempt some groups from a fall in take-home pay makes it impossible for it to argue that it can do nothing. Yet government cannot prevent everybody's take-home pay from falling, when the state of the political economy means that more people must lose rather than gain. Those who bear the brunt of cuts will react more intensely against government than those who are sheltered will react in its favor. If everyone reacts with equal intensity, for or against government, the aggregate result is political conflict.

As government becomes more involved in questions of income distribution, it is more likely to face demands to promote income equality. The ideological argument in favor of making incomes more equal (or at least, less unequal) is older than Socialism. The overloading of the political economy makes the idea salient. But to make equality of income the goal when take-home pay is falling threatens to make a government more enemies than friends. By definition, half the population receives more than the median national income. Thus, any move toward income equality relatively disadvantages half the population. When take-home pay is rising, it is possible to promote equality the easy way, by making above-average incomes rise slower than below-average incomes. When take-home pay is falling, income equality can only be achieved if above-average earners suffer an absolute cut in take-home pay. The more money that is transferred to below-average income groups and the greater the number benefiting the greater the number of persons whose above-average income is significantly lowered.

The political conflicts threatened by equalizing income are not properly described as "class" conflict. Income differences are not a simple reflection of class differences; plumbers may earn more than clergymen or elementary schoolteachers, and farmers' incomes vary widely. Within the labor movement, there are jealously guarded income differentials between members of more and less skilled unions. Families with only one wage-earner usually have less than families where two or three members are in paid employment. Income redistribution threatens to divide society between those who *identify* with the haves, quite possibly a majority, against those who identify with the have-nots. When take-home pay is falling, there would be no fiscal dividend of growth to increase the income of the have-nots. Thus, those who gained real cash benefits would be relatively few by comparison with those who would lose money, absolutely as well as relatively. At such a juncture, citizens who found government *intentionally* reducing their take-home pay would have an immediate and intense economic incentive to nullify its policy. For a disaffected individual to take up arms in the literal sense would risk property and life. A safer and more direct alternative is to undermine political authority by a display of civic indifference.

The more intense the pressures upon take-home pay, the greater the pressure upon individuals to turn their backs on parties and policies that have failed to look after their interests in the past and to do what pays them best. In the words of a City of London banker advising a major client, "This is anti-British and derogatory to sterling, but on balance, if one is free to do so, it makes sense to me." [4]

Citizen indifference pays cash dividends if individuals organize their work to suit their own needs, and not the needs of government for tax revenue. One way to do this is to demonetize labor, thus legally avoiding any occasion for tax. Another way is to take a job where the pay is tax-free, that is, paid in ways that facilitate illegal tax evasion. While government in political bankruptcy has a special need for economic growth, it may find that the biggest growth is in the shadow economy hidden from the tax collector.

When a worker must pay in tax one-third or more of every extra pound or Deutsche mark earned, and a business or professional man upwards of one-half, there are immediate advantages in earning benefits that will not be taxed. In every country a company car is not only a status symbol, but also a tax-free gratuity for employees. Major restaurants in major cities fill up with businessmen eating large and unhealthy expense account lunches because the food is "free." Low-paid workers in high-tax countries may become victims of the "poverty trap." The post-tax take-home pay of such workers may be little different from untaxed unemployment benefits. The moral is, in a high-tax political economy, it doesn't pay to be paid in money.

Demonetizing labor legally reduces individual liability to taxation, while increasing effective earnings. The growth of do-it-yourself household work not only reflects individual tastes in leisure pursuits, but also the economic advantages of unpaid work. For example, a person faced with a $1,000 bill for painting his house needs to earn about $1,500 before tax to pay this bill. By doing his own house-painting, even if it means taking time off work to do it unpaid, the average citizen would be better off at the end of the year. The two weeks salary fore-gone will come off the top bracket of taxable income, and no tax will be due for the unpaid labor devoted to painting one's own house.

Tax evasion is very different from tax avoidance. It is a cash phenomenon, but cash that is kept outside the official econ-omy. From the government's point of view, tax evasion is ille-gal. From an individual's viewpoint, it is extralegal, that is, no business of government—whatever the laws may say. Politi-cally, tax evasion *contracts* the government's power, creating a shadow economy that it cannot regulate, because no one wants government to know what is happening there.

As a government faces more and more difficulties in making the official national product grow, the shadow economy grows. For example, in Britain workers in the building industry have formed themselves into unincorporated subcontracting firms selling labor for lump sums to large construction companies. These small firms operate from fictitious addresses, and work-ers paid in cash give false names to evade tax inspectors. The estimated loss of tax revenue to the British government from building work done "on the lump" has been up to £20 million annually.

Tax increases are an immediate incentive to citizens to col-lect their take-home pay in the shadow economy. A penny earned in the shadow economy is worth anything from 50 to 100 percent more than a penny earned after payment of taxes. By definition, illegal activities are not accurately recorded in government statistics. In the rueful words of a British Inland Revenue official, "If we knew how much tax evasion was going on, it wouldn't be evasion." [5] The indications are that tax evasion is already substantial or becoming significant in every major Western nation.

Italians have the most experience and expertise in evading taxes. One reason is political: Italians have always had a much higher degree of disaffection from government than is normal in Anglo-Saxon Europe. Another is administrative: archaic and complex taxes are collected by complex and archaic means. Periodic attempts to reform the Italian tax system in 1951, 1962, and 1971 have only emphasized the strength of popular resistance to paying taxes as levied. For example, after the government increased the Value Added Tax in 1975, it estimated that 39 percent of sums due were not paid. The government would have gained more money if it had left the tax at the old rate, and collected all that was legally due it. Upward of one in six Italian workers engage in black work (*lavoro nero*), earning money not reported for tax purposes. Often the work is a second job, held in addition to a job qualifying the individual for state welfare benefits. An estimated 27 percent of total income is not declared to the taxman in Italy today. If Italians paid taxes on all that they earned, tax rates would have to be cut to avoid a massive drop in take-home pay.[6]

In France, government has long been lax, allowing citizens to evade taxes by underreporting income. One French explanation is political: "Most citizens are small evaders; therefore, there is a majority to oppose strong detection, enforcement, and penalty, since everyone sees clearly what he would lose in tax but only dimly that he could gain through the global budget."[7] In the 1970s, the common program of French Socialists and Communists called for a vast expansion of public expenditure. But this could only be paid for by cutting take-home pay, whether through raising tax rates or collecting taxes on previously unreported earnings. Doing this would not necessarily win the left popular support. Instead, left-wing ambitions to tax and spend more on public policy could invite political bankruptcy. Rather than accept a cut in take-home pay, Frenchmen might become strongly indifferent to authority in order to make new taxes ineffectual.

In Anglo-Saxon countries, tax evasion has historically been relatively low. This gives added significance to evidence of growing tax evasion, especially in Sweden and Britain, where the overloading of political economies has placed greatest pressure upon take-home pay. In Sweden, extremely high marginal tax rates have led to growing popular tolerance of tax evasion. A survey of public opinion by the government's own Central Bureau of Statistics found that approximately three-quarters of Swedes endorsed a series of statements excusing tax evasion, and one-third indicated that they themselves had evaded taxes illegally.[8] In Britain tax revenues are rising six times faster than officially ascertained underpayment of tax. This figure can be interpreted to mean that Britons are becoming more compliant as taxes rise—or that the British Inland Revenue is becoming less successful at detecting evasion. The latter is almost certainly the case. Because of concern about tax evasion in the 1970s, the German government has introduced new laws, requiring employers to report more detailed information about payments to individuals, including casual labor. In America, existing federal laws against tax evasion have become more significant, as the number of criminal charges and convictions has more than doubled from 1970 to 1975.[9]

The growth of black work is particularly significant, because social acceptance is required for success. When tax evasion is confined to actions by a solitary individual (e.g., a farmer or salesman falsifying tax deductible expenses), it is not subject to social scrutiny. But when workers ask to be paid in cash in order to avoid tax, this requires the cooperation of those employing them. For every person employed in black work at least one more person, the employer, must actively connive in supporting tax evasion, and a larger number knowingly countenance it.[10]

The dependence of contemporary governments upon tax revenues gives ordinary citizens a check upon politicians additional to the vote. A vote can only substitute one party for another in government. When the evidence of a quarter-century shows that the costs of public policy rise regardless of the party in office, voting is not sure to protect an individual's take-home pay. However, the same individual can effectively frustrate government's wish to spend more on public policies by refusing consent to taxation. Individual citizens can no longer expect to overthrow a regime by dressing up like red Indians, as did eighteenth-century American colonists. But they can undermine political authority by altering the slogan "No taxation without representation" to "Poor taxation with poor representation."

Civic indifference to taxes touches the authority of contemporary government at a tender point. While a government can continue to collect substantial sums in taxes, it cannot manage the economy efficiently or effectively if an increasingly large portion of economic activity is hidden in the shadows. Nor can it predict the consequence of its policies if instead of complying with laws citizens adopt a "catch me if you can" attitude.

To press demands upon citizens to pay more and more taxes, when take-home pay is falling, is to assume that the loyalty of citizens is absolute and unconditional. But the history of France and Italy offers ample evidence that there are many things that citizens will not do simply at the state's command. Weak regimes may have survived *because* they were not fully effective against those who withheld their full consent. The flouting of Prohibition in the United States in the 1920s (not to mention the nonenforcement of post-Civil War civil rights measures until a century later) did not lead to the overthrow of American government, but it did demonstrate a limit of government's effectiveness.

Today, the case for expecting citizens to make political authority conditional rests upon a cardinal assumption of economics, namely, that individuals behave rationally. If individuals are economically rational, and if government reduces their take-home pay, then individuals may avoid or evade its authority, even to the point at which government becomes politically bankrupt.

MAKING PUBLIC POLICY SACROSANCT

The closer political bankruptcy comes, the greater the pressure upon politicians to declare a clear and public choice between making public policy sacrosanct or protecting take-home pay. From an economist's perspective, the choice may appear unimportant, for money is money whoever controls it. Taking more money from the national pie to meet the costs of public policy squeezes take-home pay, but it does not reduce the total amount of money in society.

Politically, the choice between advancing public policy or defending take-home pay raises fundamental issues about power in society. From a Marxian point of view, the existing allocation of economic power between government and the private sector gives inadequate power to the state. From the viewpoint of another nineteenth-century thinker, John Stuart Mill, the achievement of the Marxian ideal would mean that "not all the freedom of the press and popular constitution of the legislature would make this or any other country free." [11]

Political collectivists accept that no society can indefinitely consume more than it produces. They resolve difficulties by advocating the continued growth of government programs. The case for doing so, even at the cost of an absolute cut in take-home pay, has positive and negative elements. In Europe, most proponents of giving absolute priority to public policy start from a general ideological preference for collective action by the state. In the United States, the starting point is often a wish for a specific public benefit; it is the sum of these wants that could force down take-home pay. At a time of world economic recession, there is also a negative case. The mixed economy is said to have failed to deliver the goods, and promoting private benefits through a growth in take-home pay is said to be no longer practicable.

The justifications for collectively controlling the national product can be drawn from many different political philosophies—Socialist, Communist, Nationalist, Catholic, or Fascist —or a combination of these values. Each of these ideologies emphasizes the importance of society as a whole, rejecting the liberal belief in the individual as the central figure in society. Individuals are submerged in a collective entity, whether described as a class, a nation, defenders of the faith, or a *Herrenvolk*. Since man is a social animal, these philosophies consider it desirable as well as necessary that citizens should flock together and draw their greatest satisfactions from collective activities.

In the contemporary Western world, Socialism is the chief political ideology making public policy sacrosanct.[12] Socialists argue that government power represents the only resource that the mass of the population has to offset the advantages of wealthy individuals and leaders of corporations controlling major national resources. By oneself an ordinary citizen cannot fight "the system." But by shifting conflicts to the political arena, masses of individuals can prevail, whether through public ownership of economic resources, or regulating private industry by laws said to be in the public interest. From this perspective, the choice is not between more government or less government, but rather between "strong government for the few and the rich, or strong government for the unrich and the many." [13]

The practice of party politics means that the simple principles and dogmas of political philosophy are not the sole basis for action by European Socialist parties, nor are Socialist policies adopted only by nominally left-wing governments. For example, the United States has no Socialist party, but the liberal wing of the Democratic Party often adopts so-called Socialist programs, that is, measures intended to promote the welfare of economically disadvantaged groups. In Germany, a Social Democratic government has strong inhibitions about the extent of collective economic action, influenced by the experience of Weimar inflation and the totalitarian Third Reich.

The proponents of collectivist political views argue that public policy should always be given priority. Public expenditure is assumed to be desirable, because it is public, that is, determined by government. An individual is responsible only for himself and a family, and thus considered biased by selfish motives, just like a private enterprise responsible only to its shareholders. By contrast, public institutions are assumed to be responsible for the public interest, that is, the collective interest of all members of society.[14]

In an era when such individualist figures as the lone frontiersman and the self-sufficient peasant are ideological anachronisms, masses and classes are seen as the crucial building blocks of society, and government as the architect designing what society should be. From a collectivist perspective, increasing the interdependence of individuals is more than a fact of life in a technologically complex era; it is also considered a good in itself, encouraging common values and communal solidarity through that overarching institution of society, the modern state. Collectivists endorse the anticipated equalization of take-home pay resulting from the growth of public policy as one more step on the road to a society in which individuals have more and more in common with their fellow citizens.

To shift control of the national product from the market place to government does not of itself give individual citizens greater control of their own lives. Instead of depending upon their own efforts in the market place, individuals become dependent upon government decisions for the determination of their wages, the amount of education their children can receive, and welfare services. Individuals also become increasingly dependent upon government to decide how goods and services are to be paid for when they can no longer be bought and sold in the market place.

The collectivist belief that individuals can satisfactorily control their lives through government rests upon a simple nineteenth-century liberal faith in elections determining what government does, as well as who governs. Elitist assumptions are often implicit in proposals to make public policy sacrosanct. In a democratic era, however, few nominal friends of the people are prepared to be frank enough to state publicly, "We know what is best for them"—even if this is a fair inference from their behavior. (Cf the discussion of Keynes' politics in Chapter 6.) Ironically, collectivists who denounce control of corporations by shareholders as a nineteenth-century laissez-faire myth do not recognize that it is equally a myth to assume that popularly elected big governments can precisely reflect the preferences of all citizens.

A generation of research into voting behavior has demonstrated that the electorate can only deliver crude judgments about who should govern, and not judgments about what government should do. In an American or French presidential election, a voter can only choose between two individuals contesting the country's top political office. With multiparty competition in Parliament, it is not always known in advance of an election which parties will form a coalition government. Moreover, in every Western nation, at least 40 percent of the electorate votes *against* the government of the day; sometimes it is more than the proportion voting for the government. In the extreme case of Britain, no governing party has won as much as half the vote since 1935; and in Italy, the dominant Christian Democratic Party has averaged only 39 percent of the vote in eight postwar elections. At most, a duly elected government can claim the moral authority to speak for a plurality of those voting. It can only claim to speak for a notional "will of all" if it abandons free elections for the institutions of a one-party state.[15]

Words such as "democracy" and "participation" are symbols that obscure the distribution of power in large organizations, whether private corporations or government. However sincerely politicians try to do what the people want, they are no more able to make government produce goods tailored to every individual's satisfaction than is a mammoth private organization such as the Ford Motor Company or ITT. At best, big organizations can make decisions that satisfy most people most of the time. The move from the private to the public sector alters who makes the decisions, but does not change the fact that, in any large organization, the major decisions are made by relatively few officials. Pyramids of power remain pyramids of power, whatever flag flies from their top.[16]

Two decades ago, an American journalist, W. H. Whyte, wrote *The Organization Man*, indicting the increasing dependence of American workers upon the private companies that employed them.[17] Whyte did not denounce giant employers for alleged cruelty, but for their generosity and readiness to make workers part of a collective community of company men. Such companies were said to threaten individuality by imposing common standards of behavior upon their employees, influencing how they lived, and even what they thought. Whyte argued that an individual's identification with an organization, like a gray flannel suit, should be something that a person could take off as well as put on in the course of a day. It should not be a demand for total allegiance and conformity.

Today, citizens are increasingly dependent upon a single central organization—government—for their choice of livelihood, as well as the amount of their take-home pay. The state regulates entry to leading professions, and to less skilled occupations as well, such as taxi-driving and hairdressing. It also puts the force of law behind trade unions negotiating closed shop restrictions affecting manual workers. Directly and indirectly it employs up to one-third of the national work force.

When the government allocated only a small fraction of the national product, individuals had much reason to worry about its power being too little rather than too great. As the government controls a larger and larger share of the national product it becomes the central power in society. A basic assumption of the mixed-economy welfare state is that private hands as well as public hands should control a substantial share of the national pie.

While self-styled progressives fight the battles of yesteryear against private enterprises, the growth of government makes it the dominant or even the sole provider of many goods and services in society today. In Europe, the centralization of economic power in government has meant the decline in alternative sources of money to support education, culture, or philanthropic institutions. Government is the primary or sole guarantor of art and music, of schools, universities, libraries, and health services. In place of a pluralistic society, in which private resources could complement or countervail against public power, there is today a concentration of power in government hands. More exposure to government makes citizens increasingly conscious of the distinction that Alfred Marshall, the great English economist, made between "Government all wise, all just, all powerful, and government as it now is."

As government controls more and more of the national product, citizens are not so much impoverished financially as they are turned into members of a totally dependent society. For example, if levels of public spending as a proportion of national product were to continue to increase, whether on trends of the past five years or the past twenty-five years, then by 1985 the costs of public policy would be equivalent to two-thirds to three-quarters of the national product in Britain, Germany, Italy, and Sweden; and to about three-fifths in the United States and France. (Cf. Table 2.1.) In such circum-

[216

stances, what an individual receives is not so much what is chosen in an admittedly imperfect market, but what is granted by laws written and administered by similarly imperfect legislators and bureaucrats. Pensioners and the unemployed may be relatively fortunate, for government at least gives them money to spend as they wish. Most citizens have to take the services that government offers them, whether they like them or not.

With the best will in the world, lawmakers cannot avoid the fact that a welfare state concerned with up to 200 million people is inevitably a bureaucratic maze of institutions and entitlements, and not a "caring" institution, like a community organization run by volunteers. Replacing market power with bureaucratic power is not intended by proponents of more and more public policies. It may nonetheless be the consequence. As Assar Lindbeck points out, "It may be possible to make a strong case against either markets or bureaucratic systems, but if we are against *both* we are in trouble. There is hardly a third method for allocating resources and coordinating economic decisions, if we eliminate physical force." [18]

Technically, it is possible to establish a totally dependent society, with virtually the whole of a family's income in the form of benefits that the state provides in cash and kind. For example, Russian citizens pay low income taxes, and many of their basic needs are met by state-provided goods and services, including housing, transportation, and vacations.[19] Pay is also low because Russians do not need (or are not allowed) to buy many goods and services. Instead, those who serve the state and party well are given privileged access to goods and services. Russians who want better houses or holidays are not meant to earn more money, but to do what the state will reward from its monopoly of consumer goods.

While the creation of an increasingly dependent society can be justified by collectivist political values, it is not free of all political costs. In *Four Essays on Liberty*, the Oxford philosopher Sir Isaiah Berlin has identified what must be given up in return for collectively provided goods:

> To avoid glaring inequality or widespread misery I am ready to sacrifice some or all of my freedom. I may do so willingly and freely, but it is freedom that I am giving up for the sake of justice or equality or the love of my fellow man. I should be guilt stricken and rightly so if I were not in some circumstances ready to make this sacrifice. But a sacrifice is not an increase in what is being sacrificed, namely freedom, however great the moral need or the compensation for it. Everything is what it is: liberty is liberty, not equality or fairness or justice or culture or human happiness or a quiet conscience.[20]

To continue to debate the advantages and disadvantages of dependence upon government as the case for or against a laissez faire economy is to become stuck in the categories of a century ago. Today, we are far from the world of laissez faire, as viewed through the eyes of John Stuart Mill, Charles Dickens, or Karl Marx. The greatest political innovation of the twentieth century is not the welfare state, but the totalitarian society.

PROTECTING TAKE-HOME PAY

The chief reason for putting take-home pay first is political: to maintain the authority of government. By contrast, making public policy sacrosanct involves a real risk of political bankruptcy. Protecting take-home pay means that no individual need be made worse off in terms of take-home pay, and as long as there is at least a modicum of economic growth, public policy can continue to grow.

Throughout a quarter-century of treble affluence, politicians have not had to think about protecting take-home pay. It was doubly safeguarded. First of all, it was made secure by a historically high rate of growth of the national product. Secondly, it was secure because the growing costs of public policy took a relatively limited share of the national pie. And as long as the national pie continues to grow, there is no necessary reason why take-home pay should decline. Even during the world recession of the 1970s, the national product has continued to grow.

To protect take-home pay in present circumstances, the governors of major Western nations only need limit the future growth of public policies; no Western government need spend less on government programs than today. Italy, Britain, and Sweden need to put the brakes on rising costs of public policy immediately. And the United States, France, and Germany must be prepared to do so in the future, if the costs of public policy continue to grow as in the past. But slowing down a rate of increase is not nearly so difficult as trying to reverse the direction of public policy.

Not a single penny need be cut from public spending to protect take-home pay. This point is usually overlooked by advocates of particular welfare policies or of a general collectivist philosophy. It is also overlooked by critics of the welfare state, who pursue such chimeras as the eternally balanced budget, or a return to a minimalist pre-1914, pre-1939, or pre-1950 state. It is easy enough to understand why those who dislike the welfare state would like to see public spending cut. But it is misleading for defenders of the welfare state to confuse a slow increase in public spending with a real cut.

Confusion is sometimes caused because proponents of welfare programs suffer from "one-eyed" beneficence. They can see the benefits of the programs that they promote, but cannot see the costs. It is the job of others to worry about where the money comes from. In aggregate, there is never enough money to pay for all the programs pressed upon government, however meritorious each individually may be. Every government must determine which programs should *not* be financed by public funds, as well as which deserve to be among the costs of public policy.

Verbal sleights-of-hand are often employed to turn increases in public spending into cuts. The process is as follows. Most major programs encourage a host of political expectations for improvements. To hold spending constant in real terms from year to year requires spending more money. But to spend less than is demanded by interest groups is to fail to meet expectations, whether well-founded or otherwise. Thus a government that proposes spending tens of billions more may be attacked for alleged "cuts" in public policy, that is, not spending all that is demanded of it.

When government increases spending on a given policy, the ordinary person would expect its supporters to be satisfied, because they are better off than before. But some social psychologists argue that benefits can create a sense of relative deprivation, if what is given is less than what was demanded or expected, and at the extreme, the resulting frustrations could lead men to rebel. Economists by contrast react to the limits of the economy by asking how ordinary people adjust their preferences, given that they cannot have everything they want at once.[21] Opinion surveys show that in the world of the 1970s, citizens do not expect to get everything they want from government; some people even expect to get things that they do not want, such as rising prices and more unemployment. Individual expectations of the political economy are flexible and reversible, rather than rigid.*

A slowdown in the growth of public spending, take-home pay, or both should not be confused with an end of affluence. An affluent society is defined by its level of mass consumption and not by the satisfaction of all wants. Affluence is not deter-

* See Chapter 10.

mined by how quickly living standards change; it can persist even when the economy grows slowly or not at all. When the national product of major Western nations fell in 1975, they did not cease to be affluent. Nor would a decade of continuing growth make a poor country such as India or Indonesia affluent by the material standards of Western nations. Short of ecological doom or economic collapse, rich Western nations will remain affluent for the foreseeable future, whether or not their governors feel rich or feel poor. The least and the most that the events of the 1970s require is rethinking affluence.

HOW TO PUT THE BRAKES ON

Simply stated, protecting take-home pay requires that, under certain specified circumstances, government should spend a little more rather than a lot more money. It is a matter of putting the brakes on rising costs and not of putting the engine of government into reverse. Identifying what to brake is easy; the crucial costs are the policies that account for most of the spending of the modern welfare state. Identifying how to brake is much harder, for this requires the government marshalling a force equal and opposite to the force of its own inertia commitments.

In every major Western nation there is a Big Six of public policies that together claim more than half the total budget. In order of size, in a typical Western nation, these are pensions, education, health, defense, industrial and trade policies, and interest on the national debt.* If governors are to put the

* The following paragraphs are based upon detailed breakdowns of data summarized in Table A3.1.

brakes on public spending in a big way, they must limit the growth of policies that are highly popular or essential by definition. It is virtually impossible for government to effect big savings by putting brakes on smaller programs, for the sums spent on the thousand and one programs that account for the rest of the public budget constitute much less than half the total costs of public policy. Big cuts in small programs can cause political controversy out of all proportion to the small effect they would have on an overloaded political economy.

Pensions rank first in spending significance in every major European country, accounting for as much as one Deutsche mark in every six spent by the German government. In the United States, pensions rank third because of the relatively great importance of defense and education. Pensions cannot easily be limited in number, because they are an open-ended commitment of the welfare state. As long as people live in retirement, a pension is due them. Increased longevity increases the total number of people of pensionable age. Moreover, there are lobbies in every Western nation to reduce the age of retirement, not only out of solicitude for the elderly, but also to provide more jobs for younger workers when unemployment is a problem. The only way in which government could be sure to contain pension costs would be to withdraw guarantees to proof pensions against inflation and increase them with rises in the real standard of living.

Education ranks close to pensions in spending significance; it is first or second in importance in every major Western nation except Germany, where it is a close third. In the United States, education accounts for one in every six dollars spent by government. The pressure to increase spending in primary education in the near future will be moderated by the absolute decline in the birthrate in the first half of the 1970s. Pressures upon colleges and universities are likely to continue, for the baby boom of earlier years is still working its way through the youthful population; demand for further education can rise everywhere into the 1980s. Insofar as birth rates do level off,* the chief pressure to increase spending is likely to come in the form of demands to improve the quality of education by spending more per pupil on the best educational practices.[22]

Health services rank third in cost on average, with significant variations from country to country. In the United States, government spends less on health than on any other major public policy, whereas health costs rank second in Germany and in France and Sweden tie for second place. Health services, like pensions, are open-ended commitments to provide for those in need. An individual's need for health lasts through a lifetime, unlike education, which is primarily for the young, and pensions, exclusively for the elderly. The more that doctors succeed in prolonging life, the more this adds to the cost of health services, for the chronic sick have a persisting and intense need for relatively expensive health services. In theory, preventive medicine would best contain rising costs. But many of the things that can be done to keep individuals in good health must be done by individuals for themselves and cannot be secured by legislation. Only America still has to make the biggest decision about the claims of health on the public purse: whether or not to have a national health service.

Defense has been overtaken by social policy as the biggest claimant on the public purse, ranking fourth overall among the Big Six of public policies. Only in the United States and Britain (where Northern Ireland has kept the British Army in action through the 1970s) does defense spending claim as much or more than a major welfare policy. The relative decline in the significance of defense has not meant an absolute cut in such spending. In the Cold War decade of the 1950s defense

---

* Falls in birthrates in the first half of the 1970s are uneven, ranging from a 1 percent reduction in total births in France to a 30 percent reduction in Germany. The shortfall could easily be made up by a rise in birthrates in subsequent years. The increase in the number of young persons reaching the age for higher education in the 1980s is surer, reflecting births already recorded in the 1960s.

was a first priority of many governments. Today, a different international climate encourages the containment of defense spending, and domestic social programs have greater political claims to the fiscal dividend of growth. The technological obsolescence built into contemporary defense is sure to maintain steady pressure for more military spending. Major Western governments at best can hope to limit the growth of defense spending; the scope for major cuts has probably been exhausted.

A variety of programs intended to promote trade and industry rank fifth in importance, in aggregate taking up more than one-tenth of the total cost of public policy. In every major Western nation, government provides a variety of benefits to industry, and spending on roads and communications indirectly promotes trade and industry. Some of these policies show up in the losses of nationalized industries, and others are implicit, like tax allowances for investment. Insofar as these programs can rightly be described as investments, in the recession of the 1970s there is a case for spending more to make the national product grow faster.

Debt interest ranks sixth in significance, except in overloaded Britain, and in the United States, where it claims more than public spending on the health of citizens. Paying interest on the national debt is a first charge on public policy, even though it is a relatively small charge. If a government defaulted on interest payments it would have great difficulty in financing annual expenditure and in raising new loans to pay back old loans when they mature. The cost of government borrowing is under pressure to rise, for the longer inflation continues, the higher the rates of interest that borrowers will want.

The surest way to keep costs of public policy from rising is to avoid the introduction of new programs. A new program has proponents, but unlike an existing program it lacks an entrenched cluster of beneficiaries, within as well as outside government. Once enacted, new policies attract entrenched supporters, and costs can balloon up in size. The Food Stamp program of the United States Department of Agriculture, introduced on an experimental basis at a cost of less than half a million dollars in 1961, is an extreme example of how a new program can swell. By 1966 the program was costing $70 million, an increase of 1400 times in five years. By 1976, it cost $5.6 billion, an increase of 80 times in a decade.

Because politics today is about what is new, politicians are rarely content to act as custodians for established programs. Politicians want to do things, and almost always the things they want to do cost money. In such circumstances, brakes can best be kept on the upward trend in public spending if the policies that government adopts do not provide individual benefits with costs rising in proportion to benefits. Cautious activists could adopt policies that have a cost ceiling, whether high or low, so that their new law does not push public spending up a little more each year.

A cost-free way to legislate is to repeal established laws. Decriminalizing abortion or the use of soft drugs such as marijuana actually allows government to spend less money on law enforcement by having fewer laws to enforce. Many of the major goals of the permissive society assume that government should intervene less rather than more in society's affairs. Applying a similar approach to the regulation of trade and industry could similarly lead to savings in administrative costs within government, as well as money saving by those being regulated.[23]

Insofar as politicians want to make people do things, a government can offload the cost of carrying out public policies onto private budgets. A law that compels every motorist to carry insurance against the cost of automobile accidents protects citizens, but the money that individuals pay for car insurance is not regarded as a tax, but as a fee for a market service. Moreover the sums that insurance companies pay out each year are not charged against the government's budget.

Can Government Go Bankrupt?

The compulsion of legislation secures the principal aim of public spirited politicians. Leaving the implementation of the policy to market forces—profit-making, cooperative, or even government-owned insurance companies—allows individuals to shop around for the particular service that most suits them, rather than compelling them to accept whatever service a national law mandates.[24]

One obvious way to put a ceiling on recurring costs is to adopt policies that do not recur. An advantage of celebrating a Bicentennial or a Royal Silver Jubilee, or hosting the Olympic Games, is that whatever the cost, it is a one-off event. By definition, a Bicentennial celebration can only happen once every 200 years, and at most a monarchy can celebrate its twenty-fifth anniversary four times a century. Whatever a host country spends in four years on the Olympics, its budgeters have the consolation of knowing that it is disqualified from acting as host again for another quarter-century or longer.

Another way to put a ceiling on recurring costs is to promote collective goods that provide benefits at more or less fixed costs. Whereas building community theatres for local entertainment has a cost roughly proportional to the number of entertainers and spectators involved, the cost of a collective good such as a nationwide public television network is nearly constant, however many or few people watch its programs. Policies that provide individual benefits proportionate to cost have a tendency to escalate, whereas policies involving collective goods have a ceiling.

If a policy generates revenue, claims upon the public purse can be limited by increasing user charges if costs escalate. Every major Western nation makes revenue charges for some services, just as it gives away others. For example, public libraries are usually available free of charge, whereas swimming pools and motorways are often subject to user charges, and municipal restaurants and cinemas almost invariably collect money from those who use their services. In the United States and Britain, art museums rarely make an entrance charge, whereas in Continental Europe, such entrance fees are normal. When forced to choose between alternative policies, a government that favored a policy that generated revenue, especially revenue that covered annual operating costs, would be less vulnerable to overloading in future.[25]

Putting the brakes on established spending commitments is far more difficult, as Chapters 5 and 6 demonstrated. In theory, the most effective way to prevent costs rising would be to abolish some existing programs. American proponents of so-called "sunset" laws believe that this would happen if major laws automatically expired every five years, unless specifically reenacted. The assumption is that a program appealing in prospect to a legislature may not command a majority after its effects have been witnessed. But American experience with program evaluation has demonstrated that policies once established are not abolished, whatever an evaluation may show, because of the support institutionalized within as well as outside government.[26]

To put the brakes on public spending requires strengthening the hand of institutions much concerned with the risks of overloading the political economy. In every major Western nation the central bank fulfills this role. Changing the power structure of the political economy to strengthen the central bank's influence would almost certainly affect its direction. A country's central bank is important because it influences the nation's money supply and interest rates, as well as being responsible for managing its balance of payments with other lands. By its nature a central bank responds to market pressures. When a nation's currency begins an international decline, the central bank must seek foreign credits to make good the balance of payments deficit. When a government decides to increase its deficit to expand its public programs, the central bank must borrow money to cover the resulting gap. The more overloaded a political economy, the harder the task of central bankers. Central banks thus have an institutional interest in their government avoiding policies that threaten political bankruptcy.

Politically, the crucial question is the extent to which a central bank is the creature of the government of the day, or has sufficient autonomy to adopt policies independent of government. At a minimum, central banks are always likely to put a different point of view to a president or prime minister than the head of a welfare agency. The organizational interests of bankers favor policies that limit spending, just as politicians heading welfare agencies favor more spending. There are substantial differences crossnationally in the freedom of central banks to voice public criticism of prevailing government policy. Experts credit the United States Federal Reserve Bank and the German Bundesbank with more political independence than the Bank of England, the Banque de France, the Swedish Riksbank, and the Banca d'Italia.[27]

The strong point of a central bank is also its Achilles heel. A central bank can ignore a government's political calculations because central bankers are not elected. But because of this, it lacks a political base from which to disagree publicly and fundamentally with the elected government of the day. Moreover, where central bank directors are subordinate by appointment and law to the government of the day, they lack the political base to engage in public controversy. In a showdown, elected governments can claim greater legitimacy than a bank. Central banks are likely to be strongest when governments are economically weak and must rely upon central bank expertise to arrest immediately a decline in international confidence in a country's currency.

Indexing taxes reduces the supply of government revenue in an inflationary era, thus making it more difficult for a government to treat the expansion of government programs as if they were "cost free." When taxes are indexed, the deductions that individuals can claim for themselves and their family increase with the rise in the cost of living. Moreover, the rate of tax levied on a given income falls if its purchasing power falls. For example, if $10,000 of taxable income today will only buy $7,500 of goods at prices prevailing at the starting point for indexation, then taxes on the inflated income would be cut in proportion since the purchasing power of this money is less than it ought to be.

No major Western nation has properly indexed taxes for the obvious reason: to do so would cost it income effortlessly provided as a byproduct of inflation. The only government fully committed to tax indexation at present is the Australian Liberal government of Malcolm Fraser, which has leaned far to the right, in reaction against the "fiscal Watergate" of the preceding Labour government under Gough Whitlam.

In a system with tax indexation, a government can increase its revenue. But it can do so only by getting the legislature to pass a law that explicitly and publicly raises tax rates or cuts deductions. This makes both the governors and the governed conscious of the costs as well as the benefits of public policy. The government remains free to decide which to put first. The choice is not taken in ignorance, but with painful and public awareness of both the plus and the minus terms of public policy.

Any attempt to impose a mechanical legislative constraint upon the amount that public spending or the deficit can rise each year will run aground on a host of practical obstacles. First of all, a spending constraint by one level of government is of no consequence if costs balloon at other levels. For example, in the United States, the federal government often receives the blame for the increased cost of public spending, but much of the burden that the taxpayer feels is placed there by state and local government. A law that seeks to limit spending to a fixed percentage of the national product is unenforceable, because fluctuations up or down in the national product, crucial for determining whether public spending was on target, cannot be controlled by government. Similarly, any legislation attempting to limit the annual growth of public spending by a fixed percentage would be broken by relatively volatile open-ended spending commitments, such as unemployment benefits. Equally, any attempt to limit annual deficits to a fixed sum of money or percentage would founder, because the actual size of the year's deficit is not only influenced by a government's own decisions, but also by how much tax revenue the economy generates. The uncertainties of public expenditure are only marginal. But controls can be effective only if they operate at this unpredictable margin, because it is spending at the margin that determines whether take-home pay falls in an overloaded economy.

The most optimistic view of containing public expenditure presupposes an equilibrium, in which any tendency for the political economy to go "too far" (i.e., become overloaded) sets up a reaction to contain the costs of public policy and take-home pay. From this perspective, the timing of decisions is crucial. Politicians are not expected to worry about the costs of public policy when things are going well. Only when take-home pay is threatened or a body like the International Monetary Fund must be satisfied will politicians be prepared to put on the brakes. Measures that were previously politically impossible become politically acceptable in an emergency.

Unfortunately, the definition of an emergency is very subjective. Because of its past history of inflation and economic collapse, the German government is most ready to guard against risks to its political economy, notwithstanding its relative strength among Western nations. By contrast, neither the Italian, British, nor Swedish government, each nearing big troubles, chose to put on the brakes immediately after the 1973 oil crisis made it clear that this "temporary" economic difficulty would intensify their serious long-term problems.

When the British government finally faced up to the state of its overloaded economy in 1976, as an emergency measure it imposed a system of cash limits on the cost of public policy. The object was not to prevent any increase in spending, but to keep the increase within limits. All public agencies were expected to keep their total spending within cash ceilings authorized at the beginning of the year, and not to claim additional money because of unexpected cost increases or easily justified cost overruns. Within a year, cash limits showed results. The British Treasury found that public spending was 5 percent below the expected cash ceiling.[28]

By definition, emergency measures are meant to be of short duration. A freeze or squeeze can be sustained for a matter of months, or perhaps a year or two. Whether it can become permanent is a very different question. The very need to adopt emergency procedures is evidence that those meant to be controlled have previously been successful in circumventing restrictions. Moreover, Keynesian arguments can be invoked to criticize too little spending and too small a budget deficit, when an economy is thought to need the stimulus of a larger public deficit to achieve more economic growth. For example, no sooner had the British Treasury published evidence of underspending in autumn 1977 than it announced that it was conducting an investigation to see why it had not spent more, to fend off critics wishing to stimulate the economy by more public spending.[29] By January 1978, with a general election in the offing, the British Treasury could return to laxer ways, announcing that public spending in the coming year should rise by anything from 2.5 to 6.7 percent.[30]

The distance between treble affluence and political bankruptcy is not great. In the course of a year or two, an affluent economy can become so overloaded that take-home pay is cut, and an overloaded economy can, by a short period of restraint, once again see take-home pay rising.

Limiting the growth of public spending delays but does not deny an increase in the benefits of public policy. To argue that spending delayed is spending denied is to imply an absurd proposition, namely, that government should do at once every-thing demanded of it without any budget constraint. No gov-ernment anywhere in the world can accept such a view. Even in the best of economic circumstances, a government must order its spending commitments, deferring some to make sure that there will be enough money in hand to meet others. When a political economy is overloaded, more spending claims are likely to be delayed, and delayed with good reason.

For better or for worse, the achievements and nonachieve-ments of public expenditure control—from the growth-oriented years of the Kennedy and Johnson Administrations to the Carter Administration's hopeful talk of balanced budgets—are a cau-tion against expecting too much from any one new public fi-nance technique. After all, within two years of the British Public Expenditure Survey Committee being hailed by a knowledgeable and sceptical expert as the "one major reform of modern times . . . to control spending several years into the future," another knowledgeable expert described the same in-novation as an example of the "breakdown of control." [31]

No set of procedures or principles by itself can contain the growing costs of public policy. A government can only reduce the risks of political bankruptcy if its leaders are prepared to show the political will to limit growth. If the will is there, the means can be found to safeguard public policy as some Western nations have demonstrated in the 1970s. If there is no political will to act, no amount of institutional tinkering can secure a government from the risk of political bankruptcy.

CHAPTER 10

First Things First, or Money Isn't Everything

> The object of government is not to promote efficiency but to preclude the exercise of arbitrary power.
>
> Supreme Court Justice Louis D. Brandeis

TRADITIONALLY, the first concern of government was establishing order in society. Today, the first concern of government is maintaining consent. In political terms, making authority legitimate comes before making people rich. Money means a lot, but it does not mean everything. And citizens can worry as much about protecting themselves from government as they do about advancing their interests through government.

The first rights that citizens sought to establish were civil rights, those procedural and substantive guarantees of liberty summed up in the phrase "the rule of law." [1] Civil rights collectively secure individuals the benefits of public order and freedom from the arbitrary powers against which Mr. Justice

Brandeis warned. Political rights—the right to vote and partici-
pate in representative institutions—have only been achieved in
the past century. Whereas the rule of law emphasizes the need
for government to act effectively, the franchise emphasizes popular consent to authority. The twentieth century has also seen
government become responsible for providing many welfare
benefits measurable in money terms. The demand for civil and
political rights is finite; people can tire of voting, speaking
their views, or litigating. But the wants of citizens for health,
education, and pensions are potentially infinite.

When citizens of Western nations claim their civil and political rights, they do not expect to be told that government
cannot afford them. Nor do they expect to be offered welfare
benefits in place of the rights they seek. The history of
nineteenth-century America and England demonstrates that
government can grant civil and political rights without creating a welfare state; the history of Germany demonstrates that
providing welfare benefits is not sufficient to maintain a regime
that does not secure its citizens civil and political rights. The
fact that citizens today welcome welfare benefits is not proof
that these benefits would be accepted in place of civil and political rights. The black civil rights campaign of the 1960s in
America is a dramatic example of the political demand for
the "priceless" rights of the rule of law and the franchise.
The success of blacks in achieving these rights has not ended
black poverty, but it has transformed blacks from second-class
to first-class citizens.[2]

To argue that welfare benefits are the first priority of citizens is to imply their degradation as citizens. It suggests that
an authoritarian regime that knew no law except its own
force would be a good government, if it could keep its subjects
well fed, in work, and in good health. It implies that citizens
would accept the use of coercion to control wages, prices, and
investment, if this enabled a government to manage the political economy effectively. It ignores or denies the possibility

of citizens frustrating a would-be authoritarian government by voting with their feet for political bankruptcy.

For ordinary citizens, government is a means, not an end in itself. The first section of this chapter reviews the very different mixture of things that individuals can seek from government, some costing vast sums of money, and others priceless. The concluding section asks whether voters would react against a government limiting the benefits of public policy to protect take-home pay.

RIGHTS, BENEFITS, AND WANTS

When government cannot do everything, politicians must economize, not in terms of a calculus of money, but in terms of a political calculus of first things first. Only if politicians learn to discern the essentials in a welter of political desires can they be secure against the risk of political bankruptcy.

The everyday rhetoric of politics unfortunately confuses the things that citizens claim from government as of right with contingent benefits and putative wants. Social scientists can add to the confusion by treating all activities of government as if they were of equal importance, and then averting their gaze from such essential activities as policing and prisons to concentrate upon what is desirable but not strictly essential, such as the provision of health services. Only by discriminating between different activities of government can we begin to identify those concerns that government *must* put first.

First of all, government must see that individuals receive their rights as citizens, in order to exercise authority with consent. To deny some individuals their rights is to classify them as second-class citizens, and to encourage their indifference or disaffection. The rights that citizens can claim from a government are set forth in the constitution that charters political authority. The constitutional enumeration of rights makes explicit what citizens can expect from government, and the legal means by which these rights can be pursued. For a government to deny individuals their constitutional rights is to be guilty of unconstitutional action, and to invite citizens to do the same, thus doubly breaching political authority.

The rights guaranteed citizens in national constitutions are few, and rarely refer to the policies or issues that threaten contemporary economies. For example, the Preamble of the United States Constitution emphasizes the promotion of justice, domestic tranquility, and common defense; concern with "the general welfare" is a vague addendum. The Bill of Rights refers to civil and political rights, and not to welfare issues. Similarly, the Constitution of the Fifth French Republic promises its citizens institutions founded on the common ideal of liberty, equality, and fraternity. The 1949 German *Grundgesetz*, in nineteen articles, guarantees its citizens a host of civil and political (but not welfare) rights that the Third Reich denied. Individuals may also claim other rights derived from God, the nature of mankind, or the political philosopher or social scientist of their choice. But if they are not specified in a constitution, these claims cannot be treated as lawfully equal to the claims that the constitution has recognized as their due.

Because the fundamental rights of citizens concern civil and political questions, they are cheap to provide, and do not threaten the overloading of contemporary political economies. For example, no modern state will ever become overloaded by the money cost of law enforcement. For a Western government to deny citizens civil and political rights would be to violate the terms on which citizens grant allegiance to authority. No government proposes to do so today, nor is there any economic reason why it need do so.

[236

The benefits to which citizens are entitled by statute law are far more numerous than basic civil and political rights, and account for the great bulk of the spending of the mixed-economy welfare state. They remain, however, discretionary policies; citizens are entitled to many benefits by statute, but they do not enjoy them as of constitutional right. The distinction is crucial. A government has no choice but to grant citizens their constitutional rights; but a government decides whether or not to adopt a proposal entitling citizens to a given benefit. Once enacted, it may increase or reduce the money spent to provide these benefits, expand or contract the conditions entitling individuals to a benefit, or, in the extreme case, repeal a law granting benefits. After a benefit is granted by law, a government is bound to distribute it to each citizen with an entitlement under the act, because each citizen has the civil right to equal treatment under the law.

As long as a country can produce sufficient wealth to pay for the generous provision of discretionary benefits, their proliferation presents no hard choices to the government of the day. The contemporary welfare state goes far beyond the minimalist standard of welfare services necessary to prevent destitution, the ideal of early twentieth-century architects of the welfare state, when mass poverty was the problem. Today, politicians are concerned with distributing the fruits of treble affluence by increasing both discretionary welfare benefits and take-home pay.

The language of rights is the language of obligation, but the language of benefits is the language of bargaining, in which citizens may lose as well as gain advantages. For example, the benefits that citizens receive from government as parents, home-owners, motorists, or pensioners may fluctuate up *or* down in value. To treat every law as if it gave citizens an irrevocable constitutional right forever to enjoy a public benefit at a fixed cost would be to fetter the living to the dead.

The wants that citizens can enunciate (or that vote-seeking

politicians can demand in their name) are potentially infinite. Every election campaign shows politicians prepared to give a courteous hearing to the demands of many different groups for government's help. The fact that many wants are voiced does not mean that government can meet each and every want that is voiced. The sum total of these wants is far more than the total size of the national product.

Government cannot legislate to meet infinite wants with a finite national product. One of the arts of governing is saying no politely to clamant pressure groups. Another skill is identifying tasks that government is not capable of carrying out, and which may even be beyond the scope of schools, churches, or faith-healers to realize. In their everyday lives, citizens know that their finite earnings cannot satisfy infinite wants. They are not so foolish as to expect to receive all that they might want.

Individual wants cannot be equated with rights, for everybody wants things that government is not yet committed to provide, and may never establish as a benefit in law. To confuse wants and benefits with rights is to make the latter an indiscriminate category embracing every law on the statute books and every draft bill in the pocket of a lobbyist. Moreover, it implies that citizenship is little more than the byproduct of benefits (or bribes) from government, expanding in meaning as well as in cash value with the growth of government spending.

The activities of government can be ranked in a hierarchy. First come the relatively few things that citizens claim as of *right*, like the right to vote or to speak their minds freely. While these rights are not costly in money terms, granting them at one time cost privileged minorities political power. Secondly, there are *benefits* to which citizens are entitled by law. The great bulk of public policies, including the major spending programs of the welfare state, are among these popular but not strictly necessary activities of government. Third in significance are *wants,* whether expressed by individuals, pressure groups or public officials. At any given moment, political controversy concentrates great attention upon the possible translation of wants into public benefits by legislation. The result is that some wants are incorporated by law as benefits, while others are not.

In an overloaded political economy, protecting take-home pay requires government to discriminate carefully between wants and benefits; questions of rights do not weigh heavily in the budget calculus. Inasmuch as government does not need to cut public spending to be secure against the risk of political bankruptcy, time-honored benefits can be treated almost as if they were rights, that is, the existing spending commitments of the welfare state can be sustained with little risk. But by the same token the assertion of new wants must be scrutinized more severely for cost implications before being given the hard-to-revoke status of enacted benefits. In a world of finite resources, a government inevitably must refuse to endorse many wants as the price of protecting established benefits.

Today, welfare benefits extend far beyond basic rights, but they do not offer everybody everything they might want. For example, every Western nation provides its citizens with far more education that is absolutely necessary for citizenship. The minimum education needed to exercise political rights can be very little; some Cabinet ministers of the 1945–51 Labour government in Britain had left school at age eleven, and in the Italian Chamber of Deputies today there are a few representatives with even less formal education. Government today guarantees each citizen at least eight years of education. But education is like a piece of string; it can be of almost any length. The potential quantity and cost of education is not limited to a statutory minimum.

Every major Western nation now makes it possible for each citizen to complete secondary school without paying fees. But teenage pupils are not paid cash grants to attend secondary school. Young people are expected to forego the wages that they might otherwise earn as their share of the social cost of secondary schooling. Every country discriminates in providing the benefits of higher education; there is never enough to match all wants. There are a limited number of university places, and within universities, a limited number of places for those who want to follow well-paid, high prestige occupations, such as medicine. Examinations not only give some students the qualification that they wish, but also deny it to those who fail. The benefits of education are real and widespread, but they are not absolute rights in any Western nation today.

Every European nation provides citizens with a wide range of health benefits: medical, dental, and eye treatment; hospital care, and often cash payments when absent from work due to sickness. The range and terms of benefits vary slightly from country to country within Europe. For example, France and Sweden require citizens to pay a portion of the costs of routine medical treatment, but Britain does not. Such differences in specific benefits do not make Englishmen more fully citizens than Frenchmen or Swedes. Equally, Americans have not been deprived of constitutional rights of citizenship because Congress has not enacted a national health service along European lines. Important as a health service may be, it is a subject of political controversy, and not a constitutional right.

No government offers citizens as much health care as they might want. There are shortages of specialist doctors and facilities. Economic considerations limit the availability of expensive medical technology such as kidney machines, and personnel and organizational difficulties limit access to specialist medical treatment. Citizens too may refuse treatment that doctors think they need, such as psychiatric counselling or, if religious principles dictate, treatment for organic illnesses. Even the best national health service cannot guarantee every citizen the right to a maximum length of life, as it can guarantee a right to vote.

The pension policies of major Western nations are not based upon a notional doctrine of the right to life. If they were, they would be confined only to those needing a pension to avoid starvation, and cash benefits could be geared to minimum subsistence standards. Pensions are paid at rates above the minimum necessary to sustain life. In European nations, there is an explicit attempt to relate pension payments to what a worker has earned during his or her working life, and to increase pensions when the standard of living, as well as the cost of living, rises. Unlike the right to vote. the same pension benefit is not paid equally to each citizen. Moreover, no government is prepared to give pensioners all the money they might want. The potential wants of the elderly are greater than existing pension programs can finance. Some elderly persons must supplement state pensions with private resources or, like citizens of working age, do without some things they want.

The benefits of the contemporary welfare state are as popular as they are costly and widespread throughout society. There is no effective political demand for an absolute reduction in public spending. But there can never be enough money in the public purse to supply all the wants of citizens. To attempt to meet all the potential wants for education, health, and pensions would only back a government into political bankruptcy. Whether a government puts public policy or take-home pay first, it will always have enough money to meet the basic rights of citizens, but it will never have enough to meet all the wants that may be voiced in their name. Legislation cannot overcome the limitations imposed upon government programs by the economic laws of scarcity.

THE PRIORITIES OF ORDINARY CITIZENS

When politicians are faced with the need to limit the costs of public policy, they may reply that the voters will not stand for it. It is assumed that voters always want more from government, even if this leads to political bankruptcy.[3] But the history of the twentieth century demonstrates that in peacetime as well as wartime, masses of individuals *will* accept low material living standards without rebelling against government.

Studies of how ordinary people evaluate their lives show that life satisfaction is high, notwithstanding the world recession of the 1970s. Among the nine nations of the European Community, 79 percent of respondents reported themselves satisfied with their lives in 1973. Four years later, in spite of the economic problems that had arisen meanwhile, 75 percent continued to report satisfaction.[4] Americans similarly show a high degree of life satisfaction. The readiness of individuals to draw satisfaction from life is not confined to rich industrial nations. In Africa and Asia, surveys find that there too individuals report they are satisfied with their lives.[5]

Individual life satisfaction does not depend upon the performance of government, for Europeans express specific dissatisfaction with major institutions of their society. Whereas 75 percent report that they are satisfied with their own lives, 66 percent express dissatisfaction with their present financial situation.[6] In the United States too, private satisfaction and public dissatisfaction coexist.[7]

If anything, the economic troubles of the 1970s have made citizens more cautious about protecting what they have. In 1977 a majority of Europeans gave first priority to fighting rising prices and keeping order. While a majority (55 percent) of Europeans endorse gradual reforms, from 1970 to 1977 the proportion of citizens staunchly in favor of the status quo has risen from 15 percent to 32 percent. At the same time, the proportion favoring radical change has remained below 10 percent. The rejection of radical change is as strong among manual workers as it is in the middle class.[8] The increase in defenders of the status quo occurs not only in prosperous Germany, but also in economically overloaded Italy. The presidential elections of 1972 and 1976 similarly demonstrate widespread caution in the American electorate. At least nine out of ten voters would support a policy of protecting take-home pay and gradually increasing spending on government programs.

Individual citizens are not primarily concerned with maximizing their material advantages. If this were the case, there would be a rapid movement of labor within the European Economic Community, with individuals changing countries in pursuit of better pay, moving from England and Italy to flood prosperous societies such as Germany with immigrants. In fact, only harsh deprivation in economically declining societies has led numbers of people to uproot themselves and emigrate to better themselves economically.

As individuals move through the life cycle, they are likely to become even less concerned with making more money. The greatest pressure to earn money falls upon young married couples with young children, for family claims are then greatest, and material resources limited. By middle age, individuals appear to find a niche in life, whatever their economic circumstances. Public employment, unionization, or unemployment benefits insure an individual basic economic security. Once an occupational pattern is fixed, a person has a limited chance to rise occupationally. In exchange for union dues and an occasional vote, individuals can delegate responsibility for maintaining living standards to others, and concentrate upon what is most important to themselves.

The explanation for these findings is simple, yet important in its implications: the greatest concerns of individuals are insulated from the overarching institutions of society. If we could do a systematic content analysis of what ordinary people talked about, we would almost certainly find that the weather, children, or sports was more frequently a subject of discourse than talk about politics, and phatic communion more common than reasoned analysis of society's ills.

Life satisfactions are independent of changing material standards of living, because the things that most concern individuals—their family, friends, and health—are not immediately affected by fluctuations in the national economy. The primary concerns of most individuals in major Western nations today are face-to-face relationships with family and friends, and not the things that most concern economists, political scientists, and sociologists. Only in a totalitarian society does government invest political meaning in everything that an individual wants or does.

Time and again, when people are asked to evaluate different domains of life, individuals report that they are most satisfied with what is immediate to them—their family, friends, the place they live, their health, and their job—and least satisfied with those things for which major institutions of society are responsible, e.g., government, the economy, and law and order. Individuals generalize their judgment of life from face-to-face experiences, and not from the impersonal achievements of major social institutions.

Yet in a modern society of up to 200 million people, no individual can live outside the reach of government as did Robinson Crusoe on a desert island. Like it or not, individuals in their daily routines do depend upon the institutions of the mixed-economy welfare state. In the words of a contemporary political philosopher, "Just as small-scale humanly comprehensible groupings are essential, so are large-scale humanly incomprehensible ones." [9]

The views of ordinary people about the political economy are not only important to individuals but also to policy-makers. Politicians may claim that popular election is proof that they already know what people think. Economists tend to make *a priori* assumptions about how individuals behave, and reckon that their assumptions are valid across time and space. However, many commonly voiced assumptions about the attitudes of ordinary citizens toward the political economy are contradicted by the evidence.

The most familiar commonplace is that individuals expect a continually increasing flow of public and private material benefits. In the words of a British Chancellor of the Exchequer, they may "riot in the street" if these expectations are not met.[10] But a major European-American survey of public opinion refutes the simple-minded assumption that all citizens inevitably expect more and more material benefits. This survey, *Aspirations and Affluence,* conducted in 1968, at the height of a decade of treble affluence, found big differences in economic expectations within the United States, Britain, and Germany. A plurality of people in each nation considered that their living standard had been rising in the past four years; but in no country did half the population say they expected living standards to improve in the next four years, and in Germany only 24 percent expected more prosperity in the four years ahead. The proportion expecting living standards to rise steadily in the future as well as in the past was low, ranging from 6 percent in Germany to 35 percent in the United States.[11]

The presence of contrasting expectations within the electorate gives politicians great leeway in determining economic policy. At the height of the economic boom of the 1960s, the *Aspirations* survey found the balance of expectations within each country tipped towards optimism, but not by much. In Germany, those expecting continued growth outnumbered the pessimists by only 11 percent, in Britain by 17 percent, and in the United States by 35 percent: the "don't knows" and those uncertain about future prosperity held the balance.[12] A majority expected living standards to rise at some times and remain steady at others. Popular expectations at the height of treble affluence are best described in negative terms: living standards should not fall.

A second assumption refuted by the evidence is that citizens everywhere have the same expectations about the political economy. There are significant differences in outlooks between nations, as well as within them. These differences reflect contrasting historical experiences and current conditions; they also make it easier for some governments to act promptly to guard against political bankruptcy. For example, in the 1968 *Aspirations* survey, Americans can be characterized as combining an expectation of change for the better with a history of prosperity, Germans as enjoying prosperity without expecting it to continue automatically, and the British as assuming continued prosperity without the material evidence to justify this. In 1976, after an absolute fall in the national product of major nations, there remained striking national differences in views of the economy. At one extreme 89 percent of Italians saw economic conditions worsening, a view taken by only 22 percent of Germans.[13]

Thirdly, and most importantly, individual attitudes do not remain static when economic conditions change. The world recession of the 1970s has caused ordinary citizens everywhere to adapt their expectations about the political economy in keeping with its altered performance. At the beginning of 1972, Europeans and Americans were, on balance, optimistic about the immediate economic future (see Table 10.1). Except in Germany, the proportion expecting economic conditions to improve was greater than those expecting conditions to worsen. The shock given to the world economy by dollar devaluation and its immediate aftermath had not penetrated popular awareness. At the beginning of 1976, pessimism prevailed everywhere except Sweden, which had suffered least in the general contraction of national economies in the preceding year. By the start of 1978 the picture was different again:

pessimism had generally declined; even if the present was far from ideal, citizens saw evidence that the worst was behind them. The turnaround was most marked in Britain, where 53 percent expected 1978 to be better, as against 18 percent fearing that it would be worse. The swing to pessimism was most marked in Sweden where 50 percent expected the coming year to be worse, as against 25 percent expecting things to be better.

TABLE 10.1
Expectations for the Coming Year:
The Volatile 1970s

	1972	1976	1978

The entry for each country registers the percentage saying that they think the coming year will be better, minus the percentage saying they think it will be worse.

	%	%	%
America	+35	−47	+15
Britain	+14	−50	+35
France	+7	−48	+6
Germany	−23	−42	−9
Italy	n.a.	−44	−9
Sweden	+25	+25	−25

Sources: Gallup *Political Index* (London), (December 1971), no. 137, p. 221; (December 1975), no. 185, p. 15; and (January 1978), no. 210, p. 21. Supplemented by Gallup Poll files.

The views of that hypothetical being, economic man, depend upon the conditions of the moment, and upon the passport that he carries. The readiness of public opinion to alter in accord with short-term changes in national economic circumstances is illustrated by the fact that in each major Western nation a majority has been optimistic in at least one year in the 1970s, and pessimistic in another. At no time has public opinion within all six countries come down on the same side at the same time.

In Britain, there is evidence of a new phenomenon: "a revolution of falling expectations." Since 1960, a plurality of Englishmen have usually expected the economy to be in difficulty in the coming year, and they have not been disappointed. Between 1973 and 1977, the numbers expecting a higher standard of living fell, as did the numbers believing themselves entitled to a higher standard of living. In this period of declining take-home pay, Englishmen reported that they needed less extra money to get by on than four years before, another sign of declining expectations.[14]

Overall, individual citizens have a realistic view of the political economy of which they are a part. At any given time, some expect their conditions to improve, a smaller number expect conditions to worsen, and a third group—often the largest or decisive—reckons it will stay the same. Past prosperity does not lead people to expect prosperity to continue indefinitely, and recession causes popular expectations to reverse. Ironically, a simple-minded politician who sought to give people what they expected today would deliver rising prices, higher taxes, and unemployment!

Hyperthyroid politicians, anxious to leave their mark upon government by doing something (and almost invariably, something that costs money), cannot blame voters for making them spend and spend without constraint. The initiative for public spending is with government, and not with ordinary citizens. So too is the responsibility for making up national accounts. Politicians who ignore the reversal of economic fortunes in the 1970s convict themselves of the inflexibility and unrealism they attribute to voters. Not to adapt to changing circumstances reduces political effectiveness, and risks citizen indifference resulting in political bankruptcy.

If politicians face up to the limits of political economy, the difficulties of the 1970s can have a beneficial effect. Citizens have learned from the fact of failure that there are limits to the benefits that government can provide at a cost that they are prepared to pay. The limitations of government evident today give politicians a vested interest in promoting realistic, even cautious plans for the future growth of government programs.

Risk is inevitable, but failure is not. There is nothing in the constitution of any Western nation that compels it to try to consume more than it produces. But there is much in the specific incentives of politicians and in the inertia commitments of government that makes it easy for governors to continue increasing the costs of public policy, hoping like Mr. Micawber that something will turn up. But the future of political authority in major Western nations cannot be secured by trusting to Dame Fortune. It can be secure only if governors are prepared to face the future consequences of past actions, and prevent the total cost of individual public programs from adding up to too much. If governors are unwilling to protect citizens' take-home pay, they may radicalize those who in the past have looked to government to advance their interests. The chief threat to political authority today does not come from an old-fashioned confrontation between left and right; it is the prospect of citizens gradually becoming indifferent to government, thereby pushing it into political bankruptcy.

APPENDIX

THE FOLLOWING PAGES consist of tables giving more detailed supporting statistical information for the argument of the book. Each table is referred to where it is most relevant in the main text, and can be linked to a specific chapter by the number that introduces it; for example, Appendix Tables 2.1–3 refer to questions discussed in Chapter 2.

TABLE A 2.1: THE GROWTH OF THE NATIONAL PRODUCT, 1951–1976

The data in this table document the growth of affluence in the past quarter-century, as measured in currencies of constant purchasing power. Column 1 shows the annual average growth in the Gross Domestic Product, and column 2 shows the total increase in the national product from 1951 to 1976. On both measures, Germany has grown most, and Britain least. The 1976 value of the national product is given in column 3, and the value per person is given in column 4. While the United States has the largest total national product at current exchange rates, both Germany and Sweden register a higher standard of living in terms of per capita Gross Domestic Product.

Appendix

TABLE A 2.1
The Growth of the National Product, 1951–1976

	(1) Average Percentage Growth in GDP Per Annum	(2) Total Percentage Increase	(3) Gross Domestic Product (in millions), 1976	(4) Per Capita GDP, 1976
America	3.3	121	$1,573,700	$7,315
Britain	2.8	102	£116,600	£2,087
France	4.8	235	Fr F 1,456,700	Fr F 27,527
Germany	6.1	310	DM 1,019,600	DM 16,579
Italy	4.8	230	Lire 128,463,000	Lire 2,286,232
Sweden	3.7	154	SKr 285,400	SKr 34,730

Sources: OECD, *National Accounts of OECD Countries, 1950–1968* (Paris: OECD, 1969), table 2 for each country. OECD, *Main Economic Indicators* (October 1977), app. A.

TABLE A 2.2: THE GROWTH OF PUBLIC POLICY, 1951–1976

Public spending is the best single indicator of the growth of public policy. Table A 2.2 shows how substantial the increase has been in the past quarter-century. Column 1 gives the annual average growth in the cost of public policy, and column 2 gives the total increase from 1951 to 1976, using the Gross Domestic Product deflator to make calculations in terms of money with a constant purchasing power. Italy shows the fastest annual rate of growth in public policy and total growth, and Britain the least. The 1976 cost of public policy, reported in column 3, is highest in total in the United States, but not so much higher as America's population might suggest. As column 4 shows, Sweden ranks first in the amount of government

[252

spending per head (about $4,500), and the United States ranks fourth.

TABLE A 2.2
The Growth of Public Policy, 1951–1976

	(1) Average Percentage Growth Per Annum	(2) Total Percentage Increase	(3) The Cost of Public Policy (in millions), 1976	(4) Per Capita Cost, 1976
America	5.3	245	$597,230	$2,776
Britain	4.3	185	£62,657	£1,121
France	8.8	589	Fr F 719,350	Fr F 13,593
Germany	8.1	498	DM 510,810	DM 8,306
Italy	9.4	820	Lire 64,566,000	Lire 1,149,100
Sweden	7.0	445	SKr 174,550	SKr 21,235

Sources: OECD, *National Accounts of OECD Countries, 1950–1968* (Paris: OECD, 1969), table 7 for each country. OECD, *National Accounts of OECD Countries, 1975,* vol. 2 (Paris: OECD, 1977), table 7 for each country; *1976,* table 7 figures preliminary.

TABLE A 2.3: THE GROWTH OF TAKE-HOME PAY, 1951–1976

The money that an individual earns after taxes are deducted is usually larger than the benefits received from public policies, but it is growing more slowly. The steady annual growth of take-home pay is shown in column 1, and the total increase in the past quarter-century is shown in column 2. In both instances, Germany leads, and Britain brings up the rear. When allowance is made for population growth, as in column 3, then Germany still ranks first in the total growth in take-home pay per capita, and the United States moves to last place, because

Appendix

of its postwar population explosion. (The figures in columns
1–3 are all based on constant value currencies, derived by use of
the Gross Domestic Product deflator.) By contrast, column 4
shows the United States ranking first in the total cash value of
take-home pay per capita in 1976, with Italy at the bottom.

TABLE A 2.3
The Growth of Take-Home Pay, 1951–1976

	(1) Average Percentage Growth Per Annum	(2) Total Percentage Increase	(3) Percentage Per Capita Increase, 1951–1976	(4) Per Capita Take-Home Pay, 1976
America	2.7	105	48	$5,619
Britain	2.1	67	51	£1,412
France	4.3	212	147	Fr F 21,226
Germany	4.5	254	175	DM 11,436
Italy	3.9	179	135	Lire 1,657,100
Sweden	2.5	80	56	SKr 20,696

Sources: OECD, *National Accounts of OECD Countries, 1950–1968* (Paris:
OECD, 1969), tables 1 and 7 for each country; OECD, *National Accounts of
OECD Countries, 1975,* vol. 2 (Paris: OECD, 1977), table 7 for each country;
vol. 1, pp. 9, 25, 27, 35, 47, and 53; *1976,* tables 1 and 7 preliminary.

TABLE A 3.1: HOW THE COSTS OF PUBLIC POLICY ARE APPORTIONED

The relative importance of different types of public policy is
demonstrated in this table. Column 1 shows that social policies
take by far the largest share of the budget in every major Western nation. Column 2 shows that a substantial but variable

fraction of the budget, ranging from one-sixth to one-third, is
devoted to policies intended to mobilize economic resources.
While defining policies are necessary for the survival of a government, column 3 shows that their claim to public spending is
usually limited, and even in the United States, where defense
spending is disproportionately large, they account for only 29
percent of the total costs of public policy.

TABLE A 3.1

*How the Costs of Public Policy Are Apportioned ***

	Percentage Devoted to:		
	(1) Social Policies	(2) Mobilizing Economic Resources	(3) Defining Policies
America	44	27	29
Britain	54	23	23
France	61	16	23
Germany	56	27	17
Italy	45	35	20
Sweden	56	24	20

* For a full definition of the three categories, see Rose, "On the Priorities of
Government," *European Journal of Political Research* 4 (1976): 3.

Sources: OECD, *National Accounts of OECD Countries, 1975,* vol. 2 (Paris:
OECD, 1977), table 1 for each country. Bureau of the Census, *Government
Finances 1974–75* (Washington, D.C.: Government Printing Office, 1976),
tables 5–6. Central Statistical Office, *Annual Abstract of Statistics, 1976*
(London: HMSO, 1977), table 360. INSEE, *Annuaire Statistique de la
France, 1976* (Paris: INSEE, 1977), tables 7.1–7.10, and 15.2. *Statistisches
Jahrbuch für die Bundesrepublik, 1976* (Stuttgart: Kohlhammer, 1977),
tables 21.4, 22.4. Bundesministerium der Finanz, *Finanzbericht, 1976*
(Bonn: Bundesministerium der Finanz, 1976). Banca d'Italia, *Relazione
Annuale, 1975* (Rome: Banca d'Italia, 1976), tables 1, 4, and 7. Statistiska
Centralbyrån, *Statistiska Årsbok för Sverige, 1976* (Stockholm: Statistiska
Centralbyrån, 1976), tables 295, 296, 445, 464, 465, and 470. Statis-
tiska Centralbyrån, *Kommuneras Finanser, 1975* (Stockholm: Statistiska
Centralbyrån, 1976), tables 1–4.

TABLE A 3.2: THE EXTENT OF INDIVIDUAL
BENEFITS FROM THE WELFARE STATE

Any attempt to estimate the total number of individual beneficiaries of public policy can only yield approximate figures.
By concentrating upon major social policies with readily identifiable beneficiaries, this table provides a minimum estimate
of the scope of benefits provided by the welfare state. Column
7 shows the total number of major social benefits provided; in
every European country, they are equivalent to more than one
per citizen, and in the United States they are equivalent to
four benefits for every five Americans. Columns 1 through 6
record the proportion of the population receiving particular
benefits. Health and sickness benefits are of greatest importance in every European country, because the need for such
care is independent of age. Education normally ranks second
in importance, because of the cumulative effect of the "baby
boom" since World War II.

TABLE A 3.3: THE EXTENT OF DEPENDENCE
UPON GOVERNMENT FOR TAKE-HOME PAY

The public sector is the largest employer of workers in every
major Western nation. The data in columns 5 and 6 show that
the proportion of employees directly or indirectly employed by
government ranges from 29 percent in America to 58 percent in
Sweden. The data in columns 1 through 4 indicate the different national patterns in the employment of public sector
workers. Column 1 shows that central government is the chief

TABLE A 3.2

The Extent of Individual Benefits from the Welfare State

	(1) Education	(2) Health and Sickness Benefit	(3) Pensions	(4) Other Income Maintenance	(5) Children's Allowances	(6) Special National Programs	(7) Total Benefits
		Percentage of Population Receiving a Benefit:					
America	28	9	11	17	0	14 [a, b]	166,000,000
Britain	21	46	16	8	9	32 [b]	75,000,000
France	25	35	19	6	21	13 [b]	63,000,000
Germany	21	51	18	8	11	3 [b]	70,000,000
Italy	23	32	18	26	20	9 [b]	63,000,000
Sweden	21	98	13	15	17	28 [b, c]	16,000,000

[a] Food Stamps
[b] Housing assistance
[c] Labor market policies

Sources: Bureau of the Census, Statistical Abstract of the United States, 1976 (Washington, D.C.: Government Printing Office, 1976), tables 156, 157, 182, 466, 488, 496, 497, 534, 563, and 1281; Central Statistical Office, Annual Abstract of Statistics, 1976, tables 46, 66, 124, and 130; Central Statistical Office, Social Trends, 1975 (London: HMSO, 1976), table 2.3; Institut National des Statistiques et des Etudes Economiques, Annuaire Statistique de la France, 1976, tables 7.6, 7.8, 7.12, 7.14, 7.15, 8.10, 9.1, and 10.7; Statistisches Bundesamt, Statistisches Jahrbuch für die Bundesrepublik, 1976, tables 5.4, 6.1, 12.3.2, 21.4.2, 21.5, 21.7, 21.8, 21.9, 21.10, 21.11, and 21.13; Istituto Centrale di Statistica, Annuario Statistico Italiano, 1976 (Rome: Istituto Centrale di Statistica, 1976), tables 47, 48, 53, 55, 57, and 58; Statistiska Centralbyrån, Statistiska Årsbok för Sverige, 1976 (Stockholm: Statistiska Centralbyrån, 1976), tables 288, 291, 292, 313, 323, 328, and 361.

TABLE A 3.3

The Extent of Dependence upon Government for Take-Home Pay

	(1) Central Government	(2) Local Government	(3) Nationalized Industries [a]	(4) Private Sector Suppliers to Government [b]	(5) Total Number of Government Employees	(6) Percentage of All Employees
		(Thousands of Employees)				
America	4,400	11,600	1,300	8,000	25,300,000	29
Britain	2,200	3,000	1,900	2,300	9,400,000	38
France	2,400	1,200	1,500	2,000	7,100,000	33
Germany	1,200	2,600	1,600	2,500	7,900,000	30
Italy	2,200	1,800	1,300	1,900	7,200,000	38
Sweden	800	700	300	500	2,300,000	58

[a] Excludes joint stock companies with government as sole or principal owner.
[b] Estimated by dividing the difference between government final consumption expenditures in Gross Domestic Product (OECD, National Accounts Statistics, 1974, vol. 2, table 1, line 2) and Gross Domestic Product coming from producers of government services (ibid, table 3, line B.6) by the average output per industrial worker (calculated from ibid., table 3, line A.11) divided by national employment figures for industry obtained from the national sources listed below.

Sources: Bureau of the Census, Statistical Abstract of the United States, 1976, tables 440, 445; Central Statistical Office, National Income and Expenditure, 1965–1975 (London: HMSO, 1976), table 1.10; Institut National des Statistiques et des Etudes Economiques, Annuaire Statistique de la France, 1976, tables 4.1, 15.2; Statistisches Bundesamt, Statistisches Jahrbuch für die Bundesrepublik, 1976, tables 14.11, 22.10.3, and 22.10.4; Istituto Centrale di Statistica, Annuario Statistico Italiano, 1976, tables 330, 359, and 360; Statistiska Centralbyrån, Statistiska Årsbok for Sverige, 1976, tables 253, 255, and 256.

employer of workers in France, Italy, and Sweden. Column 2 shows that local government is the chief employer of workers in the United States, Britain, and Germany. Nationalized industries are relatively important sources of employment in France and Germany; see column 3. Private sector suppliers to government are important in every major Western nation, and especially so in the United States; see column 4.

TABLE A 4.1: THE SOURCES OF TAX REVENUE

Income tax, social security levies, and sales and excise taxes are the three principal sources of revenue in every major Western nation. But the proportion that each raises to meet the costs of public policy varies substantially from nation to nation. Column 1 shows that Sweden raises the largest fraction of

TABLE A 4.1
The Sources of Tax Revenue

	(1)	(2)	(3)	(4)	(5)	(6)
	Income Tax	Social Security Contributions	Sales & Excise Taxes	Property Tax	Corporate Profits Tax	Other Taxes
(as a Percentage of Total Tax Revenue)						
America	34	23	16	12	11	4
Britain	36	17	25	10	8	4
France	11	42	33	-	8	6
Germany	30	35	24	-	5	6
Italy	15	42	32	-	7	4
Sweden	46	19	25	-	4	6

Note: - = 0.1 percent or less.

Source: OECD, *Revenue Statistics of OECD Member Countries, 1965–1974* (Paris: OECD, 1976), tables 7, 13, 15, 17, 35, 36, 39, 47, 50, and 51. Calculated from 1974 data.

revenue from income tax, and France raises the least. On the other hand, France and Italy raise the largest proportion of their revenue from social security taxes, and Sweden and Britain raise the least (column 2). Sales and excise taxes are most important in France and Italy (column 3). Because Continental European countries do not normally levy property taxes, only the United States and Britain have entries in column 4. In every major Western nation, corporation profits tax is relatively unimportant; it is smallest in Sweden, and relatively most significant in the United States.

TABLE A 8.1: THE CHANGING VALUE OF NATIONAL CURRENCIES IN THE INTERNATIONAL MARKET PLACE

In the 1970s, the floating (that is, freeing) of national currencies from fixed exchange rates has led to major short-term up and down fluctuations in the value of national currencies relative to each other. Cumulatively, it has resulted in major shifts, with the Deutsche mark rising steadily against all currencies, and the lira falling. Column 1 shows the value of each national currency at 100 in 1970, the year before exchange rates became volatile. Column 2 shows that the currencies of Germany, France, and Sweden have risen in value against the dollar, and British and Italian currencies have fallen. Column 3 shows the overall change of each national currency, adjusted to allow for the relative importance of major nations in world trade. European nations have been better able to protect or improve the value of their currency *vis a vis* the dollar than against all trading countries; for example, whereas the lira has depreciated by 28 percent against the dollar, it has depreciated by 41 percent on a worldwide basis.

TABLE A 8.1
*The Changing Value of National Currencies
in the International Market Place*

	(1) Value in 1970	(2) Change in Value Against Dollar (1970–1978)	(3) Change in Value Against International "Basket" of Currencies (1970–1978)
America	100	Not applicable	−19
Britain	100	−20	−35
France	100	+18	−4
Germany	100	+80	+55
Italy	100	−27	−43
Sweden	100	+12	−2

Source: International Monetary Fund, *International Financial Statistics* 31 (May 1978): 5, national tables. (The 1970 figures are annual averages, the 1978 figure is as of March.)

NOTES

Introduction

1. Quoted in Sar E. Levitan and Robert Taggart, *The Promise of Greatness* (Cambridge: Harvard University Press, 1976), p. 3. Johnson's views were encouraged by his Chief Economic Advisor. See Walter W. Heller, *New Dimensions of Political Economy* (New York: W. W. Norton & Co., 1967).

2. See a report to the Trilateral Commission by Michel J. Crozier, Samuel P. Huntington, and Joji Watanuki, *The Crisis of Democracy* (New York: New York University Press, 1976); R. Emmett Tyrrell Jr., ed., *The Future That Doesn't Work: Social Democracy's Failures in Britain* (Garden City, N.Y.: Doubleday & Co., 1977); Alain Peyrefitte, *Le Mal Français* (Paris: Plon, 1977); and Wilhelm Hennis, Peter Graf Kielmansegg, and Ulrich Matz, *Regierbarkeit*, vol. 1 (Stuttgart: Klett-Cotta, 1977).

3. Roland Huntford, *The New Totalitarians* (New York: Stein and Day, 1972).

4. Peter Nichols, *La Scelta Italiana* (Milan: Garzanti, 1974).

5. *Wird die Schweiz Unregierbar?*, a symposium of the *Schweizer Monatshefte* 55 (1975):4.

6. See Erwin K. Scheuch, *Wird die Bundesrepublik Unregierbar?* (Cologne: Arbeitgeberverband der Metallindustrie, 1976), pp. 39ff.

7. For example, the Federal Republic of Germany still pays benefits to the families of soldiers who fought for the Third Reich, and makes financial reparation to Jewish victims of that Reich. See G. Stapler, K. Hauser, and K. Borchardt, *The German Economy: 1870 to the Present* (New York: Harcourt, Brace, Jovanovich, 1967), p. 212.

8. See e.g. David S. Landes, *Bankers and Pashas* (Cambridge: Harvard University Press, 1958).

9. See Stephen A. Schuker, *The End of French Predominance in Europe: The Financial Crisis of 1924 and the Adoption of the Dawes Plan* (Chapel Hill: University of North Carolina Press, 1976). After defaulting on loans in 1934, Newfoundland surrendered its Dominion status and returned to being a British colony until it joined Canada in 1949. See Richard Gwyn, *Smallwood: The Unlikely Revolutionary* (Toronto: McClelland & Stewart, 1972).

10. Because of its subordinate status, New York City's financial affairs are not directly comparable to the problems of independent countries. See e.g. Martin Shefter, "New York City's Fiscal Crisis: the Politics of Inflation and Retrenchment," *The Public Interest* 48 (Summer 1977): 98–127; and Attiat F. Ott and Jang H. Yoo, *New York City's Financial Crisis: Can the Trend be Reversed?* (Washington, D.C.: American Enterprise Institute, 1975).

Notes

11. For an influential statement of this view, see S. M. Lipset, *Political Man* (Garden City, N.Y.: Doubleday & Co., 1960).

12. This is the remark of a Kennedy staff man, though it best characterizes the behavior of Nixon staff men. Quoted in Thomas E. Cronin, *The State of the Presidency* (Boston: Little, Brown & Co., 1975), p. 17.

13. Quoted in Joseph Kraft, "An Insider's View of London Summit," *International Herald-Tribune* (Paris), 16 May 1977. Cf. Richard Simeon, ed., *Must Canada Fail?* (Montreal: McGill-Queen's University Press, 1977).

14. J. M. Keynes, *The General Theory of Employment, Interest, and Money* (London: Macmillan, 1936), p. 403.

15. *Towards Full Employment and Price Stability* (Paris: OECD, 1977), p. 14, hereafter cited as OECD, *The McCracken Report*. For a political criticism of the report, see Robert O. Keohane, "Neo-Orthodox Economics, Inflation, and the Role of the State," *World Politics* 31 (1978).

16. See Assar Lindbeck, *The Political Economy of the New Left: An Outsider's View* (New York: Harper & Row, 1971), p. 98. A widely read American book, James O'Connor, *The Fiscal Crisis of the State* (New York: St. Martin's Press, 1973), can be criticized both for mistakes in interpretation of American experience, and because European experience often contradicts its ethnocentric arguments. See James Tobin, *The New Economics One Decade Older* (Princeton: University Press, 1974), pp. 41ff; and Kenneth Newton, "The Politics of Public Expenditure Studies," *Political Studies* 25 (1977):1, 122–127.

17. Peter Jay, "Nature's Remedy or Man's?" *Times* (London), 30 September 1976; see also Peter Jay, *Employment, Inflation, and Politics* (London: Institute of Economic Affairs, 1976).

18. In a television interview with Barbara Walters, quoted in "Ford Fear of Carter Promises," *Daily Telegraph* (London), 4 January 1977.

Chapter 1

1. For a full development of the importance of noneconomic challenges as against economic challenges to political authority in Western nations, see Richard Rose, *Governing without Consensus: An Irish Perspective* (Boston: Beacon Press, 1971), chap. 14.

2. See S. M. Lipset, "The Changing Class Structure and Contemporary European Politics," *Daedalus* 18 (1966):1, 296; Joseph Schumpeter, *Capitalism, Socialism, and Democracy*, 4th ed. (London: Allen and Unwin, 1952), p. 411; and Robert Heilbroner, *Business Civilization in Decline* (New York: W. W. Norton & Co., 1976), p. 34.

3. Erwin K. Scheuch, *Wird die Bundesrepublik Unregierbar?* (Cologne: Arbeitgeberverband der Metallindustrie, 1976), p. 28.

4. See e.g. Assar Lindbeck, "The Changing Role of the National State," *Kyklos* 28 (1975):1, 23–44; and "Stabilization Policy in Open Economies with Endogenous Politicians," *American Economic Review* 66 (1976):2, 1–19.

5. Paul Lewis, *The New York Times,* 21 October 1976.

6. In devising our model we have followed the advice of Wilfred Beckerman, *An Introduction to National Income Analysis* (London: Weidenfeld and Nicolson, 1968), pp. 21ff: "In selecting a system of classification for purposes of analysing any phenomenon, one must start with some theory of what are the important distinctions that have to be drawn between different categories to be classified, and what are the important relationships between them. It may be necessary to classify transactions on a special basis devised for purposes of that particular issue." As our primary concerns are political rather than economic, our model emphasizes government control of the allocation of the national product, and not final consumption.

7. For an excellent systematic development of this problem by economists, see the study commissioned by Ireland's National Economic and Social Council: Jack Wiseman and Bernard Stafford, *The Future of Public Expenditure in Ireland* (Dublin: Stationery Office, Pri. 5337, 1976).

8. See e.g. David Smith, "Public Consumption and Economic Performance," *National Westminster Bank Quarterly Review* (November 1975), pp. 17–30.

9. See Aaron Wildavsky, *Budgeting* (Boston: Little, Brown & Co., 1975), chap. 6.

10. For a full outline of the terms employed here, see Richard Rose, "Dynamic Tendencies in the Authority of Regimes," *World Politics* 21 (1969):4, 602–628; and Richard Rose, *Ungovernability: Is There Fire Behind the Smoke?* (Glasgow: University of Strathclyde Studies in Public Policy, no. 16, 1978).

11. Citizen indifference contrasts with the characteristic act of exit described by Albert Hirschman, *Exit, Voice, and Loyalty* (Cambridge: Harvard University Press, 1970). His concern is primarily with legal choices, e.g., to work longer hours to have more pay and pay more taxes; to work less and pay less taxes; or to voice complaints about taxes. Our concern is with *disloyalty,* the missing term in his analysis. A citizen who does not accept any of the legal choices offered can make an illegal choice, e.g., to work longer hours but evade paying more taxes.

12. See e.g. the assumptions in OECD, *The McCracken Report,* pp. 16, 96, 133.

13. By contrast, disaster was once predicted if public spending exceeded 25 percent of the national product; see Colin Clark, "Public Finance and Changes in the Value of Money," *Economic Journal* 55 (December 1945): 371–389. Cf. Milton Friedman, "The Line We Dare Not Cross: The Fragility of Freedom at 60 Percent," *Encounter* 47 (1976):5, 8–14.

14. Cf. S. M. Lipset, *Political Man* (Garden City, N.Y.: Doubleday & Co., 1960), pp. 81ff.

15. See Peter Nichols, *Italia, Italia* (London: Fontana, 1975), p. 92.

16. Cf. Luigi Graziano, "The Crisis of a Liberal-Democratic Regime: The Case of Italy," (Edinburgh: 1976 World Congress of the International Political Science Association); P. A. Allum, *Italy: Republic without Government* (New York: W. W. Norton & Co., 1973); and Gino Pallotta, *Dizionario Politico e Parlamentare* (Rome: Newton Compton Editori, 1976), pp. 213, 291.

17. Cf. Mancur Olson Jr. and Hans H. Landsberg, eds., *The No-Growth Society* (New York: W. W. Norton & Co., 1973).

Notes

Chapter 2

1. For this reason we start our analysis of the postwar economy in 1951, and conclude our trend studies in 1976, the final year for which OECD had published crossnational statistics as of the time of this writing. On longer term trends, see B. R. Mitchell, *European Historical Statistics, 1750–1970* (London: Macmillan Press, 1975), Table K1.

2. Quoted in James Sundquist, *Politics and Policy: The Eisenhower, Kennedy, and Johnson Years* (Washington, D.C.: The Brookings Institution, 1968), p. 56.

3. See U.S. Bureau of the Census, *Historical Statistics of the United States: Colonial Times to 1970* (Washington, D.C.: Government Printing Office, 1975), series F4, F31; cf. Simon Kuznets, *The Economic Growth of Nations* (Cambridge: Harvard University Press, 1971), pp. 38–40.

4. On automobiles, see *United Nations Statistical Yearbook: 1957* (New York: United Nations), Table 139, figures for 1938; *U.N. Yearbook: 1975*, table 157, figures for 1974. On television sets, see UNESCO, *Statistical Yearbook: 1963* (New York: UNESCO), table 41, reporting data only from 1953; and *UNESCO Yearbook: 1975*, table 16.2, reporting 1974 data. Calculations of the distribution of goods on a family basis assume four persons per family.

5. Unemployment figures are not directly comparable crossnationally, but meaningful comparisons can be made across time within a nation. See e.g., Mitchell, *European Historical Statistics*, tables C2, K1; *Historical Statistics of the United States*, series F 1-5, D85-86; and *Statistical Abstract of the United States 1976* (Washington, D.C.: Government Printing Office), table 1459.

6. See John Kenneth Galbraith, *The Affluent Society* (Boston: Houghton Mifflin, 1958). For a similar argument, see Anthony Downs, "Why the Government Budget Is Too Small in a Democracy," *World Politics* 12 (1960):541–563.

7. On the possibilities and difficulties of measuring nonmarket goods, see e.g. Milton Moss, ed., *The Measure of Economic and Social Performances* (New York: Columbia University Press, 1973). Fred Hirsch, *The Social Limits of Growth* (London: Routledge & Kegan Paul, 1977), argues that growth figures must be discounted by the growing importance of positional goods, which cannot be increased like manufactured goods. Unfortunately Hirsch does not specify any means of measuring their magnitude. Almost certainly they affect an upper middle class minority more than the masses of citizens.

8. Daily fluctuations in exchange rates, especially the exchange rates of the dollar, make it preferable to quote each nation's economic statistics in its own currency rather than convert to a single unstable national measure. As of 15 June 1978, European currencies had the following values against the United States dollar: £1 British equalled $1.83; 1 French franc, 22 cents; 1 Deutsche mark, 48 cents; 100 Italian lire, 12 cents; 1 Swedish krona, 22 cents. Cf. Table A 8.1.

9. See Edward F. Denison, *Why Growth Rates Differ: Postwar Experi-*

ences in Nine Western Countries (Washington, D.C.: The Brookings Institution, 1967), especially pp. 314–317.

10. For a review of contrasting government approaches in the 1960s, see Andrew Shonfield, *Modern Capitalism: The Changing Balance of Public and Private Power* (London: Oxford University Press, 1965); on the 1970s, see OECD, *The McCracken Report.*

11. See Richard Rose, *What Is Governing? Purpose and Policy in Washington* (Englewood Cliffs, N.J.: Prentice-Hall Inc., 1978).

12. See Bureau of the Census, *Historical Statistics of the United States,* series F1, Y336; and for Sweden, Finansdepartment, *Riks-stat och Nasta Stasreglering,* 1875 (Stockholm: P. A. Norstedt, 1876); and Erik Lindahl, Einar Dahlgren, and Karin Koch, *National Income of Sweden, 1861–1930* (Stockholm: P. A. Norstedt, 1937), app. A.

13. Quoted in Sar E. Levitan and Robert Taggart, *The Promise of Greatness* (Cambridge: Harvard University Press, 1976), p. 25.

14. Simon Nora, *Rapport sur les Enterprises Publiques* (Paris: La Documentation Française, April 1967), pp. 13ff.

15. *Public Expenditure to 1979–80* (London: Her Majesty's Stationery Office, Cmnd. 6393, 1976), paragraph 22.

16. See OECD, *The McCracken Report,* paragraph 191.

17. See M. Donald Hancock, "Elite Images and System Change in Sweden," in *Politics and the Future of Industrial Society,* ed. Leon N. Lindberg (New York: David McKay, 1976), pp. 174ff.

Chapter 3

1. See Richard Rose, "On the Priorities of Government: A Developmental Analysis of Public Policies," *European Journal of Political Research* 4 (1976):3, 247–289.

2. See e.g. Kevin Allen and Andrew Stevenson, *An Introduction to the Italian Economy* (London: Martin Robertson & Co., 1974).

3. See e.g. Assar Lindbeck, *Swedish Economic Policy* (London: Macmillan Press, 1975). The economic difficulties of Sweden since 1977 have led the Swedish government to intervene to support companies and industries, as the British government did a few years previously.

4. See the Finer Committee, *Report of the Committee on One-Parent Families* (London: Her Majesty's Stationery Office, Cmnd. 5629-I, 1974), especially Christine Cockburn and Hugh Heclo, "Income Maintenance for One Parent Families in Other Countries," vol. 2, pp. 59–186.

5. See Caisse nationale des allocations familiales, *Results Generaux,* 1975 (Paris: Caisse nationale des allocations familiales, 1976).

6. See e.g. J. S. Fuerst, ed., *Public Housing in Europe and America* (New York: Halsted Press, 1974).

7. For an American analysis of corporate dependence, see Murray Weidenbaum, *The Modern Public Sector* (New York: Basic Books Inc., 1969); and, for the employees' view, Samuel Lubell's *The Future While It Happens* (New York: W. W. Norton & Co., 1973).

8. OECD Studies in Resource Allocation No. 3, *Public Expenditure on Income Maintenance Programmes* (Paris: OECD, 1976), pp. 85, 90. The study frankly justifies a policy opposed to popular views on paternalistic grounds.

9. OECD, *Public Expenditure*, pp. 102–104.

10. See e.g. Joseph A. Pechman and Benjamin A. Okner, *Who Bears the Tax Burden?* (Washington, D.C.: The Brookings Institution, 1974), table 4.7; and A. L. Webb and J. E. Sieve, *Income Redistribution and the Welfare State* (London: Bell, 1971). On the difficulties and results of using different measures of income distribution, a precondition of any attempt to assess income equalization, see OECD, *Economic Outlook* (Paris: OECD Occasional Studies, July 1976).

11. See Leon D. Plathy, "Aid to Families with Dependent Children: An Overview," *Social Security Bulletin* 40 (1977):10, 18; and, on the poverty trap in Britain, see A. J. Culyer, *The Economics of Social Policy* (London: Martin Robertson & Co., 1973), pp. 91–110.

12. Calculated from *US Budget in Brief, 1977* (Washington, D.C.: Government Printing Office, 1977), pp. 59–63; and Statistiska Centralbyrån, *Statistiska Årsbok för Sverige* (Stockholm: 1977), table 447.

13. See Central Statistical Office, "Effects of Taxes and Benefits on Household Income, 1975," *Economic Trends* (London: Her Majesty's Stationery Office, 1976), no. 278, 96ff.

14. See OECD, Studies in Resource Allocation No. 2, *Public Expenditure on Education* (Paris: OECD, 1976).

Chapter 4

1. Leslie Lenkowsky, "Welfare in the Welfare State," in *The Future That Doesn't Work*, ed. R. Emmett Tyrrell (Garden City, N.Y.: Doubleday, 1977), p. 164.

2. Tom Wilson, "The Impact of Inflation and Economic Growth," in *The Dilemmas of Government Expenditure* (London: Institute of Economic Affairs, Readings 15, 1976), p. 33.

3. It is usually assumed that most citizens will prefer to pay earmarked taxes (especially those for social insurance) rather than taxes going into the general revenue fund. See John A. Brittain, *The Payroll Tax for Social Security* (Washington, D.C.: The Brookings Institution, 1972), pp. 6–12; J. C. Kincaid, *Poverty and Equality in Britain* (Harmondsworth, Middlesex: Penguin Books, 1975), pp. 184–191.

4. Quoted in W. E. Leuchtenberg, *Franklin D. Roosevelt and the New Deal, 1932–1940* (New York: Harper & Row, 1963), p. 133. See also W. J. Braithwaite, *Lloyd George's Ambulance Wagon* (London: Methuen, 1957).

5. The regressive element in taxation is, however, easily overestimated. See Harold L. Wilensky, *The Welfare State and Equality* (Berkeley: University of California Press, 1975), pp. 91ff. Moreover, somewhat regressive taxes like social security can finance the redistributive distribution of benefits.

6. Cost-benefit analyses suggest from $15 to $25 billion in cash and shadow benefits may accrue annually, because of the resulting better health and amenities of Americans. See Allen V. Kneese and Charles L. Schultze, *Pollution, Prices, and Public Policy* (Washington, D.C.: The Brookings Institution, 1975), pp. 73ff; John Hamer, "Pollution Control: Costs and Benefits," in *Earth, Energy, and Environment* (Washington, D.C.: Congressional Quarterly, 1977), pp. 90, 99; Cynthia H. Enloe, *The Politics of Pollution in a Comparative Perspective* (New York: David McKay Company Inc., 1975).

7. Generally available exemptions such as those for dependents are not counted as tax expenditures. These are equivalent to $30 to $35 billion foregone in federal tax revenue. On the concept of tax expenditures, see Stanley Surrey, *Pathways to Tax Reform* (Cambridge: Harvard University Press, 1973); for annual data, see *Statistical Abstract of the United States* (Washington, D.C.: Government Printing Office, 1976), table 385; and for reservations see *Special Analyses: Budget of the United States, 1979* (Washington, D.C.: Government Printing Office, 1978), pp. 148–174.

8. See Roger Choate, "Profitability Not a Taxing Business," *Times* (London), 17 November 1976.

9. Calculated by the authors from *Statistical Abstract of the United States*, 1976, table 385.

10. This is the view of a British poverty expert, Brian Abel-Smith, "Social Security and Taxation," in *Taxation Policy*, eds. Bernard Crick and William A. Robson (Harmondsworth, Middlesex: Penguin Books, 1973), p. 172.

11. Quoted in John Clarke Adams and Paolo Barile, *The Government of Republican Italy* (Boston: Houghton Mifflin Co., 1966), p. 22; see also pp. 94ff. For an overview, see Vito Tanzi, *The Individual Income Tax and Economic Growth: An International Comparison* (Baltimore: Johns Hopkins University Press, 1969), especially chap. 6; and Maurice Denuziere, *Enquête sur le Fraude Fiscale* (Paris: J. C. Lattes, 1973); and Aristide Mondani, *Basi satistische e leggi assiomatiche della dinamica dell'evasione fiscale* (Milan: Universita Bocconi, 1965).

12. Calculated from data in Martin B. Tracy, "Payroll Taxes under Social Security Programs: Cross National Survey," *Social Security Bulletin* 38 (1975):5.

13. See OECD, *Revenue Statistics of OECD Member Countries, 1965–1974* (Paris, 1976), tables 16, 17.

14. See e.g., C. T. Sandford, *Hidden Costs of Taxation* (London: Institute for Fiscal Studies, No. 6, 1973), and, for comparative data, Arnold J. Heidenheimer, Hugh Heclo, and C. T. Adams, *Comparative Public Policy* (New York: St. Martin's Press, 1975), pp. 235ff.

15. Unpublished OECD research. For theoretical background, see J. Pitchford and S. J. Turnovsky, "Some Effects of Taxes on Inflation," *Quarterly Journal of Economics* 15 (1976):4, 523–539; and D. A. L. Auld and C. Southey, "The Simple Analytics of Tax-Induced Inflation," *Public Finance* 32 (1977):1, 37–47.

16. Calculated by the authors from data in *Statistical Abstract of the United States* (Washington, D.C.: Government Printing Office, 1976), table 391; *Statistisches Jahrbuch für die Bundesrepublik* (Stuttgart: Kohlhammer, 1976), table 22.13; and Central Statistical Office, *Annual Ab-*

stract of Statistics, 1976 (London: Her Majesty's Stationery Office, 1976), table 365.

17. This example is taken from Arthur M. Okun, *Equality and Efficiency: The Big Tradeoff* (Washington, D.C.: The Brookings Institution, 1975), p. 53.

18. See e.g. N. C. Kakwani, "Measurement of Tax Progressivity: An International Comparison," *The Economic Journal* 87 (March 1977):71–80.

19. Peter Wilsher, "We'll All Be Walking Wounded," *Sunday Times* (London), 6 March 1977.

Chapter 5

1. American figures can only be an estimate because of a paucity of data; in the 1880s the federal government is known to have controlled about 2.2 percent of the national product. See Bureau of the Census, *Historical Statistics of the United States, Colonial Times to 1970*, series Y-336. For Britain, see Jindrich Veverka, "The Growth of Government Expenditure in the United Kingdom since 1790," *Scottish Journal of Political Economy* 10 (1963):1, table 1.

2. Harold Wilensky, *The Welfare State and Equality* (Berkeley: University of California Press, 1975), p. 12. Gompers himself would have rejected the association of Socialism and social welfare. See e.g., his exchange with Morris Hillquit in a 1916 U.S. Senate committee hearing reprinted in Loren Baritz, ed., *The American Left* (New York: Basic Books, 1971), pp. 160–165.

3. For a classic exposition, see Anthony Downs, *An Economic Theory of Democracy* (New York: Harper and Row, 1957).

4. See e.g. Mancur Olson Jr., *The Logic of Collective Action* (Cambridge: Harvard University Press, 1965); and Fred Hirsch, *The Social Limits to Growth* (London: Routledge & Kegan Paul, 1977).

5. Reginald Maudling, a former Chancellor of the Exchequer. Quoted in D. E. Butler and Anthony King, *The British General Election of 1966* (London: Macmillan, 1966), p. 5.

6. German parties are trying to export their political skills and campaign know-how to other countries in the Mediterranean, Latin America, Africa, and Asia. In the period 1963–1972, the three chief parties spent more than 268 million Deutsche marks abroad. See Alan Watson, *The Political Foundations in West Germany* (London: Anglo-German Foundation, 1976), p. 3.

7. See evidence cited in note, page 55.

8. Andrew T. Cowart and Anthony Blum, "Monetary Policy in America: Findings and Some Comparisons with the European Experience" (Washington, D.C.: Annual Meeting of the American Political Science Association, 1977), p. 26.

9. Martin Boss, "Revolution or Choice? The Political Economy of School Financial Referenda," *Western Political Quarterly* 29 (1976):1, 75–85; Mickey Levy, "Voting on California's Tax and Expenditure Limitation

Initiative," *National Tax Journal* 28 (1975):4, 426–435; J. Horton and W. Thompson, "Powerlessness and Political Negativism: A Study of Defeated Local Referendums," *American Journal of Sociology* 67 (1972):3, 485–493.

10. The argument that follows does not assume that voters operate without a budget constraint. Contrast the approach of Samuel Brittan, "The Economic Contradictions of Democracy," *British Journal of Political Science* 5 (1975):2, 139; Peter Jay, *Employment, Inflation, and Politics* (London: Institute of Economic Affairs, 1976), pp. 12ff; and the assumption of ever expanding consumer wants in Fred Hirsch, *The Social Limits to Growth.* Their *a priori* assumptions are shown to be inconsistent with survey data about Britain by James Alt, "The Politics of Economic Decline" (Ph.D. diss., University of Essex Government Department, 1977).

11. Quoted by Philip Shabecoff, "U.S. Subsidizes Nearly Everything," *New York Times*, 20 March 1977.

12. V. O. Key, Jr., *The Responsible Electorate* (Cambridge: Harvard University Press, 1966), p. 7. For our evidence on this point, see *infra*, chap. 10.

13. Cf. Otto A. Davis, M. A. H. Dempster, and Aaron Wildavsky, "Toward a Predictive Theory of Government Expenditure: U.S. Domestic Appropriations," *British Journal of Political Science* 4 (1974):4, 419–452; Peter B. Natchez and Irvin C. Bupp, "Policy and Priority in the Budgetary Process," *American Political Science Review* 67 (1973):3, 960–962; and John Wanat, "Bases of Budgetary Incrementalism," *American Political Science Review* 68 (1974):3, 1221–1228.

14. Guy Lord, *The French Budgetary Process* (Berkeley: University of California Press, 1973), p. 30.

15. Karl Heinrich Friauf, "Parliamentary Control of the Budget in the Federal Republic of Germany," in *The Power of the Purse: The Role of European Parliaments in Budgetary Decisions*, eds. David Coombes et al. (London: Allen and Unwin, 1976), p. 79.

16. *The Budget of the United States, Fiscal Year 1977* (Washington, D.C.: Government Printing Office, 1976), p. 34; *The Budget of the United States, 1974* (Washington, D.C.: Government Printing Office, 1973), p. 39; Barry M. Blechman, Edward D. Gramlich, and Robert W. Hartman, *Setting National Priorities: The 1976 Budget* (Washington, D.C.: The Brookings Institution, 1975), pp. 191ff; and Joel Havemann, "Ford Congress Seeks Handle on 'Uncontrollable' Spending," *National Journal* 6 (1975):48, 1619–1625.

17. Frederic V. Malek, *Washington's Hidden Tragedy* (New York: The Free Press, 1978), p. 171.

18. Daniel Tarschys, "The Problem of Pre-Planned Society" (Washington, D.C.: Annual Meeting of the American Political Science Association, 1977), p. 6. See also W. Dullforce, "Socialist Omelette Hard to Unscramble," *Financial Times* (London), 19 January 1977.

19. See OECD Studies in Resource Allocation No. 3, *Public Expenditure on Income Maintenance Programmes* (Paris: OECD, 1976), pp. 39ff.

20. Quoted in "Carter Asks Tax Rises, Funding Shift to Ease Social Security Drain," *New York Times*, 10 May 1977.

21. For a full discussion, see e.g. Michael J. Boskin, ed., *The Crisis in*

Notes

Social Security (San Francisco: Institute of Contemporary Studies, 1977); and Alicia H. Munnell, *The Future of Social Security* (Washington, D.C.: The Brookings Institution, 1977), especially p. 41.

22. For a wide-ranging and sophisticated catalogue of theories emphasizing producer, consumer, and supply pressures increasing public spending, see Daniel Tarschys, "The Growth of Public Expenditures: Nine Modes of Explanation," *Scandinavian Political Studies* 10 (1975):9–31.

23. See *Demographic Trends in OECD Countries* (Paris: OECD, 1974); and *Current Population Reports* (Washington, D.C.: U.S. Bureau of the Census, 1975) no. 501, p. 25.

24. See George Katona, *Psychological Economics* (New York: Elsevier, 1975), pp. 359–360; and Gabriel A. Almond and Sidney Verba, *The Civic Culture* (Princeton: University Press, 1963).

25. Herbert Kaufman, *Are Government Organizations Immortal?* (Washington, D.C.: The Brookings Institution, 1976). A pyramid decorates the cover of the book.

26. See Richard Rose, "On the Priorities of Government: A Developmental Analysis of Public Policies," *European Journal of Political Research*, 4 (1976):3, 262ff.

27. Milton Friedman, "The Line We Dare Not Cross: The Fragility of Freedom at Sixty Per Cent," *Encounter*, 47 (1976):12.

28. See Joel D. Aberbach and Bert A. Rockman, "Clashing Beliefs within the Executive Branch: The Nixon Administration Bureaucracy," *American Political Science Review*, 70 (1976):2, 461.

29. See Richard Rose, *What Is Governing? Purpose and Policy in Washington* (Englewood Cliffs, N.J.: Prentice-Hall Inc., 1978), pp. 95ff.

30. OECD Studies in Resource Allocation No. 2, *Public Expenditure on Education* (Paris: OECD, 1976), p. 23.

31. Our calculations, which omit Italy, are based upon data presented in Morris Beck, "The Expanding Public Sector: Some Contrary Evidence," *National Tax Journal* 29 (1976):1, 17.

32. See OECD Studies in Resource Allocation Nos. 2 and 3, *Public Expenditure on Education*, and *Public Expenditure on Income Maintenance Programmes* (Paris: OECD, 1976).

33. See Daniel Tarschys, "The Growth of Public Expenditures," for a review of these arguments. For an application, see Alan T. Peacock and Jack Wiseman, *The Growth of Public Expenditure in the United Kingdom* (London: Oxford University Press, 1961).

34. See James M. Buchanan and Richard E. Wagner, *Democracy in Deficit: The Political Legacy of Lord Keynes* (New York: Academic Press Inc., 1977), pp. 11ff; and for a fuller discussion of these issues, *infra*, chap. 6.

35. Buchanan and Wagner, *Democracy in Deficit*, p. 140.

36. Unpublished OECD calculations.

37. Calculated by the authors from a mimeographed background paper prepared by the Department of Health & Social Security, for the Seminar on Social Security Priorities (London), 5 July 1977.

38. Wilensky, *The Welfare State and Equality*, pp. 25ff.

Chapter 6

1. In J. M. Keynes, *Collected Writings* (London: Macmillan Press, in press), being published under the auspices of the Royal Economic Society.

2. For a discussion of the political puritanism of the time, see Robert J. Skidelsky, *Politicians and the Slump* (London: Macmillan Press, 1967); on Keynes's reaction against this outlook, see Robert J. Skidelsky, ed., *The End of the Keynesian Era* (London: Macmillan Press, 1977).

3. President Franklin D. Roosevelt could not understand Keynesian ideas even when explained to him by the master. After the English economist had spoken to him at the White House in 1934, he complained that Keynes was not a political economist but a mathematician. See Frances Perkins, *The Roosevelt I Knew* (New York: Viking Press, 1946), p. 225.

4. Roosevelt himself was ready to "out-Hoover" Hoover in the 1932 Presidential race. See "Campaign Address on the Federal Budget at Pittsburgh, Pa., October 19, 1932," *Public Papers and Addresses of Franklin D. Roosevelt*, vol. I (New York: Random House, 1938), pp. 795–811.

5. Hugh Dalton, *Principles of Public Finance*, 4th ed. (London: Routledge & Kegan Paul, 1954), p. 221. Dalton himself had his career as Chancellor collapse in 1947 in consequence of following a Keynesian-type cheap money policy.

6. Roy Harrod, *The Life of John Maynard Keynes* (London: Macmillan, 1951), pp. 192–193.

7. Cf. Harrod, *The Life of Keynes*, chap. 14; Harry S. Truman, *Memoirs*, vol. 1 (Garden City, N.Y.: Doubleday & Co., 1955), pp. 178–180; and Richard Gardner, *Sterling-Dollar Diplomacy* (Oxford: Clarendon Press, 1956), chap. 10.

8. See e.g. John Williamson, *The Failure of World Monetary Reform, 1971–74* (Sudbury-on-Thames, Middlesex: Thomas Nelson, 1977), chaps. 1–2. On deficit finance as a stimulus to inflation, see James Buchanan and Richard E. Wagner, *Democracy in Deficit* (New York: Academic Press, 1977).

9. See *Endogenous Politicians and the Theory of Economic Policy* (Stockholm: Institute for International Economic Studies Seminar Papers, 1973), no. 35, p. 52; and Lindbeck, "Stabilization Policy in Open Economies with Endogenous Politicians," *American Economic Review* 66 (1976):2, 17.

10. Nor does the formal centralization of the Soviet Union end the headaches of managing a political economy. See Alec Nove, *The Soviet Economy*, 3rd ed. (London: George Allen & Unwin, 1969).

11. Keynes himself noted the advantages in maximizing the economic output that a centralized nondemocratic state might have. See George Garvey, "Keynes and the Economic Activists of Pre-Hitler Germany," *Journal of Political Economy* 83 (April 1975):403. Garvey's article is especially revealing of Keynes's English insularity.

12. J. P. Crecine, "Coordination of Federal Fiscal and Budgetary Policy Processes," Unpublished manuscript (Pittsburgh: Carnegie-Mellon University, Department of Social Science, 1977), p. 12.

Notes

13. Compiling the price index used to deflate current prices to units of constant value involves a good many judgmental decisions about changes in the quality of products, the development of new products, and changes in consumption patterns. See e.g. Zvi Griliches, *Price Indexes and Quality Change* (Cambridge: Harvard University Press, 1971). Problems expand when crosstime crossnational comparisons are involved. See Wilfred Beckerman, *International Comparisons of Real Income* (Paris: OECD Development Center, 1966).

14. Cf. *The Government's Expenditure Plans* (London: Her Majesty's Stationery Office, Cmnd. 6721-I, 1977), p. 18; and *The United States Budget in Brief, Fiscal Year 1978* (Washington, D.C.: Government Printing Office, 1977).

15. *The Budget of the United States Government, Fiscal Year 1977* (Washington, D.C.: Government Printing Office, 1977), pp. 3, 4, 7.

16. Buchanan and Wagner, *Democracy in Deficit*, pp. 151ff.

17. *The Budget of the United States Government, Fiscal Year 1978* (Washington, D.C.: Government Printing Office, 1978), pp. 3, 4, 7.

18. See Joseph E. Pechman, "The Full Employment Budget," in ed. J. E. Pechman *Setting National Priorities: The 1978 Budget* (Washington, D.C.: The Brookings Institution, 1977), p. 420. Cf. the even more agnostic stance of Charles L. Schultze, "Federal Spending," in *Setting National Priorities: The Next Ten Years*, eds. Henry Owen and Charles L. Schultze (Washington, D.C.: The Brookings Institution, 1976), p. 327, n. 4.

19. See Sir Richard Clarke, "The Long-Term Planning of Taxation," in *Taxation Policy*, eds. Bernard Crick and William A. Robson (Harmondsworth, Middlesex: Penguin Books, 1973), p. 159.

20. OECD, *The McCracken Report*, p. 192.

21. Cf. *The Budget of the United States Government 1977*, pp. 24ff; and the preelection views of Charles L. Schultze, subsequently appointed President Carter's chairman of the Council of Economic Advisors, in Owen and Schultze, eds., *Setting National Priorities: The Next Ten Years*, pp. 323-370.

22. See *Public Expenditure* (London: Her Majesty's Stationery Office, Cmnd. 2915), (96) p. 1.

23. Österreichisches Institut für Wirtschaftsforschung, *Recent Economic Developments in the Industrial Countries* (Vienna, 1976), p. 18.

24. OECD, *Economic Outlook* (Special Supplement 19, 1976), p. 127.

25. See OECD, *Economic Outlook* 22 (December 1977).

26. Cf. Peter Jay, "The Classic Profile of National Bankruptcy," *The Times* (London), 20 February 1976.

27. Cf. Rudolf Klein, Martin Buxton, and Quentin Outram, *Constraints and Choice: Social Policy and Public Expenditure, 1976* (London: Centre for Studies in Social Policy, 1976), p. 4.

28. For a clear and relevant statement of this view, see OECD, *The McCracken Report*, chap. 1.

Chapter 7

1. OECD, *The McCracken Report*, pp. 152, 153; italics added. Cf. OECD, *Economic Outlook*, 22 (December 1977), p. 15.
2. Calculated from data on major Western nations in OECD, *The McCracken Report*, p. 147.
3. See OECD, *The McCracken Report*, p. 305. The trend line of profits has been down everywhere; in the extreme case of Britain from a "trend" level of 6.2 percent in 1960 to 2.4 percent in 1975.
4. Cf. Robert Bacon and Walter Eltis, *Britain's Economic Problem: Too Few Producers* (London: Macmillan Press, 1976).
5. For the basic economic framework, see A. W. Phillips, "The Relationship between Unemployment and the Rate of Change of Money Wage Rates in the United Kingdom, 1861–1957," *Economica*, 25 (November, 1958):283–299. For electoral analysis, see C. A. E. Goodhart and R. J. Bhansali, "Political Economy," *Political Studies* 18 (1970):1, 43–106. For a review of what has gone wrong since, see J. A. Trevithick, *Inflation: A Guide to the Crisis in Economics* (New York: Penguin Books, 1977), chap. 4, "The Rise and Fall of the Phillips Curve."
6. The Roman Empire survived Nero by centuries, and later had better periods before its final loss of authority. See e.g. Ramsay MacMullen, *Roman Government's Response to Crisis AD 235–337* (New Haven: Yale University Press, 1976).
7. For a review of different forecasting techniques, see e.g. R. K. Chisholm and C. R. Whitaker Jr., *Forecasting Methods* (Homewood, Illinois: Richard R. Irwin Inc., 1971).
8. OECD, *The McCracken Report*, p. 47.
9. OECD, *Economic Outlook* 22 (December, 1977):15.

Chapter 8

1. See Peter Hennessy, "Austerity, Rationing, the Cold War, Spies: 1946 Was Not a Very Good Year," *Times* (London), 4 January 1977.
2. "The International Scene," *Times* (London), 1 September 1975.
3. Denis Healey, quoted in "Alternative Is 'Savage Action and 3 million Jobless,'" *Times* (London), 30 September 1976.
4. Fourth Report, House of Commons Expenditure Committee, quoted in *The Scotsman*, 3 April 1976.
5. "The International Scene," *Times* (London), 1 September 1975. Cf. the comments of Daniel Bell, quoted *supra*, p. 42.
6. Studying the causes of inflation is the major growth industry in economics today. For a balanced review of cost push, monetarist, and Keynesian approaches, see J. A. Trevithick, *Inflation: A Guide to the Crisis in Economics* (New York: Penguin, 1977).
7. See International Monetary Fund, *International Financial Statistics* 30 (April 1977):8, 140, 148, 194, 332, 364, 368; line 34 in each national

table. In 1977, the money supply was contracted by four national governments concerned with the inflationary consequences of their previous policies: America, France, Germany, and Italy.

8. IMF, *International Financial Statistics*, line 65 of each table.

9. Cf. Report of the Secretary General, *Inflation: The Present Problem* (Paris: OECD, 1970), pp. 15ff.

10. For an analysis of inflation's economic effects, see e.g. David Laidler and Michael Parkin, "Inflation: A Survey," *Economic Journal* 85 (December 1975), especially pp. 743, 886ff.

11. Günter Schmölders, "The German Experience," in *Inflation: Long-Term Problems*, ed. C. Lowell Harriss (New York: The Academy of Political Science, 1975), 31:4, 210.

12. See e.g. J. M. Buchanan and Richard E. Wagner, *Democracy in Deficit* (New York: Academic Press, 1977), especially chap. 11.

13. Calculated from *The Budget of the United States Government: Fiscal Year 1979* (Washington, D.C.: Government Printing Office, 1978), p. 486.

14. Calculated from data reported in International Monetary Fund, *International Financial Statistics* 30 (1977):11, line 61 of national tables.

15. For a detailed national study of the tax consequences of inflation, see David R. Morgan, *Over-Taxation by Inflation* (London: Institute of Economic Affairs, Hobart Paper No. 72, 1977).

16. See Felipe Pazos, *Chronic Inflation in Latin America* (New York: Praeger Publishers, 1972), especially chaps. 2 and 3.

17. For an overview, see F. Pike and T. Stritch, eds., *The New Corporatism* (Notre Dame, Indiana: University Press, 1972), especially the chapter by Philippe C. Schmitter; and a special issue of *Comparative Political Studies* 10 (1977):1, edited by Schmitter.

18. See Stein Rokkan, "Votes Count, Resources Decide," in *Makt og Motiv* (Oslo: Gyldendal Norsk Forlag, 1976).

19. For an overview of wage and price policies, see OECD, *The McCracken Report*, pp. 214–219, and articles cited at pp. 33, 333ff; and Ann Romanis Braun, "The Role of Incomes Policy in Industrialized Countries since World War II," *Staff Papers* (International Monetary Fund), 20 (March 1975):1, 1–36.

20. Arnold Weber, "The Continuing Courtship: Wage-Price Policy through Five Administrations," in *Exhortation and Controls: The Search for a Wage-Price Policy, 1945–71*, ed. Craufurd D. Goodwin (Washington, D.C.: The Brookings Institution, 1975), p. 371.

21. For an excellent discussion of the coexistence of political consensus and a lack of economic consensus, see John Goldthorpe, "Social Inequality and Social Integration in Modern Britain," in *Studies in British Politics*, 3rd ed., ed. Richard Rose (New York: St. Martin's Press, 1977), pp. 84–104.

22. On the paradox of conflicting macro- and micro-rationalities, see Mancur Olson Jr., *The Logic of Collective Action* (Cambridge: Harvard University Press, 1965).

23. Cf. James S. Coleman, *Power and the Structure of Society* (New York: W. W. Norton & Co., 1974).

24. For a detailed description of the composition of this basket of cur-

rencies, see John Williamson, *The Failure of World Monetary Reform, 1971–74* (Sudbury-on-Thames, Middlesex: Thomas Nelson, 1977), p. 136.

25. Cf. Robert W. Tucker, *The Inequality of Nations* (New York: Basic Books, 1977).

26. The Watergate tape of 23 June 1972.

27. Quoted from a verbatim text of the President's press conference, *Times* (London), 3 May 1977.

28. Professor Herbert Giersch, in OECD, *The McCracken Report*, p. 248.

29. For background on the IMF, see e.g. W. M. Scamell, *International Monetary Policy: Bretton Woods and After* (New York: John Wiley & Sons, 1975); John Williamson, *The Failure of World Monetary Reform*; and Alfred E. Eckes, Jr., *A Search for Solvency* (Austin: University of Texas Press, 1975).

Chapter 9

1. A phrase of the Italianate English poet, Robert Barrett Browning, it is used as the title of an Orwellian study of Britain, Constantine Fitz-Gibbon, *When the Kissing Has to Stop* (London: Cassell, 1961).

2. See Jacques Leruez, "Macro-Economic Planning in Mixed Economies," in *Planning in Europe*, eds. J. E. S. Hayward and Olga Narkewiecz (London: Croom Helm Ltd., 1978).

3. See President Carter's reorganization message to Congress of 4 February 1977, quoted in *Congressional Quarterly Weekly Report*, 12 February 1977; and more generally, Herbert Kaufman, "Reflections on Administrative Reorganization," in *Setting National Priorities: The 1978 Budget*, ed. Joseph A. Pechman (Washington, D.C.: The Brookings Institution, 1977), especially p. 417.

4. A director of the Bank of England, W. J. Keswick, quoted in *Proceedings of the Bank Rate Tribunal* (London: Her Majesty's Stationery Office, 1957), p. 101, Q.3850.

5. Quoted in Robert Prinsky, "Income-Tax Cheating Is on the Rise in Britain as Prices Outstrip Pay," *Wall Street Journal*, 10 October 1977.

6. See e.g. A. Di Majo and F. M. Frasca, "Imposizione Personale e Distribuzione dei Redditi in Italia," *Contributi alla Ricerca Economica* (Rome: Servizio Studi della Banca d'Italia, 1975), pp. 23–74; Francesco Forte, "National Responses to the Crisis: Italy," in *The European Economy Beyond the Crisis* (Bruges: College of Europe, *Cahiers de Bruges* N.S.35, 1976), p. 19; and Censis, *L'Occupazione Occulta* (Rome: Census Research, 2, 1976).

7. Serge-Christophe Kolm, "A Note on Optimum Tax Evasion," *Journal of Public Economics* 2 (1973):270.

8. See Joachim Vogel, "Taxation and Public Opinion in Sweden: An Interpretation of Recent Survey Data," *National Tax Journal* 27 (1974):4, 509.

9. See C. T. Sandford, *Hidden Costs of Taxation* (London: Institute for

Notes

Fiscal Studies, No. 6, 1973), especially pp. 118–120; and Commissioner of Internal Revenue, *Annual Report, 1975* (Washington, D.C.: Government Printing Office, 1976), p. 59.

10. Cf. Burkhard Strumpel, "The Contribution of Survey Research to Public Finance," in *Quantitative Analysis in Public Finance*, ed. A. T. Peacock (New York: Praeger, 1969), especially p. 26.

11. Quoted by Samuel Brittan, " 'Cuts' in Government Spending and the Tax Illusion," in *Taxation Policy*, eds. B. Crick and W. A. Robson (Harmondsworth, Middlesex: Penguin Books, 1973), p. 38.

12. For an exposition of individualist, liberal, and Socialist models of welfare favoring the Socialist viewpoint, see Julia Parker, *Social Policy and Citizenship* (London: Macmillan Press, 1975), chap. 1.

13. Henry Fairlie, "In Defense of Big Government," *The New Republic*, 13 March 1976, p. 25. See also L. J. Sharpe, "American Democracy Reconsidered," *British Journal of Political Science* 3 (1973):1–2.

14. For the difficulties of the identifying of what is the public interest, see Richard Rose, *What Is Governing? Purpose and Policy in Washington* (Englewood Cliffs, N.J.: Prentice-Hall, Inc., 1978), chap. 4.

15. See Alex Pravda, "Elections in Communist Party States," in *Elections Without Choice*, eds. Guy Hermet, Richard Rose, and Alain Rouquié (London: Macmillan Press, 1978).

16. For a discussion of the very real problem that arises from this fact, see James S. Coleman, *Power and the Structure of Society* (New York: W. W. Norton & Co., 1974).

17. See William H. Whyte Jr., *The Organization Man* (New York: Simon & Schuster Inc., 1956).

18. Assar Lindbeck, *The Political Economy of the New Left: An Outsider's View* (New York: Harper & Row, 1971), pp. 32–33. A major political weakness of Fred Hirsch's *Social Limits to Growth* (New York: Twentieth Century Fund, 1976) is that he recommends government intervention to reduce competition for positional goods without considering how this would avoid all the problems of bureaucratic centralized decision-making.

19. See Karl Hulicka and Irene M. Hulicka, *Soviet Institutions: The Individual and Society* (Boston: Christopher Publishing, 1967); and cf. Paul Hollander, *Soviet and American Society: A Comparison* (New York: Oxford University Press, 1973).

20. Sir Isaiah Berlin, *Four Essays on Liberty* (London: Oxford University Press, 1969), pp. 125–126.

21. Problems of relative deprivation, inherent in any modern society, inevitably remain. But relative deprivation is not absolute deprivation. See T. R. Gurr, *Why Men Rebel* (Princeton: University Press, 1970); and W. G. Runciman, *Relative Deprivation and Social Justice* (London: Routledge & Kegan Paul, 1966).

22. See OECD Studies in Resource Allocation No. 2, *Public Expenditure on Education* (Paris: OECD, 1976).

23. See e.g. Paul W. MacAvoy, ed., *The Ford Administration Papers on Regulatory Reform* (Washington, D.C.: American Enterprise Institute, 1977).

24. Cf. Charles L. Schultze, *The Public Use of Private Interest* (Washington, D.C.: The Brookings Institution, 1977).

25. The ramifications of user charges are interesting, both theoretically and practically. For a booklength argument in their favor, see Arthur Seldon, *Charge* (London: Institute of Economic Affairs, 1977). The very novelty of user charges makes expanding their coverage politically unpopular, and like indirect taxes, they could have an inflationary effect if greatly expanded or increased.

26. See Aaron Wildavsky, "The Self-Evaluating Organization," *Public Administration Review* 32 (1972):5, 509–521; and Carol H. Weiss, *Evaluation Research* (Englewood Cliffs, N.J.: Prentice-Hall Inc., 1972).

27. See the conclusions of an unpublished paper by Michael Parkin, reported in "Masters of Money," *The Economist* (London), 10 December 1977; and the heavily documented assessment of John T. Woolley, "The Politics of Central Banking: Comparisons from Recent Experience" (Washington, D.C.: Annual Meeting of the American Political Science Association, 1977).

28. Cf. *Cash Limits on Public Expenditure* (London: Her Majesty's Stationery Office, Cmnd. 6440, 1976); Maurice Wright, "Public Expenditure in Britain: The Crisis of Control," *Public Administration* 55 (Summer 1977):157ff; and Terry Ward, "Cash Limits and the Shortfall in Public Spending," *Times* (London), 3 October 1977.

29. "Concern in Shortfall in Government Spending," *Times* (London), 19 December 1977. See also, Melvyn Westlake, "Hand in Hand Down Separate Roads," *Times* (London), 15 December 1977. Unexpected shortfalls in American federal spending in 1976 and 1977 are described as "curious" and "mystifying" by Joseph A. Peckman, "The Federal Budget in Review," in *Setting National Priorities: The 1978 Budget*, ed. J. A. Pechman (Washington, D.C.: The Brookings Institution, 1977), pp. 53–54.

30. See *The Government's Expenditure Plans 1978–79 to 1981–82* (London: Her Majesty's Stationery Office, Cmnd. 7049, 1978).

31. Cf. Aaron Wildavsky, *Budgeting: A Comparative Theory of Budgetary Processes* (Boston: Little, Brown, 1976), p. 366; and Maurice Wright, "Public Expenditure in Britain," p. 143ff.

Chapter 10

1. For historical surveys of the evolution of different citizen claims upon government, see e.g. T. H. Marshall, *Citizenship and Social Class* (Cambridge: Cambridge University Press, 1950), chap. 1; Reinhard Bendix (with Stein Rokkan), *Nation-Building and Citizenship* (New York: John Wiley & Sons, Inc., 1964), pp. 74–104; and Stein Rokkan, *Citizens, Elections, Parties* (Oslo: Universitetsforlaget, 1970).

2. See the discussion of data reported in Richard Rose, *What Is Governing? Purpose and Policy in Washington* (Englewood Cliffs, N.J.: Prentice-Hall, Inc., 1978), p. 22; and Richard Rose, "On the Priorities of Citizenship in the Deep South and Northern Ireland," *Journal of Politics* 38 (1976):2, 247–291.

3. For a clear statement of this view, see e.g. Samuel Brittan, "The

Notes

Economic Contradictions of Democracy," *British Journal of Political Science*, 5 (1975):2.

4. See *Euro-Baromètre* (Brussels: Commission of the European Communities, 1977), no. 7, p. 13.

5. See Richard Easterlin, "Does Economic Growth Improve the Human Lot: Some Empirical Evidence," in *Nations and Households in Economic Growth*, eds. Paul A. David and Melvin W. Reder (New York: Academic Press, 1974); and Angus Campbell, Philip E. Converse, and Willard L. Rodgers, *The Quality of American Life* (New York: Russell Sage Foundation, 1976), pp. 152ff.

6. See *Euro-Baromètre* (1977), no. 7, p. 8. See also Ronald Inglehart, "Political Dissatisfaction and Mass Support for Social Change in Advanced Industrial Society," *Comparative Political Studies* 10 (1977):3, 455–472.

7. Campbell et al., *The Quality of American Life*. Note also that citizens appear satisfied in personal encounters with public officials, but not in generalized judgments of government. See also Daniel Katz, Barbara Gutek, Robert F. Kahan, and Eugenia Barton, *Bureaucratic Encounters* (Ann Arbor: Institute for Social Research, University of Michigan, 1975), and Commission of the European Communities, *Science and European Public Opinion*, pp. 188ff.

8. See Commission of the European Communities, *Science and European Public Opinion* (Brussels, 1977), p. 98; and for 1970–1977 data see *Euro-Baromètre*, no. 7, p. 12. For breakdowns of responses by social classes, see Ronald Inglehart, "Political Dissatisfaction and Mass Support," pp. 466, 469.

9. Henry Kariel, *The Promise of Politics* (Englewood Cliffs, N.J.: Prentice-Hall, 1969), p. 52.

10. Denis Healey, "Alternative Is 'Savage Action and 3m Jobless'," *Times* (London), 30 September 1976.

11. See G. Katona, B. Strumpel, and E. Zahn, *Aspirations and Affluence: Comparative Studies in the United States and Europe* (New York: McGraw-Hill Book Co., 1971), pp. 44ff. and pp. 204ff.

12. Katona et al., *Aspirations and Affluence*, p. 48.

13. See *Report of the Fourteenth Economic Survey Among European Consumers* (Brussels: Commission of the European Communities, 13 December 1976), table 1.

14. See Opinion Research Centre survey, reported in "Do the British Sincerely Wish to Be Rich?," *New Society* (London), 28 April 1977; and Gallup *Political Index* (December, 1978), no. 185, p. 19.

INDEX

Index